African Americans in White Suburbia

African Americans in White Suburbia

SOCIAL NETWORKS & POLITICAL BEHAVIOR

Ernest McGowen III

Published by the University Press of Kansas (Lawrence, Kansas 66045), which was organized by the Kansas Board of Regents and is operated and funded by Emporia State University, Fort Hays State University, Kansas State University, Pittsburg State University, the University of Kansas, and Wichita State University.

Library of Congress Cataloging-in-Publication Data
Names: McGowen, Ernest, III, author.
Title: African Americans in white suburbia : social networks and political behavior / Ernest McGowen III.
Description: Lawrence, KS : University Press of Kansas, [2017] | Includes bibliographical references and index.
Identifiers: LCCN 2016055777| ISBN 9780700624164 (cloth : alk. paper) | ISBN 9780700624171 (pbk. : alk. paper) | ISBN 9780700624188 (ebook)
Subjects: LCSH: Suburban African Americans—Politics and government. | Suburban African Americans—Social networks. | Suburban African Americans—Race identity. | Suburbanites—Political activity—United States. | Suburbanites—Social networks—United States. | Group identity—United States. | United States—Race relations.
Classification: LCC E185.615 .M3534 2017 | DDC 305.896/07301733—dc23
LC record available at https://lccn.loc.gov/2016055777.

British Library Cataloguing-in-Publication Data is available.

Printed in the United States of America

10 9 8 7 6 5 4 3 2 1

The paper used in this publication is recycled and contains 30 percent postconsumer waste. It is acid free and meets the minimum requirements of the American National Standard for Permanence of Paper for Printed Library Materials Z39.48-1992.

Contents

African Americans in White Suburbia

1. The Unique Story of the Suburban African American

To say that African Americans have had a tumultuous history in the United States would be an understatement. Even before the founding of the republic, being black meant your labor was not your own and your body could be assaulted with impunity. Even with the end of chattel slavery, mainstream society (the government and individuals) denied blacks access to the political and social structure of the country by both law and practice. It may be just as much of an understatement to say blacks have not made tremendous social and economic progress in the centuries that followed. This book will tell the story of one particular subset of that group—suburban African Americans.

Suburban African Americans find themselves caught between the two worlds of high socioeconomic status (SES)[1] and low race status. Above-average income has afforded the opportunity to move to the suburbs; however, there has been a history of hostility and exclusion based on race that is not lost on the learned. Educational accomplishments have opened occupational opportunities in the most prestigious firms and businesses, yet their new coworkers have neither the same upbringings and interests, nor the same political ideologies and preferences. Suburban African Americans have abundant political resources to influence government, but lack available political choices and candidates who speak to their racial ideology.

However, there are places more welcoming, with people of similar cultures and upbringings, and political elites working toward the type of racial changes they desire. In the traditional municipality, these places are just a short drive away, in the historic African American neighborhood. The question asked in this book is how does this suburban environment, especially the racial makeup of one's neighborhood and social networks, affect the political behaviors of suburban African Americans who have strong racial identifications and policy preferences aimed at aiding the racial group writ large?

In the following chapters I will show that being one of the few blacks in the neighborhood and workplace makes suburban African Americans feel the discomfort of minority status more acutely. This, in turn, makes them more likely to view their social interactions in these situations as disagreeable and even hostile to their racial identity. As a result, they seek out more agreeable networks that reinforce their racial identity.[2]

Suburban African Americans can easily find these networks in the majority-black institutions of the historic inner city. Cultivated and refined over centuries, these institutions, such as black churches or civil rights organizations like the NAACP, have dedicated themselves to uplifting the collective group in the face of discrimination. Exposure to these norms will move suburban African Americans toward group-based behaviors even if those behaviors go against their material self-interest. Thus, they will even hold opinions *more* racially radical[3] than their urban coethnics. This is because their suburban residence and constant minority status will heighten the salience of their racial identity and its role in their political behavior decisions.

Differences among African Americans and whites based on environment lead to the motivating research question of this study. How does the metro suburban environment, with its racial disparities and close geographic proximity to majority black institutions and neighborhoods, shape the political behaviors of the African Americans who live there? In some ways, suburban neighborhoods are no different from other environments in that they impact behavior by shaping the informal and formal opportunities to engage in politics. Informally, the people who constitute one's neighborhood (and relatedly, one's workplace), and their demographics, will affect the universe of information to which the individual will have ready access. Social environments cut the cost of acquiring information, which might be conveyed through a conversation at a dinner party or the bumper sticker affixed to a neighbor's vehicle. Instead of having to seek out information and interpretation from multiple outlets, the embedded network inhabitant will have information brought to them by other network members. Additionally, networks filter this information for consonance. For the most part, people's networks are comprised of people with whom they have something in common. (However, not every network has the same level of agreement and inhabitants are not always able to choose network partners with impunity, as the review of the literature will show.) Therefore, social network theory suggests that information of interest to an individual should also be of interest to most of the group. This affinity for network members makes proffered information more credible and suggests that the individual will shape his or her (political) behaviors toward the prevailing norm of the network.

Formally, one's neighbors are also fellow political constituents. Those political ties determine the policies of political jurisdictions and the actions of electoral candidates. Higher income and education levels in suburban neighborhoods suggest that these areas will be more Republican. This setting may be great for African American residents on economic issues like taxes. However, it means that on social issues, like race, there is a chance that even the Democratic candidate's stance will be more conservative. The people with whom suburban African Americans share racial ideologies may be in a different political jurisdiction for the majority of electoral contests. Yet, just because suburban African Americans cannot vote their interests does not mean they cannot still work to advance them. They could participate by donating money or volunteering to help elect a coethnic running for mayor of the city. In chapter 5 the findings show this to be the case: suburban African Americans engage in more alternative political behaviors than suburban whites and urban African Americans.

Viewed as a collective, African Americans have made large socioeconomic gains that have translated into more residential mobility and occupational prestige, especially in contrast to the political and social environment of the 1960s and 1970s. Gone is the time when state-sanctioned segregation relegated blacks to less prestigious majority neighborhoods in the central city. Yet, present-day suburban African Americans can easily find themselves as one of only a few blacks in their neighborhood. For African Americans who identify closely with their race and culture, this isolation can have a psychological and political effect. Minority status may make one less likely to post the only Democrat sign on the block for fear of exclusion from a social setting. The suburbs are a place that has historically been hostile not only to African Americans' residence, but even to their mere presence in the neighborhood. Moreover, suburban neighborhood institutions like churches and volunteer organizations will be much less likely to focus their efforts on racial and ethnic minority issues and populations. Fortunately, for the suburban African American these racially focused networks and institutions are just a short drive away.

That minorities of any stripe will seek out reinforcing networks has a long lineage in the literature, as chapter 2 will show. However, these previous studies have not focused specifically on suburban African Americans. This is a subgroup with strong norms of group solidarity. However, they have a socioeconomic separation from others in the group and a geographic separation from the historic group-based institutions that have cultivated the culture since emancipation. Examining these citizens provides a set of unique circumstances that will surely augment our understanding of the relationship between environment and participation. The implications of researching this population are obvious and important. America is shifting geographically, and more African Americans are moving to the suburbs. At the same time, many contemporary issues cleave along racial lines. If these suburban African Americans identify more with their class than race, as some scholars have suggested, the amount of attention the mainstream pays to racial issues may lessen.

My assumption for this project is that suburban African Americans will not find the networks in which they spend the most time—their neighborhoods and workplaces—conducive to their racial identity and therefore will not look to them for normative signals or information shortcuts. Instead, they will seek out networks in the central city, such as a black church or a historic African American civil rights organization, or even a barbershop. They will also choose participatory behaviors that can better aid their group and reinforce their racial identity, even if they come at a higher resource cost when compared to simple voting.

THE RACIAL STATE OF THE AMERICAN METRO-SUBURBS

According to William Frey of the Brookings Metropolitan Policy Program and his analysis of the decennial censuses from 1990–2010, the percentage of African Americans living in the suburbs has risen steadily. In 1990 the share of blacks in large metro areas living in the suburbs was 37 percent; it increased to 44 percent in 2000, and 51 percent in 2010 (Frey 2011).[4] Frey says that blacks contributed the majority of suburban population growth in fourteen of the largest metro areas (though this compares to thirty-six areas for whites and forty-nine areas for Latinos). He attributes this shift in African American neighborhood residence to a phenomenon termed "black flight" (Frey 2011, 6), which has connotations similar to "white flight" but describes slightly different concepts and underlying motivations. As opposed to fleeing racial integration and declining property values, Frey attributes black suburbanization, in part, to "the group's economic progress in recent decades, particularly [among] younger blacks" (Frey 2011, 10).[5] However, Frey suggests that this increase in African American suburban residence may not necessarily lead to less segregated neighborhoods, as the whites who formerly lived in the suburbs are now moving even farther out into the "exurbs" (Frey 2011).

The Frey article provides a nice aggregate snapshot of African Americans in the suburbs before the individual level analysis in the following chapters. However, a point needs to be made about the romanticized idea of the suburbs versus the post-2010 census reality. While most people would picture tree-lined streets, two-car garages, kids on bikes, and white picket fences, the 2010 census showed that contemporary suburbs have gotten poorer as they have gotten more racially diverse. Some of this change is attributed to population sorting due to the revitalization (or gentrification) of some major central cities. A 2010 Brookings Institution study by Stephen Raphael and Michael Stoll attributes most of the change to "job sprawl," or the movement of jobs from the central business district to the suburbs (Raphael and Stoll 2010).

African American suburbanization is heavily contingent on income. According to Raphael and Stoll, poor blacks have the lowest suburbanization rate of all racial and ethnic groups. While African Americans as a whole increase their suburbanization as jobs become more decentralized, this decentralization does not statistically increase the likelihood that poor blacks will move to the suburbs. Therefore, as the suburbs as a whole have gotten poorer, the suburban African American population has maintained a higher SES. Again, much of this has to do with higher income whites fleeing even farther to the exurbs. This is also why suburban African Americans are more likely to live in neighborhoods below their income and education levels.

The trend of lower income people moving to the suburbs seems to have missed poor blacks. All of this suggests that suburban African Americans are truly in a unique position compared to *all* of their neighbors throughout the metro area. They are *racially* different from their fellow suburban whites and *socioeconomically* different from their urban coethnics. This begs the question as to which group (neighbors or coethnics) they will most closely resemble. I find that racial identity wins the day.

THE STATE OF AFRICAN AMERICAN SOCIOECONOMIC STATUS AND POLITICAL RESOURCES

In 2010, more than half of all blacks lived in the suburbs, up 14 percent from 1990 (Frey 2011). This residential mobility has unsurprisingly mirrored the

Figure 1.1. Average Change in HS Graduation by Race, 1990–2010

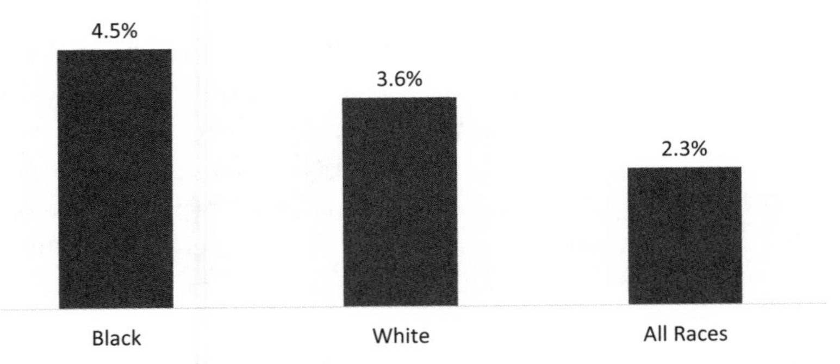

Source: Current Population Survey conducted by the U.S. Census, "Percent of People 25 Years and Over Who Have Completed High School or College, by Race, Hispanic Origin and Sex: Selected Years 1940 to 2013."

precipitous rise in SES for African Americans over the same twenty-plus-year period. Utilizing data from the Current Population Survey for every fifth year between 1990 and 2010,[6] I analyze the gains African Americans have made in terms of income, education, and occupational prestige. The upward trend is clear. From 1990 to 2010, the African American high school graduation rate jumped 18 percent (from 66.2 percent to 84.2 percent), more than twice the increase for all races combined over the same period. This equates to a five-year average increase of 4.5 percent, larger than the same measure for both whites, Latinos, and all races combined[7] (see figure 1.1). Gains in African American college graduation have been more modest, an overall increase of 8.6 percent over the same time period.

Increases in individual median income follow the same pattern. African Americans had the largest income gain of any race from 1990–2010 at $4,706 ($17,589 to $22,295), compared to a gain of $3,070 for all races ($24,495 to 27,565). African Americans also had the largest average gain per five-year period of any race at $1,176.50, compared to $767.50 for all races ($1,021.50 for whites and just $730.75 for Latinos) (see figure 1.2). While relative gains have been larger, in every year studied African Americans had lower education attainment and median individual income than both whites and the aggregation of all races.

There is some evidence that these income and education gains have translated into higher occupational prestige. In 2013, blacks made up 11.2 percent of the information workforce, 14 percent of education and health, and 16.4

Figure 1.2. Change in Median Income, 1990–2010

Source: Current Population Survey for selected years.

percent of public administration, a larger share than any other racial or ethnic minority. They also comprised 9.7 percent of the finance and insurance sector, 9.4 percent of professional and business services, and 14.2 percent of management, administrative, and waste services. All of these numbers were up from just three years prior (and also on par with or larger than their representation in the population).[8] While it is not possible to compare the workforce changes from prior decades, there is a clear correlation between SES and occupational prestige. Therefore, I believe it is a safe assumption that the movement into higher prestige, office-based jobs has followed a similar trajectory as suburban residence, given the income and education gains presented above.

With more disposable income and earning potential, it is not a surprise that racial and ethnic minorities in general, and African Americans in particular, have sought the "greener pastures" of the metropolitan suburbs. The suburban environment is one with less crime, better-funded schools, and higher property values. However, there are political consequences from such a move. Suburban African Americans will now be around neighbors and coworkers who may not share their views on partisan or particularly racialized subjects (Oliver 2010), will endure physical and possibly emotional separations from the historic coethnic community (Haynes 2001), and will be represented by governmental regimes that may be oppositional, if not downright hostile, to their most important political issues.

One of the aims of this project is to assess the consequences of these SES gains as they translate into residential mobility. This book will fit into a nascent yet rich scholarship on suburban African Americans and their political behavior. It will contribute to this line of research by examining national quantitative surveys capable of comparing the individual responses of the target group, suburban African Americans, to their white suburbanite neighbors and their urban coethnics. I also propose that our understanding of African American participation can become clearer and more complete if we study how environment, particularly neighborhood type, influences social interactions. This includes how neighborhood affects one's choices of discussion partners, the available supply of politically relevant information, and the racial makeup of social networks as well as how all of those factors influence which types of institutions and participatory behaviors will produce the highest utility.

THE SUBURBAN VERSUS URBAN ENVIRONMENT

A look at the 2012 American Community Survey (ACS) shows just how different life is in suburban versus urban neighborhoods.[9] The largest education disparities come at the bottom of the spectrum. Almost 20 percent of urbanites[10] over twenty-five years old have not completed high school compared to a little over 10 percent of suburbanites, even though high school graduation rates (26.1 percent suburban to 25 percent urban) and college graduation rates (21.3 percent suburban to 19.4 percent urban) are very similar. The major discrepancies come on income and house value, where the suburbs are clearly more affluent. Median income is more than $27,000 higher in the suburbs ($71,178 suburban; $43,680 urban), and the median home value is $41,472 higher ($225,937 suburban; $184,465 urban). Suburbs also have more residential stability, as 69.3 percent of suburban homes are owner occupied, compared to just 42.5 percent of urban homes.

When we disaggregate the numbers by race, we see the familiar pattern of suburban African Americans surpassing their urban coethnics but still falling behind their white neighbors. First, population proportions show that suburban African Americans are clearly in the minority of the three, only registering

15 percent of their neighborhood, while their urban coethnics make up a third of the city (33.7 percent) and whites are almost three-fourths of the suburbs (72.4 percent). Since suburban African Americans only make up 11.2 percent of the 4 million people in the average metropolitan statistical area (MSA), and blacks of any neighborhood type only make up 20 percent of the total MSA, most of the people suburban African Americans encounter will not be coethnics. There are important implications of this minority racial status. A suburban African American's random encounters will be overwhelmingly white, or at least multiracial. Whether it is at work, when interacting with neighbors, or even at the grocery store, the question is whether these people actually believe in, and want, the same things from government. If the answer is "no," this can be discomforting (McClurg 2006). In subsequent chapters, the data will show that there are wide disparities between what suburban African Americans and suburban whites feel on most racialized issues.

Our target group is in a similar middle position vis-à-vis their neighbors and coethnics when it comes to financial resources. While suburban African American median income cannot be measured, statistics on poverty rates show that one in five suburban blacks lives in poverty (20.2 percent), compared to 31 percent of urban African Americans and just 7.4 percent of suburban whites (see figure 1.3).

The preceding data show that the suburbs are clearly a unique environment. Suburban African American residents are caught in an interesting sandwich, one that is also mirrored geographically, between the demographics of the urban versus exurban neighborhoods. Increases in socioeconomic status and a lessening of racial barriers to residential mobility have opened up suburban living to a population for whom it was previously restricted. Yet that mobility has had consequences, including moving from an area with a rich cultural history and proximity to race-based institutions to jurisdictions where they are in the clear minority racially and politically. The question going forward is how does this minority status combine with things like racial ideology to influence suburban African American political behavior?

The extant research is clear that racial identity is a primary determinant of African American political behavior. However, we would benefit from a better understanding of the effects of social network racial makeup. The data will show that the surrounding environment truly influences these voters, at times leading them to espouse more racialized opinions and behaviors than similarly situated whites and urban African Americans.

Figure 1.3. Poverty Status by Race and Neighborhood, 2012

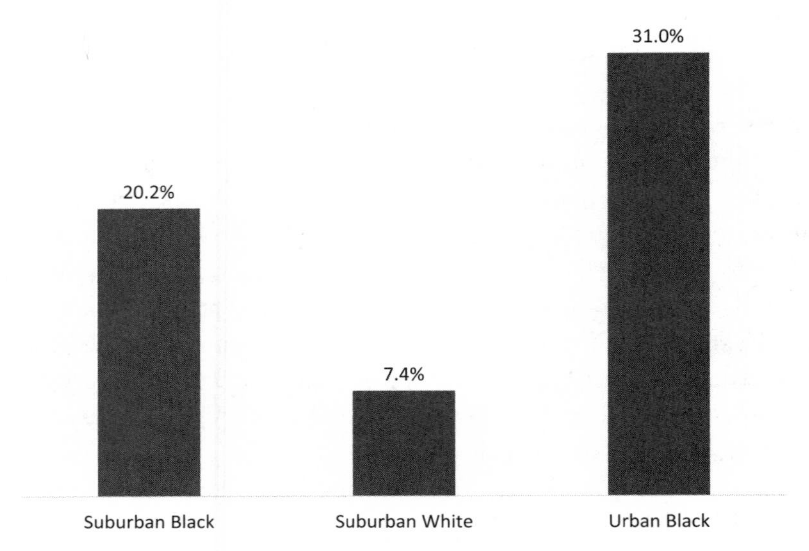

Source: 2012 Current Population Survey.

THE GEOGRAPHY OF THE MODERN AMERICAN METROPOLIS

The Philadelphia area is the picture of a typical American metropolis, both demographically and geographically. Its bustling urban core with a rich history dating back centuries is surrounded by affluent suburbs and the idyllic lifestyle they symbolize. Unfortunately, this idealized environment also holds a legacy of wide economic disparities, self-interested political competition, and racial conflict. In looking at the top twenty-five MSAs used for this chapter, Philadelphia is demographically representative of the average. It also has a particular geography that shows the differences between political and social jurisdictions and the relative ease of traveling to the majority black neighborhood with its racially reinforcing norms. As such, examining this typical area in depth will provide more context on the environments that are influencing individual behavior, a theme developed in subsequent chapters.

The Philadelphia-Camden-Wilmington MSA has on average over 3.8 million residents. Within that number, a little less than 1 million live in Philadelphia, its major central city. The remaining 71 percent live in the surrounding suburbs. The MSA is unique in that it actually covers parts of four states—Pennsylvania, New Jersey, Delaware, and Maryland—each with very different histories and governmental structures. Here we have the perfect contrast between a collective social identity—the Delaware Valley—and the many distinct political jurisdictions that determine a resident's political choices. The entire area is also typical socioeconomically. Only 8 percent of Delaware Valley residents over twenty-five years old have failed to graduate high school, while more than 22 percent have earned a bachelor's degree. Occupationally, the area is thriving. Forty-two percent of residents work in either a professional[11] or management[12] position (25.1 percent and 17.5 percent, respectively), and the unemployment rate[13] is under 10 percent. The median income of the area is also quite high at around $85,000 and almost three-fourths of the houses are owner-occupied (72.8 percent), with a median home value of $327,900. With a slightly lower median income and house value, this would be the type of area in which most suburban African Americans live.

As is the case for the suburbs as a whole, Philadelphia's suburbs are overwhelmingly white. The black population is dwarfed by almost six times the white population, 13.1 percent to 77.3 percent. A map of Philadelphia shows the extent of the racial segregation. The darker shades indicate larger concentrations of African Americans, an area that is sandwiched between the city center and the western suburbs (see figure 1.4). They are actually the largest group in Philadelphia proper (43.1 percent) but make up only 20.9 percent of the MSA. Figure 1.5 shows that the same pattern persists in terms of median income, which is not a coincidence.

The political constraint of suburban geography and its disconnect from how people live their social lives represent a major aspect of my theory. For example, if you were one of the 1,252 African Americans who lived in the 19010 zip code of Bryn Mawr (5.8 percent), there is a chance you were represented by Republican Patrick Meehan (PA-07) while other members of your same zip code were represented by Democrat Chaka Fattah (PA-02)![14] If a suburban African American is a Democrat and chooses to buy a house on the wrong side of the zip code, they might be much less enthusiastic about voting in the congressional district than coethnics with whom they may share a neighborhood grocery store. However, their SES levels suggest they have the resources and political efficacy that push for some form of participation. I hypothesize that those voters will focus their attention toward participation that yields a higher utility than voting in the local races, particularly alternatives that can help out the racial group.

Figure 1.4. Black Population Map of Philadelphia MSA Census Tracts

Source: Map compiled by author. Population data from the 2010 Census.

Figure 1.5. Median Income Map of Philadelphia MSA Census Tracts

Source: Map compiled by author. Population data from the 2010 Census.

One can see the formal political effects of suburban residence in the Philadelphia MSA. The area is covered by four states, eleven counties, and twelve congressional districts. Two residents that attend the same downtown Philadelphia yoga studio may actually have two different governors. If they happen to be from New Jersey and Delaware, the differences between their governors (Chris Christie R-NJ and Jack Markell D-DE) in party, policy, and even temperament will be large. Yet, the distance between their neighborhoods is anything but, as it is less than thirty-five miles from Wilmington, Delaware, to Camden, New Jersey, through Philadelphia. Information passed socially at the yoga studio will have the same content but divergent effects on the participatory calculus. The same piece of positive Democrat-centric information may make a Delawarean Democrat more likely to work for the statewide party, while her Democrat yoga partner from Camden may view New Jersey gubernatorial politics as a waste of effort and instead travel the five miles across the river into Philadelphia to campaign for a Democratic candidate there. At the same time, the eighty-one black suburbanites (1.8 percent) in Philadelphia's Lower Merion suburb, with a median income of $180,579, only have to travel eight miles to get to the Philadelphia NAACP chapter offices. These are the stimuli that push and pull suburban African Americans to behave in such a peculiar way. The places where they spend the most time, and have to vote, are not supportive of their racial identity, so they are pushed toward more racially reinforcing political behaviors. Luckily for most, there is a reinforcing, majority black environment with historic institutions and norms that can pull them into ideological comfort.

THE RACIALIZATION OF THE AMERICAN SUBURB

Historically, the mainstream has used the suburbs to perpetuate and crystalize the American racial hierarchy, but recently it may portend the country's journey toward a multicultural society. Originally conceived as a way to improve the lifestyles of veterans returning from World War II, and greatly aided by the new interstate highway system, the suburbs seemed like the perfect place to realize the American dream. Yet for African Americans the dream remained closed off and little was done to improve access to the symbols of this accomplishment.

Young GIs and other whites brought their ideas about racial and social integration with them to these suburban enclaves of rising social and economic status. While one should not expect an intolerant racial worldview to recede simply based on a residential relocation, the suburbanization of America is firmly rooted in governmental and personal feelings about race. This ideology, particularly the beliefs that civil society and its benefits need not be evenly distributed based on race and that racial segregation of private individuals was beyond the purview of the state, has had long-standing residential, social, and political consequences.

Government programs formalized ideas about residential racial diversity and the social desirability of minorities through departments like the Federal Housing Administration (FHA) and the Home Owners' Loan Corporation (HOLC). The government charged the FHA with evaluating government-subsidized loans for people wishing to become homeowners. Like all lenders, the government wanted to at least break even on its investments. This meant lending to people who would be able to pay back the loans, a possibility that was much more likely if the homes retained their value.

The government established a framework for evaluation in an effort to forecast which areas of the country were most likely to retain their property values. One criterion was the racial and ethnic mix of the neighborhood. The agency considered neighborhoods with more minorities riskier (as it did consider lending to minorities generally). The government designated these places in red on the FHA maps, hence the term "redlining." Figure 1.6 shows the redlining map of Philadelphia in 1937. A comparison with the 2010 Philadelphia map looks eerily similar. The darker areas—designated undesirable for lending—almost exactly mirror the census tracts with majority black populations today.[15] While arguably understandable in financial terms—the areas dominated by minorities had older dwellings, more multifamily structures, and higher crime rates—the result was unfortunate: people now conflated race with lower property values. Neighborhood racial integration could actually lower a person's net worth. This put individual buyers and sellers in a difficult position where racial intolerance and/or financial prudence would lead to the same behaviors—it was in the self-interest of both types of people to keep minorities out of their neighborhood.

In an oft-recounted scenario referred to as "blockbusting," an all-white middle-class urban neighborhood with moderate home values gets its first black family and opportunistic real estate agents take notice. Playing on the

Figure 1.6. 1937 Philadelphia Redlining Map

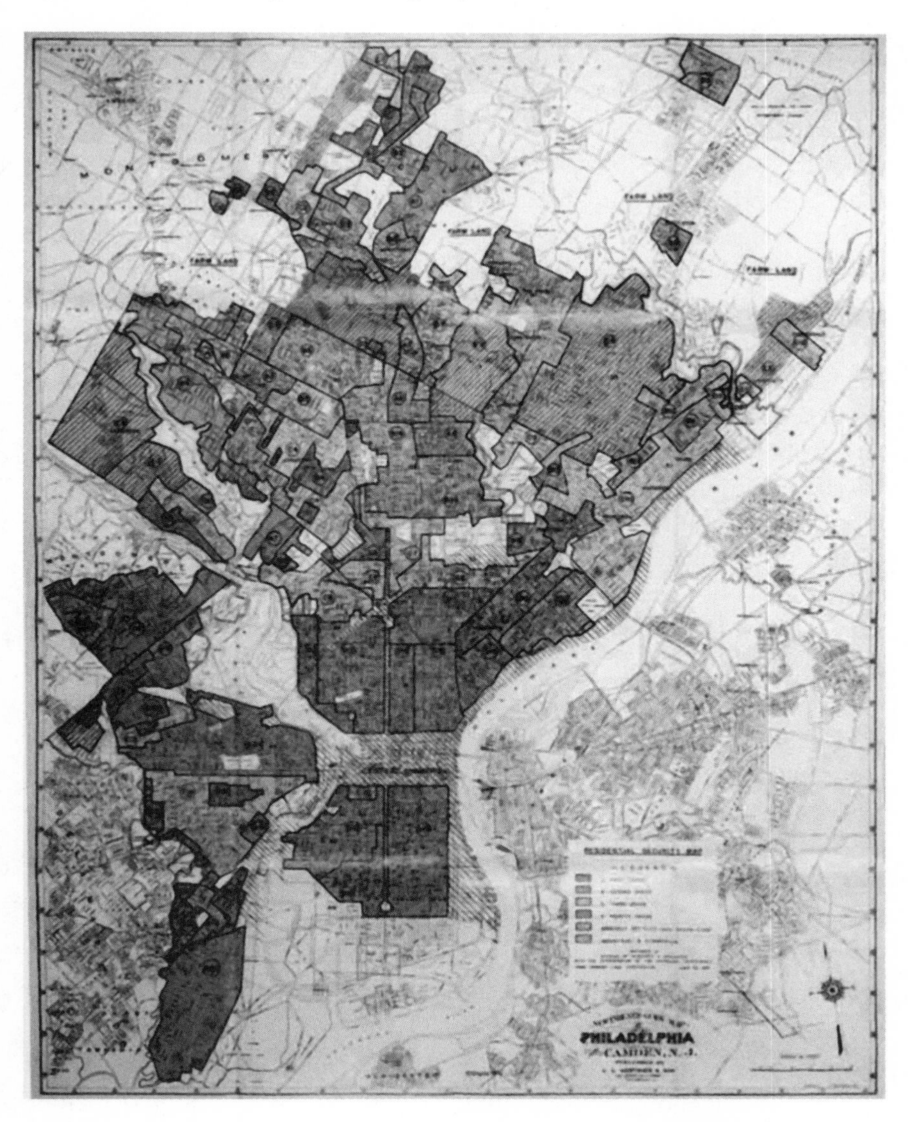

Source: Sharp (2012), thesocietypages.org/socimages/2012/04/25/1934-philadelphia-redlining-map/.

racial fears of residents, and the governmental signal that integration is fiscally detrimental, the agents approach the next-door neighbors of the black family and offer to buy their house at 100 percent of its current value. The neighbors accept the offer. The agents then sell the house to another black family at a modest profit. They then go to the next house and say, "You see there are two black families now, this neighborhood is 'changing.' You know that blacks bring filth, crime, and loud music with them. Sell your house now before your property value drops!" The agents then offer to buy the house at 80 percent of its value, turn around and sell it to another black family for 100 percent of the value, making a larger profit, then repeat the cycle. On the seller's side, things like steering (where agents push racial and ethnic minorities toward certain neighborhoods) or restricted housing covenants (where sellers agree not to sell to certain races) further made sure the inner-city segregation carried over into the burgeoning suburbs.

This intentional and unintentional racialization has had dire consequences for the subsequent generations of racial and ethnic minorities in two areas in particular: school funding and wealth accumulation. In most jurisdictions, residents fund public schools through property tax valuations. Therefore, districts with more expensive homes receive more funding and can provide a better education for their students. According to the 2012 ACS, 36 percent of houses in the suburbs were valued between $150,000 and $300,000. Only 27 percent of urban houses were worth as much. In the aforementioned Philadelphia MSA, 46.7 percent of the houses fall in the same range compared to 35.5 percent in the urban city. As a result, for the 2012–2013 school year, the Philadelphia city school district spent $6,318 less per pupil than the adjacent Lower Merion school district ($20,173 to $26,491) (openPAgov.org). The second consequence involves the accumulation of wealth. According to the Institute on Assets and Social Policy, "the number of years of homeownership accounts for 27 percent of the relative wealth growth between white and African American families, the largest portion of the growing wealth gap" (Shapiro, Meschede, Osoro 2013, 2).

This sorting has also affected our political system. With African Americans steered into neighborhoods closer to the inner cities, these areas have become much more Democratic while the whiter suburbs are much more Republican. When one's constituents are monolithic on policy issues, like taxes or government services, there is less incentive to compromise. For suburban electoral candidates of any party, this means there is little incentive to embrace a racial agenda.

The racialization of the suburbs has entrenched the racial hierarchy and geographic separation in America and affects aspects of peoples' lives from education to wealth accumulation to even political compromise. Hence, suburban African Americans are living in a previously unwelcoming environment where individual feelings and systemic politics have left them in the minority racially and politically.

A BRIEF HISTORY OF THE AFRICAN AMERICAN SUBURBANITE

African Americans' suburbanization followed a very different path than that of whites after World War II. The growing economy afforded African Americans job opportunities, like skilled trades, yet they were not able to translate these resources into suburban life outside of the city boundaries (Pattillo-McCoy 2000). Blacks moving into the middle class increasingly came to occupy what scholars refer to as "black belt" suburbs. These neighborhoods were adjacent to the historic inner-city areas but consisted of more single-family housing (Haynes 2001). The residents of those areas were also of a considerably lower income level than those in the white, government-subsidized suburbs (Schneider and Phelan 1993).[16]

Mary Pattillo-McCoy describes this evolution and its consequences in her 2000 book *Black Picket Fences* about the Chicago black belt suburb of Groveland. Two disparate environments confronted blacks who were able to move into these black belt suburbs. Occupationally, they held top-tier status by having college educations, working in professions, and owning businesses (Pattillo-McCoy 2000; Haynes 2001). They were able to afford their children extracurricular activities, unattainable even for poorer whites, like learning instruments or attending cotillion ceremonies. At the same time, they realized that economic gains did not translate into mainstream access or its privileges. They were still second-class and received harsh, even violent, treatment with impunity (Brooks 2005). This duality was likely more apparent because they still shared many institutions with their coethnics, like black churches and volunteer organizations. Black belt suburban African Americans did not respond to socioeconomic mobility by creating parallel (and more proximate) institutions, as their newly emancipated coethnics had done in the past. Instead, they directed their resources toward those places they had always relied on and supported, infusing them with new skill sets that would serve the community well when the group needed political mobilization.

Even though they had succeeded by society's metrics, they were not accepted into the (white) mainstream. Instead, they developed a unique community, essentially with one foot in each environment. One strategy for navigating these two different worlds was "code-switching" (Pattillo-McCoy 2000, 9), where one's language and mannerisms would change depending on the racial makeup of the environment. An example of the practice is using slang in majority black settings and "proper" grammar in others. Pattillo-McCoy uses this as an example of "the different worlds that whites and blacks inhabit, even African Americans with well-paying jobs or a college degree" (9). This behavioral norm produced a black middle class suburban subculture that was a mixture of "strong cultural traditions [and] economic resources" (9). One of the major points of *Black Picket Fences* is that these early 1990s African Americans navigated the discordant tugs of class and group ties, but the author concludes that high-status blacks' commitment to the traditional black agenda had not waned and that they translated this identification into analogous participation.

A year later, Bruce Haynes published *Red Lines, Black Spaces* (2001). Haynes was essentially studying the same demographic population in a markedly similar geographic environment just four states to the east: the Runyon Heights suburb of Yonkers, New York, just ten miles north of the Bronx borough in New York City. The focus of Haynes's book was also African Americans in the black belt suburbs. However, Haynes dealt more with the *divergence* of class and racial interests. He opens the book by providing a definition of community that I believe is still applicable to suburban African American populations—both what they are moving away from and what they are longing for once lost. He says that community implies more than just "place." The community is also the personal connections between people (in different geographic locations) and the historical ties that bind them. This broader sense of community is "structured, filtered, and interpreted through local institutions . . . [families, churches, schools, political organizations, voluntary civic associations] . . . , forming a multidimensional basis for group consciousness and the articulation of group political interests" (xxvii). He echoes Pattillo-McCoy's sentiment in that this community is characterized by higher resource levels, yet deprived of an unencumbered locational attainment by segregation and racial animosity.

This dual separation from suburban whites and urban African Americans fostered a unique group consciousness and solidarity. However, the shared racial identity did not preclude class divisions among the middle-class suburbanites and the lower-class blacks from the nearby historic neighborhood. Haynes describes conflicts over political representation. When the suburbanites felt being included in a district with the poorer blacks would dilute their political clout, they opposed things like plans to build lower-income housing in their neighborhood (see also Johnson 2002).

This class separation appears to be evidence of "the declining significance of race," as articulated by William Julius Wilson in his 1978 book of the same name (see also Wilson 2011). Wilson suggested that SES increases by only one segment of the black population would cause middle-class blacks to focus more on class than race. Haynes (and most subsequent research) refutes this postulate with evidence of the suburbanites' social pursuits. He describes how years earlier a long-standing neighborhood institution, the Nepperhan Community Center, moved to the majority African American area of Yonkers in order to qualify for public funding and serve more African Americans. This move did not prevent the suburbanites from using the center or its services; in fact, it heightened their racial consciousness.

> For Nepperhan residents, however, the relocation meant a trip across town to use the facility. But Nepperhaners appear to have accepted a political identification and responsibility that transcended their material self-interest. Locked into a common fate with the working class, Nepperhaners maintained the identification with the tradition of Negro uplift. Just as residents supported the rebuilding of the Nepperhan Community Center on the West side, they later became active participants and leaders in institutions like the NAACP and the YMCA, which served the black population of Yonkers (Haynes 2001, 84).

Here, the suburban African Americans are sacrificing convenience for the ability to aid less fortunate members of their extended community. They appear divided along class lines on some issues, yet in solidarity with coethnics on others. Haynes provides examples where the suburbanites' civic clubs and social/fraternal organizations would raise funds for scholarships directed at the black inner-city community. These acts laid "the groundwork for local political mobilization. . . . Social organizations gave residents a sense of having an interconnected history and future. . . . Without [which], no central community identity, racial or otherwise, would have developed" (73). One of the primary aims of this project is to bring quantitative data to this question of when the groups are together and when they split.

Written during the same time, Valerie Johnson's *Black Power in the Suburbs* (2002) provides insight into how these black suburbanites navigate class differences in their local political environment. The question for Johnson is very similar to that of Haynes; however, Johnson focuses her work on the confluence of spatial geography and racial demography. She compares the lower SES African Americans who live in the black belts, the higher SES blacks living closer to the exurbs, and the whites who have remained in these suburban neighborhoods following the white flight of the 1970s and 1980s. She finds that the white power structure exacerbated and manipulated opposing interests between the different African American classes, hindering political incorporation.

The book is set in Prince George's County, Maryland, an area east of Washington, D.C. Based on income and education levels, Prince George's is the most affluent concentration of suburban blacks in the country. More interesting (and perfect for the study of suburban politics) is that this affluence is adjacent to a lower SES black belt on the Maryland and Washington, D.C., border. Both of these black subgroups are struggling for political power against a white establishment whose numbers are dwindling due to white flight yet who maintain control over the majority of municipal offices.

Johnson wonders when class interests will trump racial interests, and more specifically, what types of issues will bring each identity to the fore? In order to exert their collective prerogatives, the author says the African American community must unify. The group will base this unity on their collective identity and group consciousness, which are the primary organizational resources needed to achieve their aims (12). Yet she challenges the idea that the African American community is a monolith, suggesting that terms like "black agenda" or "black community" gloss over the nuances between African Americans of differing SES.[17]

Johnson finds that more often than not, the more affluent African American community of Prince George's and those closer to Washington, D.C., are not united. She finds that the lack of unity is in fact highly dependent on the policy in question. When issues are explicitly racial, or focus broadly on civil rights, African Americans are in accord. Questions of class are not as simple. On class considerations, the author suggests that each community is not opposed to "subordinating" their interests in favor of their coethnics (6); however, community elites must articulate the benefits of doing so. In the instances where the community does not gel, it is the black political leaders who are not in sync.

Through her interviews with elites and voters, Johnson finds that this disunity among elites is often a result of political alliances with the white power structure or pure self-interest and personal gain. Very rarely does this disagreement flow from opposing signals within the rank and file. The words of Albert Wynn, who represented the more affluent black population, crystalizes this disunity and the policies upon which it is based: "the interests of the more affluent African Americans in the county, 'puts them at odds with the older African American community who are concerned with subsidized housing and job programs'" (100). I will test these questions quantitatively in the chapters to come.

BUILDING ON THE RESEARCH OF SUBURBAN AFRICAN AMERICAN POLITICAL BEHAVIOR

These three books are among the most exemplary and ambitious treatments of the suburban African American experience to date. They are invaluable because of their empirical designs and their temporal place, right on the cusp of the black SES increases described earlier. However, there are places where they fall short. I designed this project to fill in those gaps and go further by introducing new research questions and hypotheses to study this evolving population.

One important weakness is simply the time period. All three of these books describe populations who have changed socioeconomically and geographically since the authors collected their data. In SES terms, the suburban African American population was just emerging from the struggle of the civil rights movement and settling into their new northern and urban environments following the Second Great Migration. They were about to increase their life situations through middle-class jobs concentrated in the manufacturing and government sectors; however, society capped that improvement via the explicit exclusion of blacks and other racial and ethnic minorities from certain neighborhoods. The original survey instrument that will serve as the main data for this project, collected in 2008, is one of the most recent datasets available for this population. I also ask respondents about their suburban residence, which will be used to analyze feelings about social networks, the coethnic community, and political participation.

Less problematic than the dated nature of the data is its ethnographic format. In fact, it may be the best design for early treatments as it sacrifices generalizability for in-depth description of under-theorized questions. Ethnography is also good at examining variables that do not lend themselves to numerical quantification. For example, Johnson (2002) measures the relationship between SES, African American identity, and types of policies. In addition to discussing the specific policy issues, she also includes other "internal variables," such as the African American population size and the organizational resources within the community (8). The latter is a very broad concept that does not lend itself to obvious operationalization. Qualitative interviews can alleviate many internal validity problems[18] because the researcher can explain complex concepts, answer questions, or provide background information. Additionally, if a subject reveals an interesting (or omitted) variable in a later interview, the interviewer can recontact previous subjects for follow-up questions. The total universe of respondents also shrinks when elites are the source of data, so acquiring respondents based on convenience or ease of access is not as much of a methodological design flaw as a problem of external validity—the representativeness of the data limits the capacity to generalize.

The nature of the target population makes ethnography especially beneficial in this situation. Simple random national samples will not have robust representations of suburban African Americans. These small samples make statistical modeling particularly data-taxing—a problem I encountered in this project. To attain a critical mass of any type of African American, early national surveys employed geographic cluster sampling and focused on majority black neighborhoods since it was four times more expensive to find blacks in majority white neighborhoods (Jackson 1987; Tate 2004). The qualitative approach makes finding the geographic minorities easier. Researchers can identify them via snowball samples, where they ask respondents to provide the contact information of others like them.[19] Finally, for understudied populations, or subfields in the theory-building process, extensive ethnographies can serve as a good starting point for subsequent research by providing data on a number of disparate dimensions that researchers can quantitatively test later.

The major drawback of these types of studies is their lack of external validity. Interviews are generally not statistically generalizable to other populations with the same characteristics, and the method of administration may be less than systematic.[20] All of the surveys used for this project are nationally representative; therefore, I can extrapolate conclusions to U.S. citizens with the same demographics. Technically, the previous suburban African American studies are only representative of blacks in Chicago's Southside, the suburbs of New York, and Prince George's County, Maryland. It is highly likely that those three locales are similar to one another and to other metropolitan areas with sizable black populations, yet not every black metro resident had a statistically measurable chance of selection.

The final qualm with the previous research on suburban African Americans is that it is not explicitly political. The fields of sociology and anthropology have been invaluable for this project and provide many of the citations and assumptions for the theory. While they do address political variables and concepts, their primary aim is not to explain the political behaviors of individuals, the psychological mechanisms that affect them, or how the suburban environment influences both.

That said, there are common threads between these studies and this one, and this project does more to complement and build on earlier studies than to challenge their findings. This study centers on three primary goals in contrast to this literature. First, I will quantitatively test some of the concepts found in the previous qualitative research. Second, the study will update our picture of suburban African Americans to account for the SES gains and locational mobility that influence their political behavior decisions. Lastly, I seek to unpack the effects that social network racial makeup, feelings toward the coethnic institutions and ideologies in the coethnic community, and suburban political jurisdictions have on black political participation. I believe the theory-building nature of this project and the conclusions it draws will provide race and ethnicity scholars, and those studying political behavior generally, new theories and hypotheses for subsequent research on this burgeoning population and other minority populations following similar paths.

DATASETS

Three datasets will provide the empirical analysis: the 2008 Cooperative Congressional Election Study (CCES), the 2008 American National Election Study (ANES), and the 2004 National Politics Study (NPS). I chose these studies because they are the most recent and relevant. More recent surveys capture the socioeconomic gains of contemporary African Americans that have been allowed more access to the majority white suburbs. I attribute the unique political behaviors of suburban African Americans to this geographic shift. These datasets are particularly relevant because they deal specifically with suburban residence, social networks, and the black counterpublic spaces. Unfortunately, the numbers of suburban African Americans in each survey is below their representation in the actual electorate, so in some instances statistical analysis does not show statistically significant differences between the groups.

2008 Cooperative Congressional Election Study (CCES)

The CCES was a cooperative effort between the YouGov/Polimetrix polling firm and thirty-one universities and foundations. Each team contributed to the common content module and received fifteen minutes of original instrumentation on one thousand respondents. The content was combined with another module, to include a total of two thousand respondents. The University of Texas content of the CCES was specifically designed to assess the effect of suburban residence on racial opinions, social network interactions, views of the cultural community, and political behavior. Using the CCES presents two potential issues. I mention these not because I have problems with its use, but because the reader should be aware of them when evaluating the conclusions drawn in subsequent chapters. First, the CCES was an Internet survey. Traditionally, this means the respondent pool will have a higher SES and lower minority representation than is found in the population. However, this problem is not unique to the CCES, it is found in all survey designs. Due to an innovative sample matching technique, the CCES boasts response rates on par with more familiar random-digit-dialing telephone methods. For this analysis, suburban African Americans make up 41.6 percent of blacks in the dataset, a number slightly below census estimates, and just 4.4 percent of the entire dataset.[21]

Second, I designed some of the questions specifically for this project and therefore they have not had the reliability checks of questions repeated for more than sixty years, as with the ANES. A key question is that of suburban residence. As stated earlier, even objective definitions of the suburbs differ.

In the CCES, suburban residence is self-reported (as opposed to the ANES, where it is determined by the interviewer); therefore, the measure may not correspond with the geographic definition employed in the opening chapter. However, the self-reporting may actually be more valid. Individuals on the outskirts of the city who do all of their extracurricular activities outside of the city limits may feel (and therefore behave) like suburbanites, even if the census would not designate them as such.

2008 American National Election Study (ANES)

The 2008 ANES will supplement the CCES as it directly addresses the previous two concerns. A collaboration between Stanford University and the University of Michigan, the 2008 ANES included an oversample of blacks and Latinos to explicitly combat the lack of representation in previous designs. A full 25 percent of the 2,322 respondents are black (569). When broken down by neighborhood, 8.2 percent (191) are suburban African Americans. Having more than twice the targeted respondents allows for a more forgiving test of statistical significance. The survey has also been administered for more than sixty years, and many of the same questions were included in each iteration. It will serve as the primary instrument for the multivariate tests to assess the independent effects of suburban racial status on political participation.

2004 National Politics Study (NPS)

Conducted by scholars James Jackson, Vincent Hutchings, Ronald Brown, and Cara Wong, the focus of the NPS was on opinions in the larger African diaspora. As such, it oversamples blacks, particularly those of Afro-Caribbean descent. Of the 3,339 telephone-interviewed respondents, 756 are African Americans. Only African American respondents will be used in the comparisons. The survey also includes relevant questions on race and racial policy, including innovative questions about the racial makeup of different social networks. This includes those proximate (neighborhood and workplace) and self-selecting (church). The NPS will be used to test the social network hypotheses.

A NOTE ABOUT COMPARING ONLY AFRICAN AMERICANS AND WHITES

The racial diversification of America has brought new minority groups to the fore of our society, politics, and political science. Latinos have already overtaken African Americans as the country's largest minority group, and the gap will continue to widen. One can make the case that a work on race and ethnicity that leaves them (and Asian Americans) out is incomplete. While I recognize the validity of such an argument, I reject that claim. While it is true that most of the early work on race and ethnicity focused on the black-white binary, that does not mean scholars of any stripe have conclusively answered the questions. Additionally, the previous studies used whites as the main comparison group, and if this study is to speak to that literature, it should do the same. It is also obvious that the two groups have evolved in their relationships with one another, so a contemporary examination will do much to advance our knowledge on the subject.

Early work in Latino and Asian American politics (by necessity) took the theories borne of this binary environment and tried to apply them to their particular group. However, it soon became apparent that this was inadequate. Simply being a minority was not enough to explain the social relationships with the mainstream, the placement of certain groups, and subgroups, on the racial hierarchy, or their political behaviors. I have aimed this project at a group of people who are increasingly moving into majority white networks. With such movement comes a host of interactions, most of them against the backdrop of systematic discrimination and exclusion that was a remnant of whites having enslaved their ancestors. While I believe these theories are applicable to other minorities generally, the specifics, especially the role of the black counterpublic institutions and the evolution of a black-specific ideology, warrant an in-depth examination. This is in no way to devalue the experiences of suburban Latinos or Asian Americans, just to say that those experiences are different.

On racial questions, blacks and whites are always at the opposite extremes, with Latinos and Asian Americans somewhere in the middle. Countless studies have shown that whites have a much greater affinity toward all other major racial and ethnic groups than they do blacks. In the literature discussed in the next chapter, whites would rather live in white-Asian or white-Latino neighborhoods at much higher rates than white-black ones (Dixon 2006). The presence of blacks in white neighborhoods even makes some whites dislike their jobs (Brief et al. 2005).

This black-white binary is still very much the reality. By far, most blacks have majority black social networks; however, the next most frequent types all have this binary. Via the 2004 NPS, the next highest racial makeup for African Americans' friend groups is black-white (17.9 percent, versus 50 percent all black). In the neighborhood, the second highest category is a black-white neighborhood (9.9 percent, versus 56.7 percent all black; 8 percent are in all white neighborhoods). In the workplace, 23.7 percent of African Americans work in majority white settings versus 25.2 percent all black. This project is depicting a certain (peculiar but prevalent) environment. It asks unanswered questions and uses methods never before tested on these populations. As such, I believe it worthy to proceed in this course.

CHAPTER SUMMARY

The remainder of the chapters will proceed as follows: Chapter 2 will lay out the theoretical foundation for the hypotheses to be tested in the empirical chapters that follow. The focus will be on the relevant literatures that describe how suburban African Americans come to their participation decisions. The chapter will pay special attention to how African Americans form their racial identity and how identity is cultivated into the idea that political action is the best way to help the group or group consciousness (Miller et al. 1981). It will also show how these group distinctions influence residential segregation and perceptions of other groups. It will proceed to recount the previous research on social networks, particularly how minority status and having disagreeable discussion partners affects political behavior. From there it will discuss the cultural communities of African Americans and how their historic institutions, like the black church, advance group-conscious norms. The chapter will end with the literature on political participation, particularly the costs and benefits associated with different behaviors and how they may be used to reinforce racial identity based on one's neighborhood.

Chapter 3 will focus on social networks, including how the racial makeup of suburban African Americans' networks will determine whether they view them as welcoming networks or ones that may be hostile to their racial identities. Using independent sample t-tests (means tests) to compare averages by race and neighborhood on certain questions and ordered logistic regressions, the data show that African Americans in white neighborhoods have lower trust in various societal institutions when compared to whites in white neighborhoods. They also have very different opinions on racialized issues, like whether blacks have gotten less than they deserve from society and whether blacks face discrimination. Finally, the chapter shows that suburban African Americans do indeed think their personal views are different from those of other people in their neighborhoods and workplaces but more in line with members of their churches.

Chapter 4 will build on chapter 3 and ask where suburban African Americans will find reinforcing networks if they do not feel comfortable in their neighborhoods and workplaces. Using the same tests as the previous chapter, it will examine how often suburban African Americans travel to their cultural community and whether they actively view these areas as places where they should direct their political activity. It will also use the ideological framework of Michael Dawson (2001, 2012) to test how racially radical suburban African Americans are. While suburban African Americans do not use their cultural communities more often than suburban whites and urban African Americans (both of whom presumably live in their cultural communities), they do participate in them at a substantial rate. Suburban African Americans with strong racial identities and those that attend black churches participate more in the community than suburban African Americans with lower identity or who do not attend black churches. As to ideology, I find that suburban African Americans are not at the most racially radical end of the spectrum, but they are quite skeptical of America's commitment to diversity and racial equality.

Chapter 5 asks whether the feelings about disagreeable social networks and racially reinforcing cultural communities produce a unique strand of political behavior. It begins by affirming one of my central hypotheses about suburban African American political participation—that they do not feel comfortable in their congressional districts and therefore do not participate in them. They do not have any differences in their acquisition of political information with suburban whites and slight differences with urban African Americans. However, suburban African Americans with high racial identity do report more interest in politics, interest in the news, and read the newspaper more often. These rates are higher than those of suburban African Americans with low racial identity and even urban African Americans with high racial identity. As to actual participation, there is no difference between the groups in presidential voting, but suburban African Americans are less likely to vote in House of Representatives elections. Individual suburban African Americans with high racial identity are even more likely to have voted for president and skipped the House race, even though the amount of effort required to cast such a vote is almost nonexistent since the individual is already in the voting booth. As expected, suburban African Americans are also more likely to engage in alternative political behaviors that they can better target toward their racial group.

Chapter 6 will summarize the findings, suggest possible future avenues for research on suburban African Americans, and discuss the implications of the data for both the study of race and ethnicity and our understanding of race and geography in American society.

2. How Suburban African Americans Fit into Our Social Science Theories

This chapter will lay out the theoretical foundation for the arguments presented in the remainder of the book. There are many robust literatures that are related to the theory, but which were not specifically crafted toward suburban African Americans. The extant research examines identity, residential status, social network minority status, and group-based political behavior. However, none of this scholarship deals with the confluence of all these things in one population. This chapter will attempt to pull together all of these disparate literatures and formulate several hypotheses about how suburban African Americans make political choices and decisions.

The chapter will proceed as follows. It begins with a discussion of identity formation—specifically, why one would choose a particular demographic as his or her primary identity. It then moves to relations between whites and blacks using the framework of *Social Identity Theory* (Tajfel 1981), which attributes much of the conflict to people sorting themselves into "in-groups" and "out-groups." This affinity for one's group leads to the idea of group consciousness, the feeling that one's fate is tied to the societal perception of the larger group and therefore political participation should be directed toward the larger group, even at the sacrifice of some self-interest (Miller et al. 1981). African Americans typically register high levels of group consciousness or linked fate (Dawson 1994), because of the pervasive legacy of slavery and discrimination.

The chapter then moves on to discuss the influence of environment on behavior, particularly the influence of the type of people in an individual's social network and how certain demographics interact with one another (Huckfeldt, Plutzer, and Sprague 1993). Again, African Americans are in a unique position because they have less control than other groups over their residential environment and their neighbors. This is particularly true when African Americans try to move into white neighborhoods, as white respondents are less likely to want African American neighbors compared to Latino or Asian American neighbors (Dixon 2006). Next, it will discuss how the special context of the suburbs influences these environmental effects—specifically, how mainstream society created the suburbs to maintain racial segregation and separate resources from struggling (and increasingly minority-dominated) municipalities (Oliver 2001).

In addition to one's neighbors, social networks like the workplace or the church one decides to attend affect things like identity and group consciousness. This discussion will move to the influence of these networks on information acquisition and ultimately behavior. It will focus on the idea of homophily (Kossinets and Watts 2009; Smith, McPhereson, and Smith-Lovin 2014), which states that people prefer being in groups with others like them. This means that African Americans in majority white neighborhoods and workplaces may feel uncomfortable and seek out networks where they have more control over the racial makeups of the members, such as a historic organization working for black uplift or a black church. The chapter will then discuss the research on each of these networks and how they affect suburban African American political behavior. It will then move to a more explicit discussion of these majority African American networks and their geographic concentration, known as counterpublic spaces (Squires 2002; Dawson 2012). These areas and institutions were consciously created by African Americans to counteract their exclusion from similar mainstream institutions. Examples include fraternal organizations like the Prince Hall Freemasons. The chapter will also trace the prevalence and importance of these spaces from their creation after emancipation to their contemporary manifestations. It will then move to a discussion of the African American–specific ideologies found in these spaces and within African American individual opinions. It will place particular emphasis on the stratification of these ideologies over how to improve the lives and social standing of African Americans. Some of these ideologies, such as forming a separate black nation, are more radical than others.

The chapter will end with a recounting of the literature on African American political participation generally and what that literature may be able to tell us about how suburban African Americans will react to things like suburban politics and social network racial makeup. The extant literature has not addressed these questions, particularly using a quantitative methodology. I expect that suburban African Americans, who spend most of their time in majority white settings, will seek out those counterpublic spaces. The norms they will receive there will privilege group-based participation. This appears to be the case, as suburban African Americans are less likely to vote in their House districts but more likely to engage in alternative participatory behaviors, like attending a community meeting, which can be more directed toward the group.

The path suburban African Americans take to their ultimate participatory decisions will be one of pushes and pulls. Their racial minority status starts them at the bottom rung of the social ladder, but as they acquire more income and education they can move into better neighborhoods. Unfortunately, this means majority white social networks like the neighborhoods and workplaces that are not reinforcing to their racial identity. This environment will push them toward majority African American networks and institutions that have a history of black uplift where they can acquire group-based norms. In the end, these disparate environments adjust their participatory calculus away from simple voting and toward group-based activities that will be more rewarding.

THE FORMATION AND CONSEQUENCES OF RACIAL IDENTITY AND CONSCIOUSNESS

Identity is integral to an individual's political behaviors because it determines with whom one feels a kinship. These similarities often structure political competition. The bases of this kinship are important because the government allocates resources based on certain demographics and oftentimes policies disproportionately affect certain groups.

There are many identities open to an individual, most of which are not mutually exclusive. The same person can be an African American, a college graduate, self-employed, and a hunter. This individual can identify with any of these four characteristics. Yet some identities are more salient than others[1] and therefore more influential on political behavior. The political realities of competition over resource allocation influence these identities and their salience. These cleavages will exert an independent influence on identity choice because political success often requires collective action. Our college graduate may love fishing more than anyone in the country, but if the election deals with student loans we should expect that the educational identity may have more influence than reducing river pollution on his or her vote.

Therefore, it would make sense that the most salient identities will be those that are most durable in society *and* politics. The most durable of these identities for African Americans is race. For as long (if not longer) as the government has made policies based on social status, it has made hard distinctions based on race. These distinctions most often hurt the group holding minority status. Granted, there is no reason to think that a particular racial identity presupposes a political affiliation. However, for African Americans, the confluence of harmful governmental policies and private discrimination has meant their racial minority status almost always overlaps with lower-class economic status. Hence, policies directed at particular classes may have a disparate racial impact (which will inevitably trigger feelings among black voters that these policies fit into the category of maintaining a racial hierarchy, even though they could be rooted in the simple, and appropriate, competition over finite resources). When identity and political preference (for example, redistributive- or affirmative action–type policies) overlap, then a group member's political strategies may be inseparable from his or her identity.

For suburban African Americans, racial minority status and lower-class status do not overlap. However, if racial identity is the most salient, their political behaviors may track more with their racial preferences, even if it goes against their economic self-interest. A trove of data shows this to be the case for higher SES African Americans generally (Dawson 1994; Tate 1994). Not only do I expect suburban African Americans to fit this pattern, but I expect that spending most of their time in majority white networks will make racial identity even more salient, which will be manifest in their opinions and behaviors.

Leonie Huddy (2013) points out that racial group *membership* is different from racial *identification* because race itself is fluid. The fact that there is no biological basis for race, and that a person can be two, three, or four races concurrently, means individuals can choose how much, or even with which race, they choose to identify.[2] Therefore, Huddy defines group identification as a "more restrictive, subjective, and internalized sense of group belonging" (738), something that requires more than simple membership. The shift to using political strategies to achieve group gains then makes it a political identity (Huddy 2013).

Identity Formation

For the purposes of this study, perceived racial minority status is the primary criteria for self-categorization. The extent of one's racial identification determines reactions to social and political stimuli. A major aspect is whether this identity belongs to the mainstream (in-group) or is of marginalized status (out-group).[3] Henri Tajfel developed Social Identity Theory (SIT) in his 1981 book *Human Groups and Social Categories.* For Tajfel, identity formation depends on one's place on the social ladder. Those of the higher positioned in-group are able to attach positive qualities to group membership, while those of the lower status out-group have to work harder to find favorable characteristics attributed to their group. This search for validation is important because maintenance of the hierarchy depends on one group being "better" than another.

For most of American history, phenotype and country/region of origin have served as the major dividers between in- and out-group status. Since the mainstream power structure ascribed blacks an out-group status, they have to rally around each other and reshape the definitions of positive-valued group attributes (Huddy 2013, 740). The in-group has an incentive to make anything attributed to the out-group seem negative, especially things inherent to the group, such as skin color or hair texture. This allows arbitrary distinctions to be easily recognized and grounded in some "reality." We see this through negative stereotypes attached to African American hairstyles, dress, and music genres. Some things are so stereotyped that they signal more than just race, they signal character and behavior (as with hooded sweatshirts and criminality).

The nature of American political competition also necessitates adherence to group norms. African Americans' smaller absolute size as a group means any defection by subgroups will lessen the already low chance of influencing the government. Therefore, the group must agree on policies and strategies for their realization. The obvious issues of most agreement will be those that affect the most group members. Therefore, African Americans with higher than average SES may have to subvert their self-interest to realize the group's goals. Later sections will show this to be the case throughout history, and the empirical findings in chapters 3 through 5 will show that this is still the case.

From Identity to Group Consciousness

In their landmark 1981 article, "Group Consciousness and Political Participation," Arthur Miller and his colleagues say that identity alone is insufficient to explain how disadvantaged groups engage in cohesive political behaviors at levels higher than their socioeconomic status would predict (see also Chong and Rogers 2005). Group-conscious individuals must couple identity with a strategy for political action to influence government. Through this process, identity transitions into group consciousness. For African Americans, the cohesiveness of their preferences is based on the group's position at the bottom of the social hierarchy.

Two seminal books, Katherine Tate's *From Protest to Politics* (1994) and Michael Dawson's *Behind the Mule* (1994), found that Miller et al.'s group consciousness fits African Americans very well. The robust empirical findings in those studies were impactful and groundbreaking because they came from one of the few nationally representative, black-only surveys ever produced. Not only did both studies find high levels of group consciousness, but African Americans had a particular variant. Tate (1994) showed that as black political participation matured, transitioning from strategies of "protest to politics," the salience of race remained and trumped other demographics. Dawson (1994) articulates this as the *black utility heuristic.* "The more one believes one's own life chances are linked to those of blacks as a group, the more one will consider racial group interests in evaluating alternative political choices" (75). The heuristic is firmly rooted in Social Identity Theory and group consciousness. African American respondents categorized people into in- and out-groups and based their political behaviors on societal attributions of blame for inequalities. For Dawson, the mechanism that privileges group-based participation is derived from "the historical experiences of African Americans [that have] resulted in a situation in which group interests have served as a useful proxy for self-interest" (77). He finds that "linked fate"—whether the respondent feels as though what happens generally to the black people in the country has something to do with what happens in his or her life—does not vary much by class.

To this point, I have been using the terms "identity" and "group consciousness" somewhat interchangeably because the two necessarily flow from one another, especially using Dawson's conception. Once confronted with *political* choices,[4] identity becomes consciousness. Methodologically, I measure group consciousness or linked fate in the same way as Dawson and those who followed: how much respondents think what happens to other members of their race affects them. To investigate further the salience of racial identity, I asked an open-ended identity question in the CCES (see table 2.1). I asked respondents to choose the group to which they felt closest between their gender, class, race/ethnicity, profession/union, and an "other" category. This conceptualization does not explicitly prime race—in fact, it primes alternative identities, which should increase the chance a respondent will select one of them,

Table 2.1. Group Closeness by Race and Neighborhood

	Race	*Gender*	*Profession*	*Class*
Suburban African American	46% (0.501) 87	15.8% (0.367) 87	9.5% (0.295) 87	16.4% (0.373) 87
Suburban White	17%** (0.372) 583	25.9%* (0.438) 583	14.5% (0.352) 583	25%+ (0.433) 583
Urban African American	44% (0.500) 67	11.3% (0.319) 67	7.4% (0.264) 67	24.3% (0.432) 67

Levels of Significance: ** = 0.01; * = 0.05; + = 0.10

Source: 2008 Cooperative Congressional Election Study.

since every respondent identifies with each category in some way. The salience of race for African Americans is clear. A full 46 percent of suburban African Americans chose race as their closest group. For whites, only 17 percent chose race, a statistically significant difference. The two highest identifications for whites, gender (25.9 percent) and class (25.1 percent), were statistically significantly higher than the same identifications for suburban blacks.

Socialization and the Salience of Race

The obvious question is why racial identity is so salient for African Americans. According to the literature, it begins in childhood. David Sears and Christia Brown (2013) describe how racial orientations are formed from childhood to adulthood. What is most surprising is how early these racial orientations crystalize. Children endorse racial stereotypes and racial biases as early as age three, even before they can identify their own race or ethnicity. Black children hold a preference for white peers until about age six, after which they begin preferring coethnic playmates. African American children at this age (and racial and ethnic minorities generally) are "more likely to mention their ethnicity . . . and consider it more central to their sense of self. This [racial identity] is heavily influenced by social context—school in this case—as their identities develop earlier than for whites" (Sears and Brown 2013, 66). By age ten, children of all races show a preference for members of their own group (5). If children who are not even out of elementary school show an affinity for members of their own race, it should not be a stretch to think an African American adult walking into a majority white workplace will feel out of place and may not as readily look to coworkers as friends, much less as sources of political information (Hochschild 1996).

Racial identity stabilizes around adolescence. Expressions of outright racial stereotypes begin to decline and the individual begins to recognize a racial hierarchy in society. Individuals also begin to attach stereotypes to particular policies, such as affirmative action (Sears and Brown 2013, 7). This all comes together by high school. A person will see himself or herself as a member of a racial group, recognize the group's place in society, and begin evaluating public policies on how they help or hurt their group. This persists, in part, because the environment has repeatedly subjected the individual to information about race and appropriate behavioral practices (Sears and Brown 2013, 10).

For African Americans specifically, William Cross (1991) calls this temporal evolution *Nigrescence.* For Cross, one's childhood or adult identity is not explicitly racialized (*pre-encounter*) until confronted with a situation where society views a person as black (*encounter*) and the person must make the decision to embrace that identity characterization (or not) (*immersion*), then translates it from an identity to a lifestyle. For Cross this will be Afro-centrism—one of the more radical types of racial ideology.

This is the identity and outlook on the world suburban African Americans bring into their neighborhoods and workplaces. They recognize that the world sorts people into groups and their group is near the bottom. Whether individuals embrace the identity or not, society views them as a member of that group and attaches (mostly negative) stereotypes to them. These projections have been planted since childhood and have been solidified through the rejection of dissonant information. Recognizing this, the African American individuals will seek out ways to aid the group's position since the negative view of the collective is harmful to them personally. These actions may persist even if they conflict with the individual's material self-interest. Alleviating the psychological discomfort of being seen as inherently deviant or detrimental to society by supporting government aid to less fortunate (and stigmatized) group members may be more important to the suburban African American than paying less in taxes.

THE INFLUENCE OF ENVIRONMENT ON BEHAVIOR

In the literature, context means that one's surroundings influence their behavior. When it comes to the suburban neighborhood context, research shows that African Americans are less able to translate their income into locational prestige—in other words, they do not live in suburban neighborhoods with interracial neighbors of similar SES (Alba, Logan, and Stults 2000) and when they do move into majority white places they are far from welcomed (Dixon 2006). This environment, where minority status is obvious and in-group members may be hostile, could redouble the suburban African American's view of the world in group-based terms. I hypothesize that it will also prioritize searching for racially reinforcing information and finding racially reinforcing participatory avenues. Individuals can find both of these in reinforcing social network contexts. For Mark Joslyn (1997, 343), a network is reinforcing when there is a correspondence between predispositions (identity) and stimulus content (racial makeup of the social context) (see also Huckfeldt and Sprague 1995). When strong racial identity combines with a group-based information environment in a positive way, a network has high utility.

Huckfeldt et al. (1993, 366) describe the importance of social context this way: "Contextual theories of politics build on the argument that individual political preference is not a simple function of individual characteristics alone, but rather the complex product of an individual's own characteristics in combination with the characteristics and predispositions of other surrounding individuals." Winter (2003) describes this as the combination of situational micro and macro contexts. The *microcontext* is the immediate thing one is encountering, like the decision to vote for a candidate or the decision to engage in conversation with a discussion partner. One's reaction to the immediate is dependent on the *macrocontext,* things like race and ethnicity, or religious affiliation. One's racial minority/majority status in the neighborhood acts much like other macrocontextual stimuli in that all members encounter the same microcontext, like having to choose to turn out for an election. However, the reaction to context differs by individual in a predictable way, most often based on one's primary identification.

Three major strands of the neighborhood context literature are most relevant for this project: the exercise of personal choice in neighborhood selection, explanations of why we see persistently segregated neighborhoods, and how these areas affect the opinions and participation of their inhabitants.

Choice in Neighborhood Selection

The evidence is clear, blacks are less able to translate their income and educational levels into commensurate neighborhoods (Adelman 2005). In looking at the average income and educational levels of neighborhood residents, research shows that blacks are more likely to, all things being equal, have higher SES than their white neighbors (Alba, Logan, and Stults 2000). Since we would expect individuals to live around those similar to themselves, high-status blacks must be less able to move into high-status neighborhoods. Scholars attribute much of this inability to discrimination in the real estate and lending industries (Adelman 2005). The level of residential segregation we see today is a result of these practices. However, the exact cause of this continued segregation (on the part of individual movers) is not immediately clear. Two competing hypotheses attempt to explain it. The *spatial assimilation* model posits that racial segregation is due to economic differences between the races, while the *place stratification* model attributes racial segregation to a spatial reflection of the social hierarchy (Fischer 2008).

It is fairly obvious that historic residential patterns followed the place stratification model; however, the removal of structural discrimination must have lessened its influence. Friedman (2008) shows that there have been declines in black-white segregation[5]; however, these declines are not due to more *blacks* living with whites or vice versa. It is because there are more members of *other races* moving into previously biracial areas. Friedman also finds that these new multiethnic neighborhoods are less stable and eventually become majority-minority. Previous research also lends credence to the spatial assimilation model. That blacks cannot access the most prestigious neighborhoods may be because they have lower aggregate median income, as noted in the previous chapter. This may explain the finding that poorer suburbs are more multiracial than more affluent ones (Alba, Logan, and Stults 2000; Adelman 2005; Clark 2007).

The spatial assimilation model is not the first indication that multiple contexts (here, race and class) can overlap and have cumulative (or even conflicting) effects on social interaction (Huckfeldt, Plutzer, and Sprague 1993). Branton and Jones (2005) find that racial diversity and SES are intertwined when examining the racial attitudes of residents. In general, being around more minorities heightens whites' opposition to racialized policies. However, this effect is contingent on SES—particularly education. When whites live in a neighborhood context with larger numbers of educated blacks, they feel less racial threat and show less opposition to racialized policies. Of course, this says nothing about their perceptions of blacks and is contingent on the accurate recognition of neighborhood black education levels (see also Alba et al. 2000).

Neighborhood Integration and Racial Threat

The demographics of the larger area, one's own demographic characteristics, and the treatment a person receives from neighbors heavily influences the psychological reaction to one's residential environment (Gay 2004; Oliver 2010). Much of this reaction comes from the historic position one's group has occupied in American society, in this case placement on the racial hierarchy (Blumer 1958). In short, the effect of context is rooted in identity (Blumer 1958; Bobo 1983; Bobo and Hutchings 1996; Oliver 2001; Gay 2004).

When subordinate group members infiltrate settings based on dominant group characteristics, like African Americans moving into white neighborhoods, tensions arise. In order to promote group solidarity and justify one group having a better life situation than others, the dominant group must make the out-group objectively inferior—usually by attaching negative qualities to the group (like laziness or hypersexuality)—and make these deficiencies appear to be innate (Blumer 1958). This makes prejudice easier and assuages any guilt brought about by the reality of disparate outcomes (Bobo and Hutchings 1996).

Racial integration exacerbates these tensions when context (seemingly) strains finite resources. Scholars refer to this as *Realistic Group Theory* (RGT) (Blumer 1958; Bobo and Hutchings 1996), which states that blacks moving into white neighborhoods will meet resistance because whites will be concerned that scarce resources, like available and desirable housing, will be more difficult for other in-group members to obtain (Bobo 1983). This idea may explain why whites are most likely to prefer majority white neighborhoods to ones with more out-group members (Bobo et al. 2012). Racial diversity in one's neighborhood even makes whites view their jobs more negatively and become more hostile to workplace diversity (Brief et al. 2005).

Bobo and Hutchings's (1996) theory of *racial alienation* frames RGT in terms of the out-group. For the authors, both the dominant and subordinate groups feel intergroup hostility that manifests itself in four related but distinct ways: *simple self-interest, classical prejudice* (which is hostility based on intangible and sometimes incorrect assessments), *stratification of beliefs* (which says the more a person attributes success to individual merit the less they will view other groups as competitive threats), and Blumer's *group position* model (hostility is based on the historic racial ordering). In their extension of Blumer's framework, Bobo and Hutchings suggest that the lowest subordinate group in the hierarchy should feel the most alienation, or distance, from the mainstream, and therefore will be more likely to view other groups (even other subordinate minority groups) as competitive threats. They find that blacks have the highest levels of racial alienation and whites have the lowest. Interestingly, the influence of SES on alienation differs by race. As income rises, whites register lower levels of racial alienation, while high-income blacks feel more alienation (Bobo and Hutchings 1996; Oliver 2001; Gay 2004). Hence, the high-SES suburban African American may feel a stronger desire to seek out group-specific information and engage in group-conscious behaviors.

A related vein of research, *contact theory,* expects the opposite. Contact theory stipulates that the more contact groups have with each other, the more tolerant and accepting they become. Association should breed affinity. Yet all social contacts are not created equal and some actually breed more contempt (Oliver and Mendelberg 2000; Dixon 2006; Oliver 2010). For Dixon (2006), contact must be meaningful to the point of intimate knowledge and expressing close feelings for members of other groups. He finds that cursory contact with black neighbors actually heightens whites' prejudice (and does the opposite for whites' feelings toward Latinos and Asians). Oliver (2010) finds that the status of encountered group members matters. The contacts that lessen prejudice must be between individuals of equal status, individuals working toward a shared goal with frequent contacts, and the ability to form new superordinate identities based on the reason for the contact (21).

Taken together, the group position and countervailing contact theory may explain the complex dynamic facing suburban African Americans who move into and experience social interaction in the white neighborhood. Initially, they may expect hostility, based either on the objective reality of competing over finite resources or the subjective prejudice attached to minority racial status. However, this social situation appears tractable. As contacts become more frequent, and presumably other shared demographics (like education) become more salient, the hostility on the part of whites could dissipate. Yet, for suburban African Americans this increased contact may make race *more* salient for them and heighten racial alienation.

Of course, scholars caution against neat conclusions from either theory. For instance, Realistic Group Theory is difficult to separate from normal racial prejudice (Bobo 1983). Realistic consequences are also difficult to assess and individual threats need not be present if group threat is an equally potent influence. Meanwhile, contact theory faces the problem of self-selection. Contact may breed more tolerance because those with tolerant views are the most likely to encounter other races.

Whether the neighbors surrounding the average suburban black are actually racist is not as important as the *perception* of the racial animosity in the environment. This perception has large effects on suburban African Americans' racial ideology and life outlook. Oliver says living in an integrated neighborhood "comes at the expense of an indigenous cultural identity and creates enormous conflicts in self-perception" (2010, 8), which may lead to less social and quasi-political neighborhood involvement because blacks do not feel the same sense of community as they would in coethnic neighborhoods (Oliver 2001). Claudine Gay (2004) says integrated neighborhood contexts have conflicting effects on blacks. She agrees with Oliver that an integrated neighborhood may heighten the salience of race, as may interacting with highly educated African Americans. However, she also finds that the salience of race recedes as overall neighborhood quality improves. Higher neighborhood quality lessens racial salience because it may lead blacks to question whether discrimination actually limits their life chances (Gay 2004), though Hochschild (1996) finds that minority status makes one perceive more discrimination. I examine whether living in integrated neighborhoods actually lessens feelings of linked fate in the chapters that follow.

The Suburban Neighborhood Context

The suburbs are a unique type of neighborhood context. In his seminal 2001 book, *Democracy in Suburbia,* J. Eric Oliver describes the suburbs as places where social culture combines with the power to make government policies to create an environment that is demographically homogeneous and where the residents hold tremendous power. This power derives from their ability to "vote with their feet" (75) if they do not like the policies put forth by the governing administration or the posture toward the (usually poorer) central city. Thus, government officials have an incentive to worry more about losing a tax base than listening to the demands of vocal minorities. The effect of this structure on minorities is hardly a coincidence, since the residents incorporated the suburbs in part to shield high-SES residents from the urban political machines that focused their policies on the lower class to secure their electoral support (69).

In her recently published book *Racial and Ethnic Politics in American Suburbs* (2015), Lorrie Frasure-Yokley uses a multimethod approach to show that these issues are still at the forefront of suburban politics. She finds that the racial diversification of these areas has changed the calculus of municipal officials. The demand for services has increased, but the desire to fund them with tax levies has not. As a result, these neighborhoods are increasingly partnering with nonprofit organizations to provide social support for their new residents of lower socioeconomic status.

This desire to craft a community for one class of people has had political consequences. For African Americans, the majority of whom are of lower SES, institutionalized residential racial segregation keeps more desirable locations out of reach. Even those blacks who have been able to acquire the resources for suburban residence meet the hostility one would expect to come with racial integration. Racial minority status in the suburban neighborhood heightens the salience of racial identity and evokes a greater sense of racial consciousness (Oliver 2001).

Suburban demographic homogeneity also limits civic involvement for all residents. If everyone holds similar political preferences, there will be minimal competition and therefore less incentive to participate. Suburban African Americans are less likely to work in organizations or vote in their local environment, and they have less political interest and efficacy and feel less empowered or interested. This is because "it is unlikely that their feelings of racial community can be evoked in any politically meaningful way" (Oliver 2001, 125). However, this assumption fails to account for the readily available alternatives for African Americans that can cultivate a sense of community and are located just a short drive away in the historic neighborhoods that serve as incubators for black political thought.

The immediate question is whether these mixed-race environments actually have major effects on the perceptions of suburban African Americans. Oliver (2001, 23–24) puts it nicely, "If social contexts are shaping individual civic behavior they must be doing so indirectly by influencing the determinants of participation, . . . a place's racial composition does not make the act of voting any different, but it does change the other factors that influence whether one is likely to vote."

SOCIAL NETWORK CONTEXTS AND POLITICAL BEHAVIOR

The relevance of social networks to political behavior reaches back to Berelson et al.'s 1954 book, *Voting*, about the workings of power and influence in the small New York town of Elmira. They found that politics was a social rather than an individual pursuit; the people with whom the respondents surrounded themselves—their social networks—had a large impact on their political behavior decisions. Subsequently, Robert Huckfeldt and John Sprague (1995) wanted to know who was included in typical networks and which individuals had the largest influence. Based on their 1984 South Bend, Indiana, study, they attempted to "map" the social networks of residents to see what aspects made people more or less likely to participate.

Huckfeldt and Sprague (and those that followed) argue that social context is a major influence on network behavior. The primary role of social networks, in political behavior, is to cut the costs of acquiring information by accessing it in settings not expressly designated for that purpose. The available information is particularly useful because the receiver does not have to vet it for pertinence or veracity. The affinity between network members means the information should be beneficial to the recipient based on the credibility of the source. Network members use this information to structure behavior, in this case making participation decisions (McClurg 2003; Scheufele et al. 2004; Scott 2012). Social context mediates this information flow. The nature and content of social influence and social communication in election campaigns are fundamentally structured by the social composition of the environments where individuals reside, work, attend church, and so on (Huckfeldt et al. 1995).

Of course, not all contexts are created equal. Each involves a certain mix of people with which the individual will potentially engage in a political discussion. In the most fundamental sense, these people can be either in agreement or in disagreement with the individual on a particular subject. In each case, the network member is trying to pass on information that other members will retain. According to the *social cohesion model* (Huckfeldt et al. 1995), this retention relies on the level of trust one has with his or her network members. Retention is therefore much more likely when two discussants agree, as one will be more likely to trust someone who shares the same worldview.

Disagreement in Social Networks

A socially cohesive network is in direct contrast to disagreeable (Eveland and Hively 2009) or ambivalent (Nir 2005) networks characterized by the frequency of discussion with non–like-minded people. A sliding scale of disagreement can occur on a myriad of dimensions. For example, say there are two coworkers in a white-collar office of a metropolitan city. This city has two rival colleges, one professional football team, and biennial elections. If the coworkers attended the same college, root for the local team, and share party affiliations (scenario #1), this is an agreeable network. However, it may be the case that they both support the local team, share a party, but went to rival schools (scenario #2). By definition, this network will be less agreeable than the first as there is disagreement on one of the three dimensions of the relationship. Now say the two went to the same college and root for the local team but have different political persuasions (scenario #3). Again there is disagreement on one of the three dimensions. Scenarios #2 and #3 may have the same number of disagreeable dimensions, but the disagreements may have different levels of intensity and therefore different influences on political behavior. The disagreements in #2 may be more jovial or based on a mutual respect, dealing with identities that are strongly held but likely not fundamental to one's idea of self. The disagreements in #3 may only happen every other November, yet the clashes may be more intense since they likely deal with fundamental identities. As stated earlier, the clashes based on the most salient identities will be the strongest; however, the combination of agreeing/disagreeing members in the larger network and the bases for this characterization determine the levels of disagreement and one's reactions to it.

Disagreement is not pleasant for the individual (Festiger 1957); however, the effect of disagreement on participation is not as settled. One camp says that being in a disagreeable network makes one more likely to participate, as the individual will seek out agreeable information that can be easily retained (Zuckerman, Valentino, and Zuckerman 1994; Ulbig and Funk 1999; Scheufele et al. 2004). The other camp says disagreement could make people participate less, as the discomfort will cause a withdrawal from the system (Mutz 2002). This withdrawal happens most often for the minorities in the network (McClurg 2006). Disagreement does have an indirect effect on participation. Research has shown it increases knowledge about politics and the search for political information (Mutz 2002; Nir 2005; Eveland and Hively 2009). The relationship between network makeup and voter turnout, particularly whether it boosts or hinders participation, is unsettled. This is one of the major research questions of this project. As chapter 5 will show, the results are mixed. For suburban African Americans there does appear to be greater knowledge acquisition and engagement in participatory behaviors beyond voting. Yet, the effect on voting appears more contingent on the electoral choices.

Most social network scholars believe the perception of disagreement in a network is probabilistic (see Huckfeldt and Sprague 1995). They categorize networks as agreeable or disagreeable based on the probability that a random encounter within the network will be with an agreeable partner (see also Zuckerman, Valentino, and Zuckerman 1994; Mayhew et al. 1995). In essence, the chance of one encountering a network where a majority hold the same views is contingent on the supply of people who are available for discussion—the chance of a Republican finding an agreeable partner is much higher at a rally for lower taxes than one for more government spending.

Staerklé et al. (2011) say that any group or collective must agree on certain symbols or commonalities. These commonalities may be the nature of their association (for example, the information technology group in the firm) or more abstract (such as their political ideology). The majority demographic most often determines the definition of the group (761). The authors say that majorities maintain their dominance by resisting minority influence and marginalizing the alternative views minorities put forward. This makes the minorities uncomfortable and therefore more likely to withdraw or not express dissonant views.

Interestingly, not all network participants are good at determining the agree/disagree distribution in their networks. In general, those who hold majority status are more likely to misperceive discussion partners as agreeing. Meanwhile, there is something about minority status that makes the calculation more accurate (Huckfeldt and Sprague 1995; McClurg 2006; Scott 2012). McClurg (2006) says that the assessment of potential agreement on the part of minorities, and the realization that the probabilistic chance of agreement is lower than that for the majority, makes minorities more sensitive to the level of support they will encounter when sharing their alternative views and more cognizant of the information distribution of the group.

I believe that suburban African Americans will be more sensitive to disagreement in their neighborhood and workplace networks. If this minority perception is based on race (since there is agreement on other relevant demographics, such as neighborhood, education, and income), minority suburban African Americans may view these networks as adversarial to their identity and therefore seek out confirmatory information elsewhere. This will cause them to hold more racialized opinions and engage in group-based behaviors since these are ways they can achieve majority status and engender positive feelings about group membership.

Homophily in Social Networks

Scholars term the idea that people prefer being in groups with others like them *homophily*. Some describe homophily as one of the most stable findings in sociology and the social network literature (Kossinets and Watts 2009; Smith, McPherson, and Smith-Lovin 2014). There are numerous demographics on which to base group affinity, some of which will overlap (McPherson, Smith-Lovin, and Cook 2001; Mutz 2002). The bulk of scholarship on homophily has looked at partisanship and religion (Huckfeldt and Sprague 1988; Huckfeldt and Mendez 2008), but research has also examined network homophily in terms of age, gender, and race (Ibarra 1995; Mayhew et al. 1995; McPherson, Smith-Lovin, and Cook 2001; Smith, McPherson, and Smith-Lovin 2014). In their comprehensive survey of the homophily literature, McPherson et al. (2001) find that of all demographics measured, race/ethnicity is by far the most salient and peculiar. There is a long lineage of work that shows race to be the more homophylic of the major demographics. Most networks are more racially homophylic than they would be strictly by chance; cross-race ties are weaker, and people actually go farther to find same-race ties (McPherson, Smith-Lovin, and Cook 2001). This finding has persisted over time, even as the country is becoming more racially diverse. Mixed-race networks should be more likely, yet racial homophily has remained stable (Mayhew et al. 1995; Smith, McPherson, and Smith-Lovin 2014).

These findings substantiate the assumptions of my theory. When a suburban African American enters into a network based on many complementary and divergent identities, I believe the salience of race will make that identity a major determinant of the evolution of the group. If race is the primary categorization schema, then differences on issues dealing with race should be the main standard of minority status evaluation (Pantoja and Segura 2003). If this is true, then the reaction to disagreement in the group on racial terms may lead to a rejection of the majority racial stance and therefore cause a retreat to a more (racially) comfortable network. Findings presented in chapter 4 offer some support for this expectation.

The literature in the previous sections showed that racial makeup is a salient factor in network perception, that disagreement in network contexts is unpleasant (though it is not conclusive whether this disagreement enhances or depresses participation), and that different networks will produce different probabilistic calculations as to the potential of finding like-minded discussion partners. The question now is in which types of networks should the suburban African American be able to find agreeable discussion? If, like Scheufele et al. (2004) say, "network heterogeneity triggers post hoc information seeking" (332), then those with more SES and political resources should have an easier time finding it. If the racial makeup of the network has an inordinate influence on the perception of disagreement (Joslyn 1997), especially on racialized political issues, and one cannot change the racial makeup of one's neighborhoods or workplaces, the post hoc information seeking will be toward venues with coethnic majority racial makeups. For blacks, there are unique options established in the enclave where they can find racially similar discussion partners, such as the NAACP or predominately black religious denominations like the African Methodist Episcopal church (Harris 1999). When these institutions offer group-specific information and participatory avenues, suburban African Americans are able to exercise their group consciousness, help the group, and be more likely to receive confirmatory information.

POLITICAL BEHAVIOR BY NETWORK TYPE

The separation between types of social networks and their effects on political behavior, especially for suburban African Americans, revolves around two dimensions: homophily and proximity. I add the proximity dimension because it brings geography into the equation. The suburban African American lives in an environment that is simultaneously high in terms of locational prestige (for example, higher than average property values, better schools, lower crime rates, etc.) yet low in identity reinforcement (because of the obvious minority status and potentially hostile encounters). Hence, the probabilistic calculation will mean less like-minded discussion partners, and this baseline racial-political identity will affect participation choices.

Rationally, if individuals derive equal utility from two alternatives of the same category they will choose the one with the lowest cost. If the two alternatives are equal in cost and benefit (a rarity in reality) the choice should be random. If the two alternatives have unequal costs and the individual chooses the alternative with the higher cost, then it must have a higher utility. The greater this cost differential, the higher the benefit differential must be. If a person is going to a grocery store across town and passes multiple grocery stores on the way, the store farther away must offer something the others do not. In sheer geographic terms, the suburban African American who travels to the central city historic community to participate in its race-based institutions (having passed other more proximate places of worship or opportunities to volunteer) is incurring a higher cost and therefore must be deriving a higher utility.

Scholars have tested this idea—that individuals seek out homophilic networks—in terms of religion and partisanship (Huckfeldt and Sprague 1987; Huckfeldt, Plutzer, and Sprague 1993). They have not examined racial minority status. The extension of the probabilistic and disagreement network theories to include race suggests that when propinquity means minority status, it should drive network participants toward those networks that produce a larger utility even though they will come at a higher cost. Just as not every network is created equal, neither are the interactions within networks.

More than 80 percent of network discussants are from four sources: family, work, church, and neighborhood (Huckfeldt et al. 1995). As to network type, neighborhood discussants make up 20 percent of nonrelative partners, whereas workplace discussion partners are 33 percent of nonrelative network members (Huckfeldt et al. 1995). McPherson (2001) shows that school, work, and volunteer organizations have the most nonrelative ties.

My goals are to see if suburban African Americans will view their neighborhoods, workplaces, volunteer organizations, and churches as potential sources of agreement or disagreement, if they should accept or reject the information transmitted, and whether this will lead to more group-based behaviors.

The Neighborhood Network

The probability of the suburban African American finding agreeable neighbors on racial issues is low, given the opinion differences between racial groups. This is especially true in settings that limit interactions to smaller areas of the neighborhood.[6] Statistically, the chance of finding agreeable partners would be much higher at a neighborhood-wide civic event than it would be at a block party with residents of one's street. The recognition of minority status may be fairly easy to ascertain even without actual interactions with neighbors. People's homes are often a personal expression of their interests; a meticulously kept garden, a license plate frame of the flagship university, or a yard sign for the Democrat congressional candidate are all signals as to whether neighbors share the same passions. The history of race in suburban neighborhoods in general may heighten feelings of minority racial status and perceptions of disagreement for suburban African Americans with strong racial identities. The separation of neighborhoods by race is not simply a result of personal preference; whites have used segregation in the past to perpetuate racial hierarchies. The history of race in neighborhoods is not something suburban African Americans can ignore, but dealing with it may be a necessary reality—owning a house and having access to high-quality schools may be an acceptable tradeoff. As to participatory choices, legislatures must consider things like "traditional" community boundaries when drawing jurisdictions, such as congressional districts. But the community boundaries were put there in some cases to perpetuate the hierarchy. Districts with large proportions of suburbanites will be more ideologically conservative if for no other reason than the overlap of socioeconomic status and ideology. Furthermore, suburban candidates will have less incentive to speak positively about race since the suburban areas and districts will have fewer minorities. Therefore, the neighborhood may not be a satisfying network for racially identifying suburban African Americans to participate in. This could cause them to view the neighborhood in political terms as a necessary evil but not a source of information. I believe this will cause them to seek out more agreeable networks and reinforcing participation avenues elsewhere.

The Workplace Network

Of the four networks, the workplace may allow the least influence over choice of discussion partners. This is because minority status may actually impose negative consequences for retreating or not engaging in discussions. In the workplace, managers, not individuals, largely determine the availability of partners (Huckfeldt and Sprague 1995; Scheufele et al. 2004). The intimacy and probability of finding agreeable partners is constrained by things as broad as area of specialization (especially to the extent that certain demographics are overrepresented in some fields, such as information technology) or as small as being forced to take lunch breaks at the same time.

The perception of disagreement and minority status is a bit trickier than the probabilistic aspect. There is an argument that politics has no place on the job. However, that would be akin to saying private, non-work-related conversations about things like college sports have no place. This reasoning would be especially absurd when coworkers may spend more than forty hours a week together and may have developed a mutual affinity (about certain subjects). Perception of minority status is complicated because by virtue of holding similar job positions two coworkers of any race are likely to have similar socioeconomic statuses. In the world of overlapping contexts, they may actually have more in common with their coworkers of different races than the coethnic CEO or custodian. Yet, there may be a time when politics becomes the center of discussion and the topic is one that piques the racial identities of the group. Then the in-group members give a response that represents the median of their collective racial identity and the racial identifying suburban African American observes that he or she disagrees.

The problem is that recoiling from discussions to avoid conflict and discomfort may be detrimental to the individual, even though it has little to do with the person's job responsibilities. Oftentimes, being a "team player" is an implicit part of the evaluative process for things like raises and promotions. "Team player" is a term connoting conformity to some common set of beliefs and norms. Yet those in the majority of the network shape and maintain these beliefs and norms (Staerklé et al. 2011).[7] So, not only are the minorities steeped in this discomfort, the group may punish them for recoiling or expressing a divergent opinion (Glynn et al. 1997). Ibarra (1995) finds that minorities feel excluded from many social activities that take place after working hours. They are also the least socially integrated in workgroups.

Suburban African Americans are right to be weary of these relationships. In their recounting of the literature on racial diversity in workplaces, Brief et al. (2005) discuss how the racial makeup of a business has serious effects on the in-group members. They find that increasing racial diversity in the workplace reduces whites' commitment to the organization, lowers their job satisfaction, lowers the quality of interpersonal relationships with coworkers, and lowers their levels of trust and attraction to their peers.

The Volunteer Network

Volunteer organizations consist of participants coming together for a common cause, so finding like-minded individuals in such organizations should be much easier than in the neighborhood or workplace. In most instances, people are donating resources like time and money with little tangible individual return, only the advancement of group pursuits. The ability to seek out agreeable partners is high since one can choose with whom to associate, unlike in the neighborhood or workplace. If an individual's aim is to engage in any form of community service, and he or she does not feel comfortable with the makeup of the first organization tried, the volunteer can always find another one without much effort.[8]

The perception of disagreement in a volunteer organization may actually be difficult precisely because all are working for the same goal. Volunteer network participants will likely think they are in the majority on at least the nature of the association. If like people are more apt to work toward common goals, then they may assume agreement on other issues. However, if that common goal is something broad, like "saving the environment," then one could easily be in the minority as to which aspect of the environment should receive the most attention or which strategy the group should choose to pursue. Minority status, and therefore disagreement, is still present—it just may be more nuanced or take longer to appear. By contrast, minority disagreement by racial makeup can be determined via visual cues.

In addition, minority status may not become salient until it activates an overlapping identity. A suburban African American marathon enthusiast may have no problem belonging to an all-white running club because the purpose of the association is running. In this sense, the racial identity may be dormant (Huddy 2013). Yet, if examining all possible identities, narrowly tailored organizations, like the marathon runners, should have more *total* disagreement and a worse probabilistic makeup because the only thing in common is running, and running may not easily signal other (political) preferences. Couple this with the finding that in voluntary organizations general discussion has a positive association with political communication (Eveland Jr. and Kleinman 2011), and it is likely that the conversation will eventually turn away from marathons to the political news of the day. The turn toward political discussion may activate the "dormant" racial identity of the African American participant. This is not to say the highly racially identifying black runner will leave the group—just that the ability to choose a group does not mean there will be complete agreement.

The Church Network

The church may appear to have as favorable a probabilistic calculation as the volunteer network; however, there are denominational restrictions on churches that the other networks do not have. Theoretically, the workplace should make widgets in the most efficient way possible and the volunteer organization should choose the optimum strategy to achieve its goals. Tradition dominates church processes and resists innovation on doctrinal questions. For African Americans, the church has served as their longest continuous institution, with a tradition dating back to slavery (Brooks 2005; Dawson 2012). As political incorporation has increased in the last half-century, the church has increasingly been an agent of political mobilization. Scheufele et al. (2004) discuss the peculiarities of the church as a social network. They say it is "chiefly concerned with influencing the views, beliefs, and behaviors of their members, uniting individuals in a common world outlook . . . [and this] structural dimension of religion is closely related to a belief-based dimension, which further mitigates the ability of a church setting to promote diverse interactions" (320). In other words, because tradition governs church denominations, one may be choosing a church but not changing it. Additionally, the benefit expected from membership is more personal than collective and the primary commonality among members is adherence to this shared tradition.

The transient nature of church membership also differs from other networks. A suburban African American has to come home and see neighbors. She has to go to work. If she signs up for a volunteer activity she has to show up. But with churches, she does not have to work in the food bank or attend the voter registration seminar. This is especially true if her primary reason for membership is simply attending worship services. The church may offer networks of social interaction, but participation in them is usually not a requirement of membership.

That said, when one does choose to participate in the network aspect of the church, the probability of agreement may be very high because individuals are associating based on a shared (religious) identity that often transcends SES and is likely more salient. There is literature on the political nature of churches (McDaniel 2008; McDaniel and Ellison 2008); however, a majority of churches are not explicitly political in a partisan sense (Scheufele et al. 2004), and if one is not amenable to the level of political discussion at a particular church, another within the denomination could be chosen—or the denomination could be left altogether.

I believe each of these institutions will have a different effect on the behaviors of suburban African Americans. The key distinction for this study is between those that are most likely majority white based on suburban African Americans' SES—neighborhood and workplace—and those that they can self-select to be majority African American—church and volunteer organization.

THE BLACK PUBLIC SPHERE

Catherine Squires defines the black counterpublic as a collective of people who "(a) engage in common discourse and negotiations of what it means to be Black, and (b) pursue particularly defined Black interests" (Squires 2002, 454). Melissa Harris-Lacewell (2004) describes it as places "where African Americans jointly develop understandings of their collective interests and create strategies to navigate the complex political world" (1). A public sphere, according to Jürgen Habermas in his 1962 book, is "a setting and set of political institutions which facilitate the ability of citizens to discuss questions of common concern" (Dawson 1995, 200). The public sphere is simultaneously the physical sites where discussions take place, the ideas that spur and result from the discussion, and the places that reflect these ideas, like group-specific newspapers (Dawson 2012, 2).

The citizens to which Habermas was referring were all in a specific societal class: the bourgeois public of merchants and artisans and similar middle-class trades. Nancy Fraser (1992) suggests this makes Habermas's view of societal spheres incomplete. She says that the bourgeoisie's privileged place in society meant that other classes did not have the option to participate in the space. The public sphere itself was actually dedicated to advancing mainstream goals. In an effort to exert their preferences on the state, other groups had to set up their own institutions. Dawson (2012) calls this *bifurcation*: when dual societies develop their own norms and institutions while both are technically members of the same state. When the power dynamic is one where the dominant group consciously excludes the subordinates from mainstream civil society, the subordinates develop a counterpublic (Fraser 1992; Squires 2002) in direct reaction to the norms and behaviors of the dominant public (Dawson 2012).

Brooks (2005) says that once slaves were not given recompense in the form of the contemporarily symbolic "forty acres and a mule" and conditions were placed on their emancipation (like curfews, vagrancy laws, and the inability to sit on juries), their need for a parallel structure was clear. This "bunker mentality" is what began the perpetual adherence to the norm of linked fate that continues to define the black public sphere today.

The Black Counterpublic

Contemporary suburban African Americans are in a peculiar position relative to the counterpublic. One could make the case that their SES and the removal of formal barriers has made the mainstream sphere more accessible than ever. All but the most exclusive schools, organizations, and clubs are open to them and no major religious denominations reject their membership. However, their participation in the black counterpublic remains high.

This is presumably because of two related factors: the role of critical memory and the institutions that preserve it for the collective (Brown 1995). One can conceive of the critical memory as the pieces of evidence that undergird the racial socialization of group members. A warning about encounters with law enforcement is bolstered by personal stories of police brutality. A spurring to economic action is buttressed by tales of Madam C. J. Walker becoming the first black female millionaire despite being born just six years after the emancipation proclamation. This critical memory perseveres in the face of oppression (Squires 2002) and gives validity to constructions of race, community, and politics (Brown 1995, 150). It has persisted in the twenty-first century, though Brown and Dawson (1995) say it has become a distorted offshoot of the 1960s version that was integral to the grassroots mobilization of the civil rights movement. They believe this modern version has changed the political calculus and strategies of the counterpublic, essentially lessening the need for solidarity and exposing political differences (Brown 1995; Dawson 1995).

One explanation for this change is in the transition of critical memory into nostalgia (Baker 1995). For Baker, critical memory is the recording of strategies, efforts, and resources of past efforts that "makes decisive change always imminent" (7). The public that remembers the successes and failures of its past will always be ready to advance toward the goal. If critical memory is the recording, nostalgia is the made-for-television dramatization that writes revolutions as long-past aberrations and substitutes allegory for history (7). The fact that Walker's total collective worth was actually around $600,000–$700,000 undercuts the feel-good allegory (Gates 2013). Martin Luther King Jr.'s ideological transition in his later life undercuts the narrative of the passive King and radical Malcolm X (Baker 1995). For Baker, memories can be embellished or sanitized, but when they are viewed as disconnected from the present struggles and not seen as part of a larger pattern, the urgency is diminished and they will be less of a stimulus to mobilization. I would characterize Black History Month as part critical memory and part nostalgia. While it is a time of remembrance, only certain figures and stories receive the most attention, and those are the ones most accepted by the mainstream. Nevertheless, the fact that many African Americans without regard to age or class can recall details of that history is evidence of a collective norm and its pervasiveness.

The question of decline is one that Harris-Lacewell (2004) outright rejects and Dawson walks back from in his 2012 piece. Whether the draw of the black public sphere persists, or is even heightened in the face of geographic separation, is a major question this study will seek to answer. If these areas hold such a draw, they will serve as high-utility alternatives both visible and accessible to suburban African Americans. The prevalence of a black public sphere may lead to more group-based behaviors and even change the perception of majority white, proximate networks.

The Black Church and the Black Public Sphere

For African Americans, the black church has served as an institution whose place and purpose goes far beyond simple religiosity. Dating back to the days of American slavery, the church served as a place of strength and refuge in horrific circumstances (McAdam 1982; Morris 1984; Harris 1999; Weare et al. 2008). It also provided cover for subversive strategies to undermine slavery.[9] Post-emancipation, pastors of the church became leaders in the community, as it was one of the most prestigious occupations in the enclave attainable without formal education. In modern times, the church served as the backbone of the civil rights movement. It allowed African Americans in the community to gain resources like public speaking or management that movement leaders would call upon (McAdam 1982; Verba et al. 1995). The church also facilitated the goals of the movement by providing a long-standing and respected hierarchical leadership structure that handled ideological, strategic, and logistic issues. Politically, the church has served as a mobilizing institution. The pews include individuals who are familiar with both the pastors and the campaigning politicians, both of whom stir the congregation to action using a rhetorical frame that emphasizes group-based solidarity and aid to the less fortunate, all things that are the primary tenants of group consciousness (Morris 1984; Harris 1999). Historically, community leaders have mobilized these parishioners to aid the political and social aims of the community. Weare et al. (2008) find that church members are more dependent on organizers for mobilization than people in other types of groups.

The major point is that institutions like the black church, the NAACP, and the black press were operating simultaneously with white churches, businesses, volunteer organizations, social groups, and media outlets that would not let blacks participate, and/or were not receptive to black concerns. While this blatant exclusion is no longer the case, these black-based institutions have persisted and maintained their counterpublic posture toward the mainstream. Subsequent chapters will show large differences between suburban African Americans who choose to attend black churches and those who do not, with the former having more racialized opinions, more interaction with the cultural community, and more alternative participation.

A Brief History of the Black Public Sphere

A brief history of the black public sphere will serve to contextualize the historic inner-city neighborhoods that suburban African Americans frequent for majority-black networks and racial reinforcement. Suburban African

Americans will find normative cues and race-specific information hard to come by in their immediate surroundings even though they form the attitudinal basis for future political behavior (Huckfeldt et al. 1995). Although there are multiple aspects of the black public sphere that could be included, I will focus on three that are important to suburban African Americans: the evolution of the institutions that comprise and support the black public sphere, the ideologies and norms of thought that determined the strategies of the era, and the navigation of class differences within the group, especially for the black middle class.[10] All of these aspects are key determinants to the amount and direction of group-based participation by suburban African Americans shown in the following chapters. This evolution is what makes these areas such a draw for suburban African Americans, providing racial reinforcement, ideological consonance, and shielding from a sometimes harsh mainstream society.

The Slavery and Reconstruction Period

Blacks in America developed a collective identity and civil society during the slavery/Reconstruction era. The institutions to accomplish this were borne out of the exclusion from mainstream society and had multiple functions, as they were the only places blacks could own and organize. Dawson (2012) describes the birth of the black public sphere beginning in slavery. The nature of the plantation and the propensity to purchase whole families, who would intermarry, created a web of kin and fictive kinships that slaves relied on to survive. He says that slaves had to rely on each other to complete their tasks, but also to temper the slave owners' expectations and "work the weaknesses of the system in order to lighten their burdens while escaping punishment" (8). Essentially, if one person was being far more productive than the group, the overseer would hold others to that standard. Conversely, if one of the group was ailing, the others might have to pick up the slack so he or she could escape rebuke. These actions took coordination, and their dangerous (even deadly) nature made them impossible to accomplish unless the group had both an affinity for its individual members and a commitment to help the collective group succeed. The slaves institutionalized these kinship relationships through their religious congregations on the plantation, where they circulated rumors and ideas and refined social skills (Squires 2002). After emancipation, these relationships and institutional structures provided the foundation for the political culture that would negotiate blacks' place in Reconstruction and become the basis for things like local branches of the Republican Party (Dawson 2012, 8–9).

The black church as a counterpublic institution began in 1792 when the black members of a Philadelphia Methodist church were told they could no longer sit with the other parishioners. Instead, they were relegated to a segregated balcony, veritably excluding them from the main space of worship. In response, they formed two majority black churches. In 1794, Absalom Jones broke away from the Methodist church to form the African Methodist Episcopal church, where the formal "Articles of Association" stated that only blacks could hold leadership positions (Brooks 2005; Dawson 2012). The site of this church is only ten miles from the Lower Merion and Bryn Mawr suburbs discussed in the previous chapter. After Reconstruction, the church was not only a place of worship, but also a place where the politics of the community was formally legislated (Brown 1995, Dawson 2012).

Concurrently in Boston, Masonic lodges, one of the major social organizations of the day, were developing a similar counterpublic structure for similar reasons. A man named Prince Hall and his cohorts wanted to become Masons in order to gain entry into white society (Gregory 1995). The American masonic organization denied them entry and they had to charter under the Grand Lodge of England in 1775. Other blacks interested in Masonry forwent trying to join a white American lodge and applied to the Boston lodge for their charters. As a result, the branch of black Masons, called Prince Hall Masonry to this day, was born as an autonomous space governed by blacks (Brooks 2005). It also became clear that the aims of the black and white lodges were different. Hall and his cohort did not build black Masonry on the maintenance of secrets, but rather on "public associations that hoard special knowledge and skills . . . and protect the public interest" (73).

The normative ethos of the time was focused on transitioning from chattel to citizen with pledges of allegiance to the union and attempts to enter into the political realm (Brown 1995). Blacks were consciously forming their own civil society by making their own community holidays, holding parades on the main thoroughfares, and having picnics on the capitol square (Brown 1995; Brooks 2005). Demographically, the community was largely homogeneous. Blacks in the North were free, but in a citizenship limbo that made socioeconomic advancement from their coethnics difficult. They were also geographically compact, occupying the only neighborhoods available to them. There was some conflict within the group about the focus on slavery instead of the political and social status of freed blacks (Squires 2002).

As the decades wore on, the norms of participation and the strategies for advancement changed. In Richmond, Virginia, elites replaced mass meetings—where anyone could speak—with literary society meetings where participants prepared papers on preselected topics and designated members to speak. This more cadre (as opposed to grassroots) society separated the educated from the uneducated and gave businesspersons and professionals more control over the direction of the collective (Brown 1995).

The Great Migration Period

The Great Migration period (1915–1960) brought industrialization and urbanization to the (northern) black public. The geographic shift opened opportunities for political advancement and autonomy based on sheer numerical concentration. It also began debates within the black counterpublic about integration into society and the political direction of a public with a bourgeoning middle class. In these northern cities, blacks had already begun to organize against white oppression (Dawson 2012). These areas were ripe for a vibrant counterpublic; there was a critical mass of people for organizing, and less acute legal obstacles allowed access to some aspects of the mainstream sphere, such as economic markets (Squires 2002).

Population gains also opened access to local politics, as the urban political machine needed constituencies to amass votes. In order to capitalize on these opportunities for political organization, the black public sphere needed a structure and resources to facilitate their political incorporation. Luckily, the nascent institutions of the previous era were already in place and blacks still looked to them for acceptable norms of group behavior (Dawson 2012). Now the counterpublic was functioning on two tracks: one of political agitation in negotiating with the dominant sphere, and the other of nurturing enclaved indigenous organizations and institutions where an ideological debate was brewing. Social organizations were proliferating and Harlem, New York, was in its renaissance. While the organizations were largely invisible to the mainstream, elites could mobilize them for political purposes (Gregory 1995).

The normative debate of the day revolved around how the group could best integrate into society. Canonized as the Booker T. Washington versus W. E. B. Du Bois debates, we begin to see the first strands of long-standing ideologies that are still present, to different degrees, in black politics. Both camps felt the best way to achieve equality was through acceptance by the dominant sphere. The question was what would bring white acceptance? What is termed the Du Bois camp[11] felt that acceptance would come from showing the dominant sphere that blacks could adapt to the mainstream social and political conventions. This would presumably shed the subhuman label of slavery and achieve full access into the sphere. The Washington camp felt the best way to thrive was self-sufficiency. Blacks would participate in civil society through politics and economics but mostly stay separate.[12] On the class front, we begin to see more separation as prestigious industrial jobs become available to segments of the group. However, the majority of African Americans are not doing well. Here, the middle-class blacks who became leaders of the community clearly suppressed their self-interest to aid the larger group (Gregory 1995).

The Civil Rights Movement Period

The early stages of the civil rights movement brought about a politicization of the black public sphere institutions. Jim Crow had completely excluded southern blacks from the mainstream public sphere with a brutality that surprised observers from other regions (Baker 1995). The establishment used mobs, bombings, lynchings, cross-burnings, and other tactics to keep the counterpublic in fear and show that there was no hope of entering mainstream society. The black church now needed to recruit the foot soldiers necessary to make a grassroots, nonviolent, direct action, mass public protest movement possible (McAdam 1982). This meant breaking the educated, middle-class leadership cadre and allowing community members of all SES levels an opportunity to participate. The church was perfect for this leadership role—everyone knew where the church was located and most respected the pastor as a community leader.

Other community-based organizations also created an environment that closely linked political debate to political action (Dawson 1995, 211). Things like citizens' action councils became new arenas for debate and dialogue about societal inequalities, provided a new vocabulary and model for social mobilization, and moved people into the mainstream political sphere (Gregory 1995).

Putting a leadership face on the movement aided the group's entrance into the mainstream. This face came in the person of Martin Luther King Jr. His place as a faith leader afforded him the respect of the community members, and his attendance at the historically black Morehouse College placed him at the cusp of the contemporary dialogue on black collectivity (Morris 1984,

Baker 1995). Group members once again muted class differences because the sheer severity of Jim Crow life made it the undisputed preeminent issue for the black counterpublic.

The Post–Civil Rights/Black Power Period

As things like the Civil Rights Act of 1964 and the Voting Rights Act of 1965 dismantled the Jim Crow regime, the monolithic focus on southern oppression receded and the black public sphere began to diverge ideologically, demographically, and regionally. The clear government signal was that the mainstream public sphere would integrate. The question was just how accepting it would be and whether blacks would enter docilely, thankful for the extension, or aggressively, demanding a radical redress owed them since the emancipation era. The major institutions, volunteer organizations, and churches were unchanged, but their roles were adjusted. Using formal avenues for petitioning, lobbying government, and litigating through the courts became primary strategies. These approaches were better suited for national or regional organizations, as opposed to churches, whose power and prestige were more locally based (Baker 1995; Squires 2002). This strategy shift and new open participation—the mainstream no longer imposed sanctions on organization members[13]—facilitated the preeminent role of the civil rights organizations, like the NAACP and Urban League, in mainstream sphere negotiations.

King and the other principals soon realized that taking on the plight of the northern ghettos would be very different from the Jim Crow South. The northern blacks encountered a unique set of challenges, like acquisitive real estate owners exploiting white flight, callous labor leaders, corrupt public officials, and morally blind social welfare workers. The environment was also spatially confined, abandoned by industry, and cursed with crumbling schools, indifferent teachers, and wretched public housing (Baker 1995, 31–32). These differences from the South necessitated new strategies and heightened the salience of new ideologies. The change would come in a shift from passive resistance to a more combative stance toward the state. This rebellious community action sometimes escaped the bounds of proper protest, as exemplified by the urban riots of the time. There was also state backlash against this resistance, most notably the FBI's COINTELPRO program.

The rhetoric of Malcolm X and the Black Power ideology of the Black Panther Party exemplify this shift to a more radical racial identity.[14] The ideologies moved from what Dawson (2001, 2012) would term radical liberalism to black nationalism and/or black separatism. All three worked for the advancement of the race, but the nationalists were much more inwardly focused and much less reliant on the state. This ideological shift transformed the norms of behavior and thought away from social integration to social autonomy and brought about a renewed emphasis on black history and the group's African origins. The satellite public established black studies programs and placed an emphasis on black businesses and economic development (Baker 1995).

However, the black public sphere was in a multifaceted decline. The plight of African Americans became lumped in with the constituency politics of other marginalized groups, such as women, LGBTs, Native Americans, Asian Americans, and the Chicano movement. This new "black and brown politics" caused an inevitable fusion of two related yet distinct agendas (Baker 1995; Dawson 1995).

This era also featured a more pronounced demographic separation within the group. As African Americans principally achieved the singular goal of ending Jim Crow, questions about how best to advance the race became more prevalent. Disagreements broke down along class lines. Geographically, middle-class blacks were moving into the black belt suburbs described by Haynes, Pattillo, and Johnson. This black middle class had capitalized on the manufacturing economy and the removal of educational barriers. Subsequent generations would advance even further into the white collar and professional ranks. Meanwhile, those left in the urban ghettos became increasingly dependent on government assistance and formed an underclass within the group. Black middle-class homeowners now had an interest in another sphere of government—residential politics—and increasingly shifted their political efforts toward these aims (Wilson 1978). At the same time, conditions were worsening for blacks still in the poorer inner-city neighborhoods (Cohen and Dawson 1993; Gregory 1995).

All of these internal issues combined with an external political pushback against the civil rights regime to produce an era of black public sphere decline from the mid- to late 1980s to the millennium. The primary institutions of the time moved from those that were once counterpublic to being "fully" integrated into the mainstream through black political incorporation. However, the demands on the black politicians and the political opposition of Reagan-Bush operatives served to severely dilute the black public sphere. There was a clear shift from protest to politics as black leaders gained political positions that had to be maintained electorally, namely by steering constituents into participatory avenues in line with the conventions of the dominant sphere and civil society (Dawson 1995, 2001). Dawson says this strategic shift encouraged political passivity and installed the black political elites as a buffer between the people and the higher levels of power, which narrowed the black agenda and delegitimized protest (Dawson 1995, 2001).

It was also difficult to realize the fruits of their municipal political success, as white flight and a shifting economy left urban municipalities without the revenue to address black issues. At the same time, the need for multiracial coalitions led to a deemphasizing of racial appeals and economic redistribution (Gregory 1995; Dawson 2001). Even Jesse Jackson, who was one of the era's strongest challengers of American society, was more pro-American when compared to the King of the 1970s (Dawson 1994).

The move into the state's bureaucratic circles lessened some of the black public sphere's "bite" (Dawson 1995; Squires 2002). There was a concerted effort by the state to shift the arena of negotiation from direct action on the streets to paperwork in government offices (Gregory 1995). They now reframed societal issues like poverty into administrative problems. Even the "community" organizations the state set up to deal with the problems were dependent on the government for funding and were forced to present solutions that fit within that framework, as opposed to strategies based on community mobilization (Gregory 1995).

On the class front, members of the newly suburbanized black middle class were moving farther away from their urban coethnics socioeconomically and geographically. They also were having a much easier time integrating into the mainstream sphere, dominating the political boards and neighborhood/homeowners associations of those areas.

The previous eras may have had demographic differences, but geographically all blacks lived together, which meant two things. First, the condition of the neighborhood affected everyone without regard to class, so its condition was an important political goal. Second, a vote cast in a local election was one expressly directed toward most coethnics, even if it was simultaneously against the self-interest of the black middle class. Now, suburban African Americans are participating in jurisdictions municipally separate from the central city, with their own leadership structures, neighborhoods, schools systems, city services, and electoral districts. For suburban African Americans, votes on such issues as land use or taxes do not directly affect their coethnics in the historic urban neighborhood, and so self-interest does not have the detrimental community effect it once did and they can express this sentiment more freely (Gregory 1995).

This geographic shift began one of the greatest debates in the study of black politics. As middle-class blacks were separating from their lower-class coethnics, there was a question of whether their opinions and behaviors would also diverge. In his seminal *The Declining Significance of Race* (1978), William Julius Wilson predicted just that. In short, he showed that the evolution of the black middle class meant that class was more of a determinant of one's life chances than race. Therefore, he hypothesized black middle-class behavior would eventually mirror others in their social class rather than their race. The suburban African Americans at the heart of my study are even more separated geographically and socioeconomically from their urban coethnics than at the time of Wilson's writing. Whether suburban African Americans' opinions and behaviors will be closer to those of their white neighbors is an outstanding question. The implications of such a shift are obvious. High-SES African Americans are the members of the group with the resources—educationally, monetarily, and politically—to advance the aims of lower-status African Americans. If they no longer feel a connection to those group members, their advancement via government and/or mainstream assistance could be difficult.

Squires (2002) disagrees with Dawson (1995) about the decline of the black public sphere. While acknowledging that the black public sphere is far different from that of the 1960s, she says that there is a difference between the discursive actions of the counterpublic and any measurable successes. She argues that the continued appearance and vibrancy of multiple counterpublics shows that the black public sphere is still strong. Melissa Harris-Lacewell (2004) takes a similar tack, pointing out that there has always been disagreement within the black public sphere and that the most prominent contemporary institutions may have changed, but their role as a place to debate hidden transcripts that are ideological alternatives to dominant white discourses is an indicator of the continued role of the black public sphere (7).[15]

The Contemporary Black Public Sphere

The turn of the century has seen the primary institutions of the black counterpublic remain the same, but, again, with a slightly different connection to one another. The most accessible bridge between the people and the state is now through the political class, best exemplified by the Congressional Black Caucus and the election of Barack Obama. Obama's election to the U.S. Senate from Illinois in 2006 and the presidency of the United States in 2008 and 2012 clearly evidences the ascent of blacks in the political sphere. The civil rights and social organizations are still dedicated to a black-specific agenda and employ strategies outside of electoral channels, like protests, boycotts, and marches, though very rarely do they reach the level of civil disobedience.[16] The church has retained a more muted role in the public sphere discourse, serving as a place where rhetoric is more at variance (even hostile) to the dominant sphere and providing a ready source of political mobilization—rhetorically, logistically, and in terms of votes.

The question is whether contemporary participants hold similar ideologies to their older coethnics and if geography has an independent effect on those opinions and behaviors. For suburban African Americans, two aspects of the twenty-first-century black public sphere have received scholarly attention—the role of everyday talk in informal gatherings (informal as in nonpolitical), and the transition of the black press to black-centric websites. Melissa Harris-Lacewell writes in *Barbershops, Bibles, and BET* (2004) that the black public sphere has not necessarily disappeared, but its ideological discussions have moved to less formal settings, such as beauty salons and barbershops, where discourses about seemingly trivial things like sports teams or musical entertainers occur alongside political discussions of community issues. These institutions add another layer to the coethnic institutions sought out by suburban African Americans. Unlike a grocery store or even a volunteer organization, there is only one type of salon that specializes in African American hair. Participation in this institution is a near necessity. It is therefore the perfect cost cutter since it is also a valuable source of fresh, group-specific information.

The other black public sphere institution of particular importance to the suburban African American is the localized black press, via its evolution to black-centric news websites. Dawson (2012) describes the black press as "reflexive" because it disseminates the internal discourses of the community to the broader counterpublic and serves to present the group's case to the dominant public and the state. The black press also directs these debates, introducing new ideas into the marketplace and debunking others (Dawson 1994; Brown 1995; Brooks 2005). Beginning with *Freedom's Journal,* the first black newspaper, published in 1827, the black press was a major vehicle for publishing counterpublic information in print and under copyright so that it could not be coopted by the dominant public sphere (Brown 1995; Brooks 2005; Greenwell 2012; Lewis 2012). At times, these black press outlets have uplifted the community with positive stories, and at other times scolded it (Gosnell 1967; Greenwell 2012). The black press also has served as a challenge to the mainstream sphere. While it served a Habermasian purpose, the content of many of its writings was an outright rejection of American liberalism (Brooks 2005).

The contemporary manifestations of the black press are African American-focused websites. R. L'Heureux Lewis (2012) and Ava Thompson Greenwell (2012) have written about the place these websites, like theroot.com, thegrio.com, The Loop21 (currently inactive), and Huffington Post Black Voices, have in the current black public sphere. Their utility and demand is clear, as Greenwell recounts that 35 percent of African Americans get news from the Internet and that they prefer to spend time on websites with a black perspective. While their founders designed the websites to attract an educated middle-class audience, the communal nature of the Internet allows voices from all types of spheres to be heard (Greenwell 2012). Unlike the literary societies, academics on the site can engage the public writ large through the comment sections and by writing in a conversational tone (Lewis 2012). The role of these websites is particularly interesting for suburban African Americans. Until now, blacks had to physically access the institutions in the historic central city neighborhood, and that meant travel. If contemporary African Americans can access race-specific information from a majority white neighborhood or workplace computer, will the draw of the coethnic neighborhood and its institutions recede? I will address that question with data on group-specific media usage in chapter 5.

Black Public Sphere Ideologies

I have given cursory mention to the different ideologies of the black public sphere while recounting its history. These ideologies are strategies for black advancement that have been debated since emancipation and have evolved over the years (Harris-Lacewell 2004). Dawson defines ideology this way:

> a worldview readily found in the population, including sets of ideas and values that cohere, that are used publicly to justify political stances, and that shape and are shaped by society. Further, political ideology helps to define who are one's friends and enemies, with whom one would form political coalitions, and

furthermore, contain a causal narrative of society and the state. (Dawson 2001, 4–5; see also Harris-Lacewell 2004 and Dawson 2012)

These ideologies appear in the race-specific information and norms presented in majority-black social network institutions like the churches and volunteer organizations based in the historic urban neighborhood.[17] Suburban African Americans cannot readily find this information in the majority-white networks of the neighborhood and workplace where they spend most of their time. As these black-specific ideologies differ, so will the reinforcing behaviors. A separatist may put their efforts completely toward helping black-owned businesses, while an adherent to a more liberalist ideology may register people to vote. The thread that runs through all of these ideologies (except black conservatism) is the strong relationship between racial identity and linked fate, regardless of SES.

The major difference between the black-specific ideologies and those of the American mainstream comes in its distance from classic American liberalism. American liberalism is rooted in the privileged status of the individual, skepticism about the role of state power, and the sanctity of private property (Dawson 1995). The black public sphere, growing completely as a self-deterministic collective, rejects most of those notions. The *group* takes preeminence over the *individual* in group consciousness, the state has often been the only means of redress, and the unequal economic starting point of Reconstruction has always made the question of indebtedness central to claims against the state—be it through conventional means, such as redistribution, or radical ones, such as reparations. Dawson identifies six major black ideologies in his 2001 and 2012 works[18] and tests their prevalence in black political thought using the 1993 National Black Politics Survey. I will examine the adherence of suburban African Americans to these ideologies based on their social networks and racial identities.

Radical liberalism[19] is the most prevalent black ideology and contemporarily fits in with the shift from protest to politics. It has an activist orientation with support for a strong central state, limits on capitalism, and support for redistribution. Proponents include Du Bois, King, and Jesse Jackson (2012). Dawson finds that the adherence to a radical liberalist ideology is rooted in one's education, age, racialized worldview, social location, and embeddedness in black social networks (2001). Its more pessimistic "cousin" (2001, 125) is *disillusioned liberalism.* The disillusioned liberals understand America's promise to citizens through the U.S. Constitution, they just do not think America will live up to it because it will require upending the racial hierarchy. Their policy preferences are akin to those of the radical liberal but may be more pointed and focused on the specific race (as opposed to other poor or racial minorities). Proponents include King in the later years of his life, Malcolm X, and the Student Nonviolent Coordinating Committee (SNCC). Disillusioned liberals are encouraged by black discourse. They are the only ones that think neither major party works hard on black issues. Perceptions of black/white economic status and assessment of whites' feelings toward blacks are also strong predictors of holding this ideology (2001).

Black nationalism has been the strongest challenger to liberalism in the black public sphere, and it is obvious why, given its counterpublic roots. For the black nationalist, race structures all social interactions and takes precedence over other cleavages, such as class or gender. Black nationalists have proposed various versions of a black nation; be it self-determination within the government, a state within the state via some semi-autonomous territory (presumably in the southern United States), or a territory outside U.S. borders. This idea still has surprising traction among contemporary African Americans, as half of Dawson's sample think blacks constitute an internal black nation, not just another ethnic group (2001). There is also some support for outright separatism. Support for the poor increases with being tied to black networks and holding a black nationalist ideology. Proponents include the Black Panther Party, Marcus Garvey, Stokely Carmichael, and Minister Louis Farrakhan.

Black socialism[20] believes in the preeminence of race but also the intersectionality of race and class. This black-centric offshoot of socialism was prevalent in New York from 1900 to 1970 but disappeared later as the state cloaked their repression in the search for Russian sympathizers. Proponents include A. Philip Randolph, Angela Davis, and Amiri Baraka (2012).

The direct counterpart to the aforementioned ideologies is *black conservatism* (see Simpson 1998 and Philpot 2007 for a good treatment of black conservatism, the ideological congruence with the modern Republican Party, and its manifestations in African American communities). A major shift from liberalism is the attribution of community problems to individual and group deficiencies rather than the systematic discriminatory practices of the mainstream. Black conservatives support uplift from within instead of reliance on the state and believe economic equality is the best way to gain acceptance. Black conservatism is the least supported ideology, and adherents feel more warmth toward whites, less warmth toward the Nation of Islam, and are opposed to the view that blacks should join black-only organizations, form their own party, or form a separate nation (2001). Proponents include Booker T. Washington, Thomas Sowell, and Shelby Steele.

Lastly, *black feminism* focuses on the intersection of race and gender. White women originally excluded black feminists from their causes, so the role of race in the ideology is vital (Dawson 1995). Women are more supportive of the ideology than men, and people embedded in black networks have a more positive view toward it. Black feminists felt more warmth toward Anita Hill and are more pro-choice. Proponents include Sojourner Truth and Angela Davis.

The prevalence of these ideologies has changed throughout the history of blacks in America. Yet the data show a clear adherence to an ideology somewhere between disillusioned liberalism and nationalism/separatism for suburban African Americans.

AFRICAN AMERICAN POLITICAL PARTICIPATION

I have spent the bulk of this chapter explaining how suburban African Americans will come to participatory decisions that differ from their white neighbors and urban coethnics. In short, suburban African Americans are in a unique political and social environment that heightens perceptions of racial minority status. Since neighborhood and workplace networks are likely to be majority white, information transmitted in these social networks may not be favorable to racial issues or a racial ideology. Therefore, if suburban African Americans desire such favorable information they must find it in networks other than the neighborhood or workplace. To find favorable information, they could travel and participate in the historic counterpublic institutions like the black church, formal political volunteer organizations, and social organizations that the group can mobilize for political purposes. These black public sphere institutions will expose suburban African Americans to counter ideologies focused on racial uplift and behavioral norms rooted in group consciousness. This attitudinal environment influences their behavioral choices.

The rational choice theory of political participation, also referred to as the calculus of voting (Downs 1957; Riker and Ordeshook 1968), and its many extensions state that the decision to participate depends on the accurate calculation of costs and benefits associated with the activity. If the benefits outweigh the costs, then the rational actor should engage in an activity.[21] In addition to predicting participation based on costs and benefits, we can also compare relative costs and relative benefits to see how an actor views each behavior.

I expect that suburban African Americans will engage in group-based behaviors because they deliver more benefits despite being more resource costly (Verba et al. 1995). Voting is relatively costless, even at moderate SES levels. Political information—like the date of the election or location of the polling place—is not difficult to find and outside groups often subsidize these costs. Candidate information is also readily available. However, voting for two conservative candidates who do not discuss racialized issues in a positive way will produce a negligible benefit. Conversely, group-based behaviors, such as donating money to a coethnic candidate outside of one's jurisdiction or volunteering time at the counterpublic civil rights organization, may be more resource costly but will also produce the benefit of reinforcing one's group consciousness. I hypothesize that suburban African Americans with high racial identification will engage in the group-conscious behavior, even if it is not to the exclusion of casting a local vote. If the race/racial ideology of the candidate is the predominant factor in the decision to participate and fulfill that civic duty, suburban whites and urban African Americans have a much better chance of finding a kindred in their local election choices than African American suburbanites. I anticipate that this dearth of fulfillment will push suburban African Americans to choose group-based behaviors at higher rates than suburban whites and urban African Americans.

One can imagine a scenario where a suburban African American sees a plethora of yard signs and bumper stickers in the neighborhood supporting the Republican congressional candidate, who pundits project to win the heavily gerrymandered district easily. Then, at work, his coworkers are discussing a claim the candidate made about some (tangentially) racialized issue, such as early voting hours or fraudulent registration. Viewed through a racial lens and with heightened sensitivity, the suburban African American views the lack of a retort from the Democratic candidate as unacceptable and chooses to withdraw from that local congressional race. At the same time, he finds out when the central city NAACP chapter is training deputies to register black nonvoters. Even though becoming a deputy requires more effort, and is therefore more resource costly, the symbolic benefits and social bond with members of a like-minded political network will be large. In addition to the symbolic benefits, his or her efforts may help elect a candidate whose vote will aid the group and counterbalance the unappealing suburban candidate. It is his placement in a disagreeable network that spurs the choice to participate in a particular manner.

ENVIRONMENT AND BLACK POLITICAL BEHAVIOR

Few studies discuss the confluence of environment and African American participation explicitly, hence the need for this project. There is research on the racial makeup of cities, municipal candidates, and their influences on African American political behavior (Bobo and Gilliam 1990, Kauffman 2004), but they do not focus on suburban neighborhoods.

In their 2007 article, "Race, Roll-Off, and Racial Transition," Vanderleeuw and Sowers say that black turnout has increased because they have made gains in participatory resources and have been able to reap *tangible* benefits from political engagement. Resources include the gains in SES and efficacy following the civil rights movement. On the benefits side, the Democratic Party's shift to champion civil rights meant that blacks' preferences found representation in most electoral contests. Moreover, while on average blacks vote less than whites and are less likely to donate money, they are more likely to work on a campaign.[22] Verba et al. (1995) found that the issues that motivate African Americans to participate are also distinct. While whites focus more on taxes and economic issues, blacks care more about things like government intervention and assistance through policy areas like education, youth issues, and crime.

One of the reasons why African Americans in these areas are spurred to turn out is the behavior of black politicians that descriptively represent the majority of black inner-city areas and symbolically represent racially identifying African Americans in other areas. In Gosnell's (1967) tome on the subject, he describes the black politician as someone whose election served as a source of pride for the entire community, even if they were at times more committed to self-interest and rising through the white-dominated political structure than championing the more radical strands of civil rights. He describes how elites designed their appeals in political meetings to stir emotions, playing on the high levels of group consciousness and the threat to the counterpublic. This served to both maintain cohesion and mobilize voters. Contemporary research shows this to still be the case. Pantoja and Segura (2003) say that these appeals and norms should focus on racial hostilities and threats from the mainstream because they make minorities (Latinos in this case) more closely monitor public affairs and participate in ways corresponding to racial solidarity.

If suburban African Americans do not have the ability to vote for a black politician or in a racially salient local election, what does the literature say about their group-based alternatives? Studies with the most relevance to my theory say very little. Gosnell talks about how the counterpublic institutions mattered more to the inner-city African Americans than party organizations. In their early works, Verba and his colleagues found that African Americans and whites engage in informal political activities equally in their communities, but that African Americans are more active on civil rights even at higher resource costs. Group-based alternatives also increase African American participation, while for whites the rate stays the same.

Vanderleeuw and Sowers (2007) show the salience of racial identity and the rejection of the local races when reporting on ballot roll-off.[23] They find that when there is a racial choice on the ballot, African Americans are less likely to roll off the ballot. When education is controlled, African Americans are on average more likely to roll off than whites are. In chapter 5, I will confirm this finding for suburban African Americans, as they are more likely to skip the local congressional election, after having voted for president, than are suburban whites or urban African Americans. This study will go further by testing a variety of alternative participatory behaviors to see if suburban residence has an independent effect on the choice and to what extent phenomena like racial identification/group consciousness, social network status, and participation in the black public sphere influence that decision.

There is some indication that suburban African Americans will engage in more alternative participation. During the civil rights movement, the more affluent black belt suburbanites served as the leadership cadre for the civil rights organizations and intentionally directed their focus toward their less fortunate coethnics (Gosnell 1967). Contemporarily, the grandchildren of the aforementioned are now leaders in corporate America and occupy the same symbolic positions of prestige as the preachers of the previous eras. However, unlike those preachers who were also physically rooted in the poor communities, these new leaders actively miss that connection to the historic urban neighborhood (Hochschild 1996). Some African Americans "mourn rather than celebrate the weakening links; an ex-urbanite finds it 'difficult to maintain close ties to two communities, as much as I want to. We've got to participate in . . . [the new suburban neighborhood] as a matter of survival and so as not to be isolated . . . [But] I miss my old ties. It's painful, damned painful'" (125). The data confirm this sentiment. More well-off African Americans see more discrimination in society, including believing there has been less of a reduction in unfair treatment, expect less improvement in the future, and also are more likely than less affluent African Americans to say they have personally experienced discrimination. These middle-class blacks also feel a responsibility to the collective history and to their poorer coethnics (Hochschild 1996). In line with my theory about suburban residence, Hochschild finds that working with whites increases the black middle-class perception of discrimination (though she does not test the specific effect of neighborhood context).

All of this leads to a particular type of group-based participation by African Americans. They choose these behaviors because the norms of counterpublics in general and the black public sphere specifically encourage members to view politics in group-based terms (Gay 2004; Chong and Rogers 2005). However, group consciousness does not influence every participatory behavior equally. As expected, and hypothesized for suburban African Americans, the influence is greatest on those activities that require solidarity and a resource expenditure above simple self-interest or civic duty. Chong and Rogers (2005) find that group consciousness increased all turnout modestly but did promote voting in primaries. It had a larger effect on alternative forms of participation, such as campaign activity, petitioning officials, influencing others to vote, donating money, and participating in protests and boycotts. Dawson (2001, 2012) finds that participation in boycotts is also linked to a separatist ideology. He found that group consciousness did not promote more presidential voting, registration, or meeting attendance. However, neighborhood or social network effects were not included in the model.

This study will test those same relationships and see if suburban environment changes the equation. This is a question raised by Gay (2004), as she suggests that moving out of resource-deprived communities may erode a sense of collective identity and fate, and therefore the potential for group-based mobilization (560). The study will also explicitly test whether suburban residence has an independent influence on the African Americans who live there, particularly whether they look more like their white neighbors, with whom they share socioeconomic status, or urban African Americans, with whom they share a racial identity.

The preceding has laid the theoretical foundation for the rest of the book. The analysis will test four hypotheses:

Hypothesis 1: African Americans in majority white social networks will have very different racial opinions and hold more racially radical ideologies than whites in majority white networks and blacks in majority black networks.

Hypothesis 2: Suburban African Americans will view the networks they are in most often (neighborhood and workplace) as less receptive to their racial identity than those where they can choose their network partners (volunteer organizations and churches).

Hypothesis 3: Suburban African Americans will view the black public sphere as a norm and information transmitter. Suburban residence will have an independent influence on racialized opinions and more racially radical ideologies.

Hypothesis 4: Suburban African Americans will have an unfavorable view of their local political environment and therefore will be more likely to engage in more group-based, alternative participation.

3. Suburban African Americans and Social Networks

This chapter focuses on the effect of majority white social networks on political motivations and decision making of suburban African Americans. If the majority of white respondents in majority white social networks have a more conservative racial ideology, one should not expect a group-conscious African American in the network to receive racially reinforcing information. This disagreement in the network could cause these individuals to seek out majority African American networks. Indeed, the data show that racialized opinions are very different based on network racial makeup. African Americans in white networks would be right to assess them as nonreinforcing (or even hostile) to their racial ideology on a range of subjects and issue dimensions. These differences are also influenced by individual racial identity.

The literature shows that the networks in which one spends the most time will have the largest effect on political behaviors (Rosenstone and Hansen 1993). This is because people most often socialize with those with whom they agree. Once this agreement is established, more informed associates will pass along relevant information to other individuals, saving them the cost of seeking it out themselves. They also use this information to make political decisions and adjust their preferences. However, for some network members the situation is not so straightforward. One cannot always choose the people in his or her network. This is especially true when it comes to one's neighbors and coworkers (Huckfeldt and Sprague 1995). Those in the minority of their network on a particular issue dimension should reject the network's norms and seek out more consonant information (Scheufele et al. 2004). The research on homophily shows that race is one of the major ways people assess the majority/minority makeup of their networks. If this is the primary categorization of the network, then issues that revolve around this dimension may be particularly salient and influence the minority member's behavior. The literature is inconclusive as to the effect of minority status on the individual. Mutz (2002) finds that the minority individual recedes from political activity, while Scheufele et al. (2004) show that network-minority individuals vigorously seek out political information and therefore indirectly increase their political behavior.

The chapter will assess the effect of these networks using the National Politics Study (NPS) respondents' self-reporting of the racial makeup of their neighborhood, workplace, and church. While respondents could choose from many racial makeups, including "all races" or "black, white, and Hispanic," this analysis will be restricted to respondents in "mostly white" and "mostly black" networks. Forty-nine black respondents are in majority white neighborhoods, just 6.4 percent of the 756 blacks in the dataset. In contrast, there are 465 whites in majority white neighborhoods (50.5 percent of 919 whites) and 409 blacks in majority black neighborhoods (54.5 percent of all blacks). Since these numbers will lessen the chance we see statistically significant differences between the groups, any findings that meet the standard are consequential. As to workplace, there are 187 blacks in majority white workplaces (24.7 percent of all blacks) compared to 468 whites in majority white workplaces (50.9 percent of whites) and 179 blacks in majority black workplaces (23.6 percent of blacks). As expected, most people worship in coethnic congregations. For blacks, 454 attend majority black churches (60 percent) compared to 467 (50.8 percent) whites who attend majority white churches. Only 31 blacks attend majority white churches (4.1 percent).

Examining the racial opinion questions will allow comment on how African Americans and whites in white networks compare to past respondents. By all accounts, racism and racial prejudice are less prevalent than they were just a few decades ago. Even if there has not been an increasing intimacy between the races, expositions of "old-fashioned" racial sentiments like, "Blacks are biologically inferior," are largely a thing of the past. Evidence has shown that the group-based battles have shifted to a symbolic racism (Bobo 1983; Bobo et al. 2012; Hutchings and Valentino 2004). This symbolic racism or racial resentment (Kinder and Sanders 1996) is more rooted in the political demands of blacks, particularly whether they are pushing too hard for progress or if the basis for those demands, the legacy of Jim Crow and continued private discrimination, are urgent enough to justify government action. Elites have long mobilized their constituents on group-based terms. The responsive need for a unified collective agenda on the part of black elites, and the realization by white elites—like Richard Nixon, Barry Goldwater, and Lee Atwater—that the same issues can be counter-mobilizers for their causes, exacerbates the racialization of certain government policies (Gilens 1996, 2009; Mendelberg 2001). Examples include: welfare (Gilens 1996), school busing (Bobo 1983), affirmative action (Kinder and Sanders 1996; Bobo et al. 2012), and punitive crime policies (Peffley and Hurwitz 2002). Elites often frame these policies as being designed to disproportionately help racial and ethnic minorities. The group-based support/opposition increases when these policies are redistributive (Gilens 2009). Mendelberg (2001) shows that they even affect policies not directly tied to race, while Valentino (1999) finds that the racialization of these policies has an effect on the evaluation of (white) candidates. This trend appears to have persisted.

The hypotheses for this chapter will expound on the general hypotheses from chapter 2. Hypothesis 1: In general, blacks in white neighborhoods and workplaces will have different opinions and levels of alternative participation than whites in white neighborhoods and workplaces. Their opinions and behaviors will be more group conscious than those of blacks in black neighborhood and workplace networks. Hypothesis 1a: They will have less trust in American institutions, will have more group-conscious opinions on racial issues, and will be more likely to believe America has not lived up to its values than both whites in white networks and blacks in black networks. Hypothesis 1b: They will engage in more participation at church and receive different norms than whites in white networks and blacks in black networks. Hypothesis 1c: They will engage in more group-based participation than whites in white networks and blacks in black networks.

Hypothesis 2 will test whether suburban African Americans are able to correctly assess the discordance of their proximate networks and whether they feel the same about those they self-select. Specifically, suburban African Americans will be more likely to say their views are not in line with those in their neighborhoods or workplaces and are more in line with those in their churches and volunteer organizations.

METHODS

Means tests and logistic regressions will serve as the hypothesis tests.[1] For each question, the analysis will measure the proportion of respondents that answer a certain way for each group outlined in the hypothesis. The next step is to evaluate the differences between these proportions for statistical significance. For example, 85 percent of blacks in white neighborhoods said they voted for Barack Obama, compared to only 65 percent of whites—a difference of 20 percent. Essentially, the test measures whether a difference of that magnitude (20 percent) could arise due to chance[2] or if it is large enough that it would persist in repeated samples. Since the traditional standard of 95 percent confidence is difficult to reach given the low number of blacks in the NPS and CCES, I will also evaluate differences at the still accepted 90 percent degree of confidence as statistically significant. In addition to the means tests, I will run logistic regressions to test the effect of network racial makeup on respondent opinions. While the means tests will compare all suburban African Americans to all suburban whites, the regression will show those relationships while specifically accounting for income, education, ideology, gender, age, group identification, and home ownership.

RESULTS

The data provide strong confirmation for hypothesis 1. In general, there are large differences between blacks in white networks and whites in white networks. These differences are manifest on all issue dimensions and at times are quite stark. Therefore, it would be understandable that an African American in such a network would reject proffered information on racial issues. The same African American would likely find a more welcoming environment in majority African American networks, as the opinions are much closer. In terms of majority African American networks, blacks who work in majority white workplaces actually have more racialized opinions than blacks in majority black workplaces.

Trust in Government Institutions

As of this writing, the relationship between African Americans and the state has received much discussion. The nomination of Hillary Clinton as the 2016 Democratic Party presidential candidate has renewed discussion of punitive crime policies (such as sentencing disparities between powder cocaine and crack cocaine) and the disproportionate toll they have taken on African American communities. A well-received book by Michelle Alexander (2010) likens the prison system to a new Jim Crow regime. The government has consistently

Figure 3.1a. Institutional Trust by Race and Neighborhood

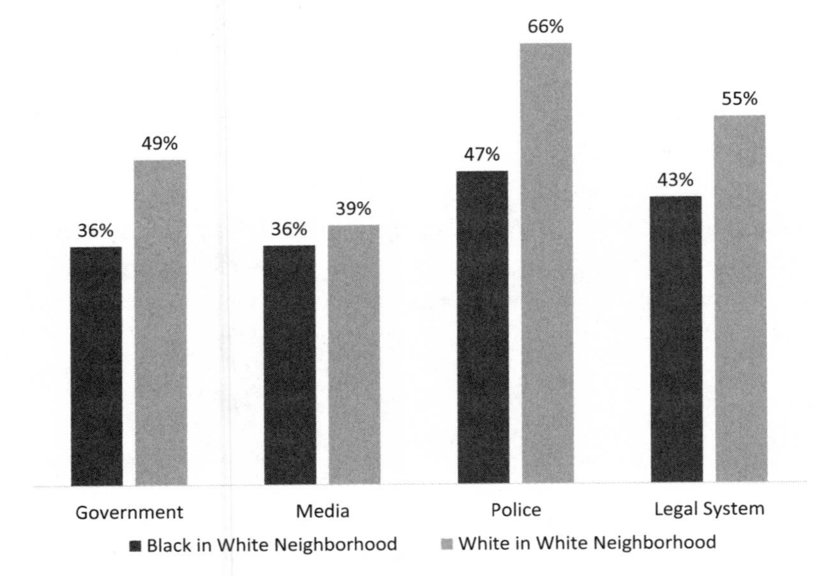

Source: 2004 National Politics Study.

cut benefits aimed at the poor, including vehement opposition to the Affordable Care Act (Obamacare), and resisted expanding Medicaid to close coverage gaps. Perhaps most impactful has been the spate of African American males killed by police, which spawned the Black Lives Matter movement. Of course, the NPS preceded all of these specific events, but as the recounting of the black counterpublic sphere showed, these issues are not new. As expected, whites in white neighborhood and workplace networks have much more trust in American institutions than blacks in white networks.

Respondents were asked about their level of trust in the government, media, police, and legal system. Across all four institutions, blacks in white networks feel less trust by an average of 12 percent in the neighborhood and workplace. The largest difference in both networks was on trust in the police. Blacks in white neighborhoods were 19 percent less trusting, with less than half saying they trusted the police, compared to two-thirds of whites in white neighborhoods (see figure 3.1a). In the workplace network, the gap in trust for the police is even larger at 24 percent (see figure 3.1b). There were no significant differences between blacks in white networks and blacks in black networks.[3]

Figure 3.1b. Institutional Trust by Race and Workplace

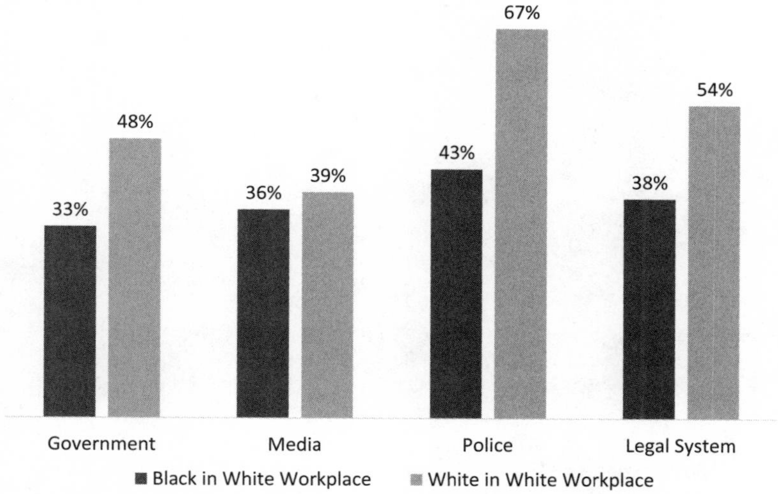

67%
54%
48%
43%
39%
36%
38%
33%
Government
Media
Police
Legal System
■ Black in White Workplace
■ White in White Workplace

Source: 2004 National Politics Study.

American Values

These differentials by race and network also extend to more general feelings about American values. As mentioned in the previous chapter, one of the major distinctions between Dawson's black ideologies is how much America has lived up to its values and commitment to equality. I would expect African Americans in majority white networks to believe America has fallen short on both counts because of socialization to these ideologies. The NPS data show this to be the case. Interestingly, the only significant difference at the neighborhood level was on the question of whether individuals can succeed in America if they work hard. On this question blacks in white neighborhoods were less likely than whites in white neighborhoods to believe this to be true.

The data are much more consistent for the workplace network. Ideologically, blacks and whites in white workplaces adhere to very different values and perceptions of America. Blacks in white workplaces are less likely than whites in white workplaces to say, "You only need to work hard to succeed in America" (64.2 percent to 74.5 percent), less likely to say it is not a big problem if some people have more of a chance at life than others (37.1 percent to 43

Figure 3.2. American Values by Race and Workplace

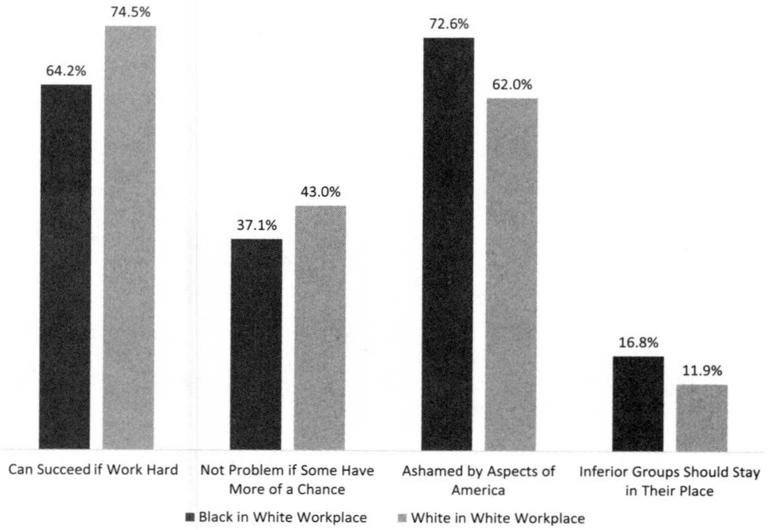

Source: 2004 National Politics Study.

percent), and more likely to say there are some things about America today that make them feel ashamed (72.6 percent to 62 percent) (see figure 3.2).

Racial Opinion

The racial opinions battery shows more pronounced differences than those for institutional trust or American values. As stated earlier, scholars have noted that racism has evolved from sentiments like blacks are biologically inferior to a more symbolic racism (Kinder and Sanders 1996) based on ideas that minority claims are illegitimate. We see evidence of this in the opinion differences on racial questions.

As hypothesized, blacks in white neighborhoods hold more racialized views than whites in white neighborhoods. A full 32 percent more blacks respond affirmatively to the question of whether African Americans have gotten less than they deserve (see figure 3.3a). These blacks are also more likely than whites to say the races will never be comfortable with each other even if they are close friends (25.6 percent to 17.7 percent). Blacks in white neighborhoods

Figure 3.3a. Race Opinion by Race and Neighborhood

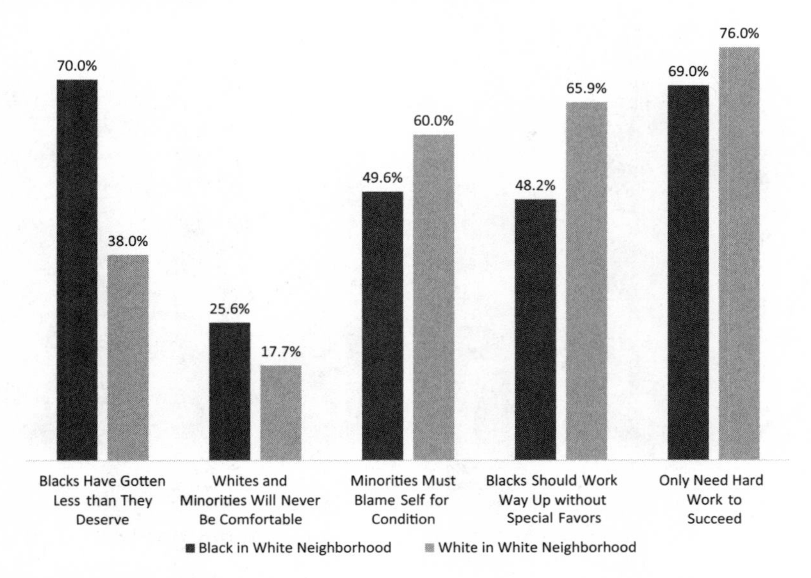

Source: 2004 National Politics Study.

are less likely than whites in white neighborhoods to think individual minorities are to blame for not doing well in life (49.6 percent to 60 percent), and they are less likely than whites to say blacks should overcome prejudice and work their way up without special favors like the Irish, Italians, and Jewish people did (48.2 percent to 65.9 percent). Whites are also more likely to say one can succeed in America with hard work (69 percent to 76 percent). In sum, whites in white neighborhoods consistently doubt African Americans' commitment to individualism and believe they have misplaced the reason for their lower status. They also believe African Americans should not expect the state to rectify disparities.

The two groups also have a very different outlook on race and discrimination in their lives. Almost two-thirds of blacks in white neighborhoods say they have personally faced discrimination or unfair treatment because of their race (62 percent). This compares to only 20 percent of whites in white neighborhoods. When asked whether blacks face discrimination, 82 percent of blacks in white neighborhoods say yes, compared to 68 percent of whites. Most interestingly, only 15.9 percent of those blacks think most whites want to give blacks a better break, compared to 42.6 percent of whites who feel the same. Blacks

Figure 3.3b. Race Opinion by Race and Neighborhood

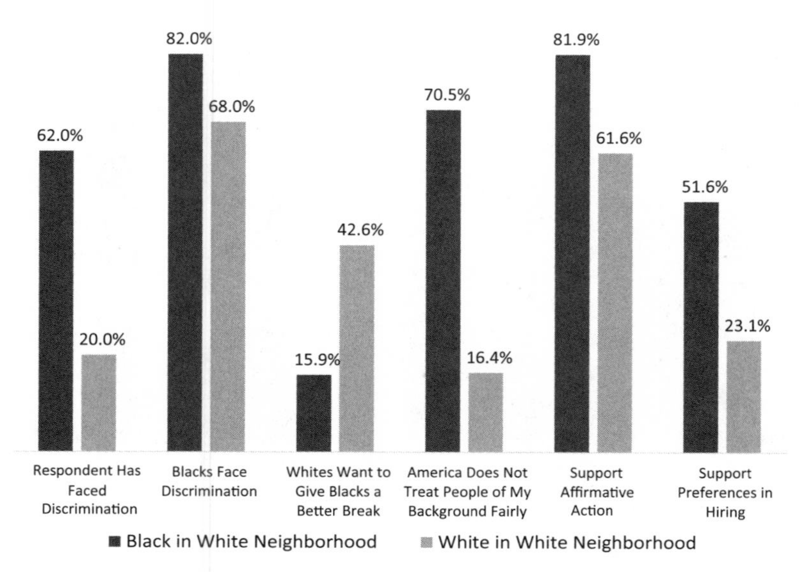

Source: 2004 National Politics Study.

in white neighborhoods are also more likely to recognize disparate treatment in society. A full 54 percent more blacks than whites in white neighborhoods say American society has treated my race unfairly, and 20 percent more blacks than whites believe affirmative action is a way to correct disparities. This recognition extends to policy, as 28.5 percent more blacks in white neighborhoods favor preferential treatment in hiring (see figure 3.3b). When thinking about minorities' perceptions of their networks, almost 85 percent of African Americans in white neighborhoods think whites want to keep them down or do not care about them (the alternative choices to the question of whether whites want to see blacks get a better break). With such a level of distrust, why should those African Americans feel comfort in their neighborhood networks?

African Americans in white workplaces would also be correct in assuming their average network interaction will be with someone who differs on racial issues. A black respondent in a white workplace is 28 percent more likely than whites in white workplaces to say blacks have gotten less than they deserve (69 percent to 41 percent) and more likely to say the races will not be comfortable with each other, even if they are close friends (35.1 percent to 17.7 percent). Blacks are actually close to (though statistically distinct from) whites in white

Figure 3.4a. Race Opinion by Race and Workplace

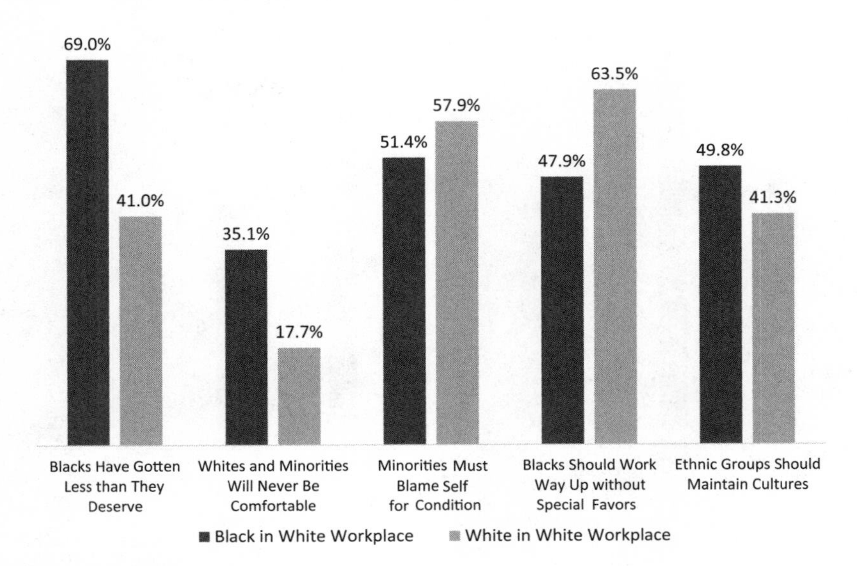

Source: 2004 National Politics Study.

workplaces on the issue of individual blame (51.4 percent to 57.9 percent), but the wide gap returns on whether blacks should have to succeed without special favors (47.9 percent to 63.5 percent). Interestingly, blacks in white workplaces are more likely to say blacks should maintain cultural distinctiveness (49.8 percent to 41.3 percent). This falls in line with the more racially radical of Dawson's ideologies, again an expression of a black separatist identity (see figure 3.4a).

The same pattern emerges when discussing discrimination. About two-thirds of blacks in white workplaces say they have personally experienced discrimination, compared with one-fifth of whites (67 percent to 21 percent), and they are more likely to think blacks face discrimination (84 percent to 70 percent). They are also less likely to say that whites want blacks to get a better break (24 percent to 41.8 percent). There is still the recognition of disparate treatment by society based on race. More than three-fourths (77.4 percent) of blacks in white workplaces, compared to only 16.7 percent of whites, say their race has been treated unfairly. These blacks consistently hold a more racially radical position on affirmative action than whites in white workplaces (88.3 percent to 60.1 percent), though overall support does go down when preferential treatment in hiring is assessed (52 percent to 24.2 percent). They are also

Figure 3.4b. Race Opinion by Race and Workplace

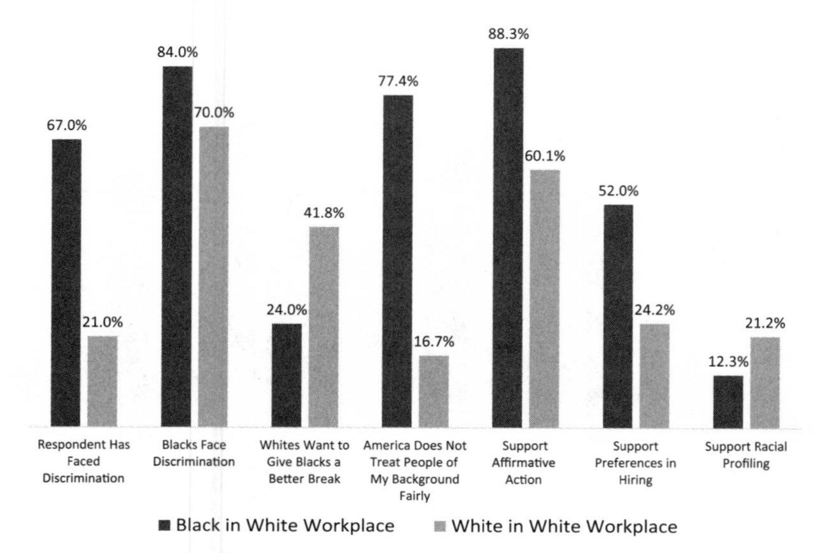

Source: 2004 National Politics Study.

less likely to support racial profiling by the police (12.3 percent to 21.2 percent) (see figure 3.4b).

The implications for suburban African Americans individually, and for racial policies in general, are obvious. For the individual, although the degree of differences between blacks and whites varies with the survey question, whites and African Americans in the same types of networks have very different perceptions of race in society. If the majority of one's network members hold these views, they will share information shaped by these norms. In addition, the frames attached to stories will differ greatly. An article passed on about a police shooting may precede a comment about the culpability of the subject. A member may follow a quote from an African American politician demanding the government help blacks in the inner cities with a comment that blacks complain too much. Observant suburban African Americans would be remiss not to think this will govern the policy decisions of their network members. Essentially, these people are not trying to help African Americans; in fact, they think African Americans' claims are illegitimate. Recognizing this uphill battle may heighten the desire and urgency of suburban African Americans to help their own group. Since they cannot do this by voting in their local elections,

I hypothesize they will turn to alternative participatory behaviors. The next section shows just that.

Political Behavior

Ideologically, blacks in white neighborhoods are more liberal and more Democratic than many of their neighbors. On a scale from 0–100, where 0 is extremely liberal and 100 is extremely conservative, the average score for blacks is 44.9, compared with 53.4 for whites. On a seven-point scale of partisanship, where 1 is strong Democrat and 7 is strong Republican, blacks average 2.27 (solidly Democratic), whereas whites average 4.47, the equivalent of "leaning Republican."

Although blacks and whites in white neighborhoods and workplaces have very different levels of trust in American institutions, feelings about America, and racialized opinions, there is not much difference in their actual political behaviors. That said, the hypothesized differences do emerge on political participation directed at the group. While there was no difference in turnout, campaigning for a candidate/party, talking to people about voting, or attending campaign events, blacks in majority white neighborhoods were more likely than whites in white neighborhoods to have given money to a campaign (35 percent to 24 percent) (see figure 3.5a). The survey did not probe the recipients of the contributions. However, participating by making a donation is consistent with the idea that these African Americans will direct their participatory efforts to elections that are more reinforcing of their racial preferences. Couple this finding with the fact that these African Americans are more than twice as likely to have campaigned for a minority candidate (13 percent to 5 percent), and there is reason to believe being a minority member in a neighborhood network leads to more group-based participation.

Blacks in white workplaces are also more liberal (43.4 to 52.2) and tend to lean Democrat (2.08 to 4.41). For workplace networks, blacks and whites are similar in the more "neutral" behaviors, though in this case there was no statistical difference in terms of donating money. Yet again, we see significant distances on more group-specific behaviors. More than twice as many blacks in white workplaces say they campaigned for minority candidates (13 percent to 5 percent). These blacks were also statistically more likely to prefer same-race leaders (51 percent to 42 percent), a strong sign of a racially radical ideology (see figure 3.5b).

Figure 3.5a. Alternative Participation by Race and Neighborhood

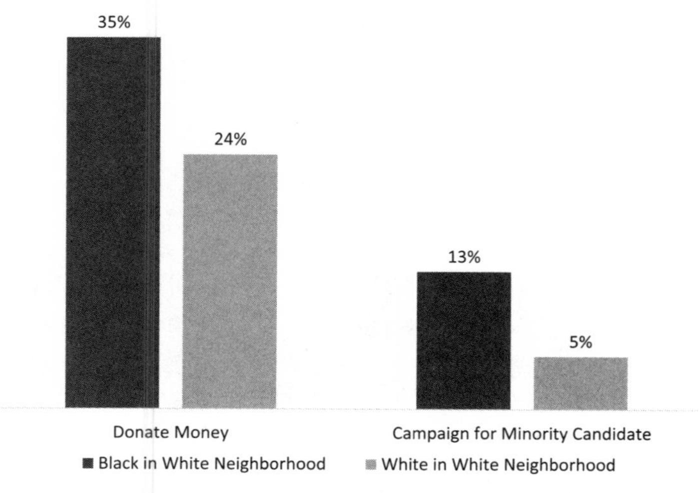

Source: 2004 National Politics Study.

Figure 3.5b. Alternative Participation by Race and Workplace

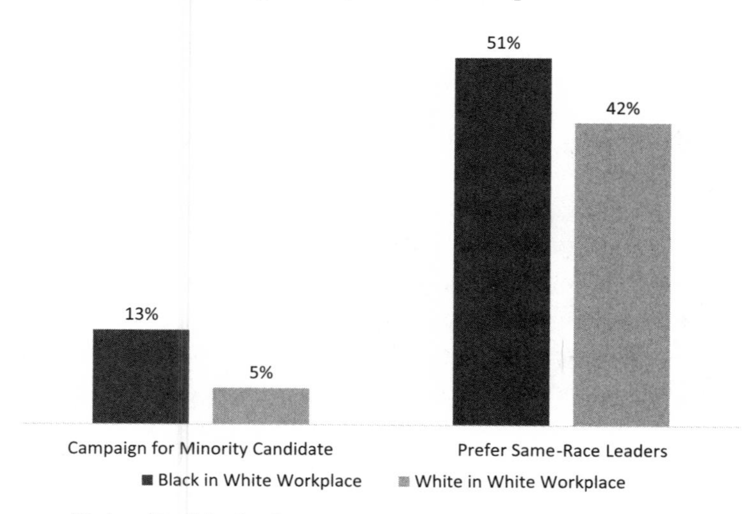

Source: 2004 National Politics Study.

The gravity of this finding cannot be overstated. It is unlikely that people in racially mixed networks would advocate same-race descriptive representation, and if the African American in the white workplace also lives in a white neighborhood (as 77.7 percent of them do), where they likely do not even have the choice of a coethnic leader, this desire is illuminating. They do not appear content with their electoral situation and long for political choices that reinforce their racial identity.

Religious Opinion and Participation

A clue as to why opinions and behaviors differ by racial minority neighborhood status may come from the role of the church as a political institution. Again, there are more differences in the workplace network than in the neighborhood, but the differences in both are robust. Blacks in white neighborhoods and workplaces are more likely to describe themselves as religious, and attend church more frequently than whites in white neighborhoods and workplaces (see the appendix). Yet the most interesting findings come in the very different norms and information each group receives in their churches. These differences may provide some rationale for the divergent opinions seen on the previous issue dimensions. As to norms, not only are blacks in white networks more likely to have heard about politics in church (see figure 3.6a), blacks in white workplaces are more likely to have their clergy spur them to take action on a political issue[4] and are almost twice as likely to have their clergy exhort them to vote (18.2 percent to 9.8 percent) (see figure 3.6b). These are specific behavioral norms presented by community leaders, and they unsurprisingly mirror the traditional role of the church in the black counterpublic.

The content and focus of this church network information is different as well. If suburban African Americans use majority black networks to get reinforcing information, the church (as expected) appears to be an excellent place to find it. Blacks in white networks were more likely than whites in white networks to have heard sermons on the economy, police, Iraq/War on Terror, and race. The largest gaps for each network type are on sermons about the police. Across both networks, around 40 percent of blacks in majority white networks heard such a sermon, compared to only 10 percent of whites.

Two things are of note. The symmetry between distrust in police and who hears about them in church is telling and provides support for the theory.

Figure 3.6a. Church-Based Participation by Race and Neighborhood

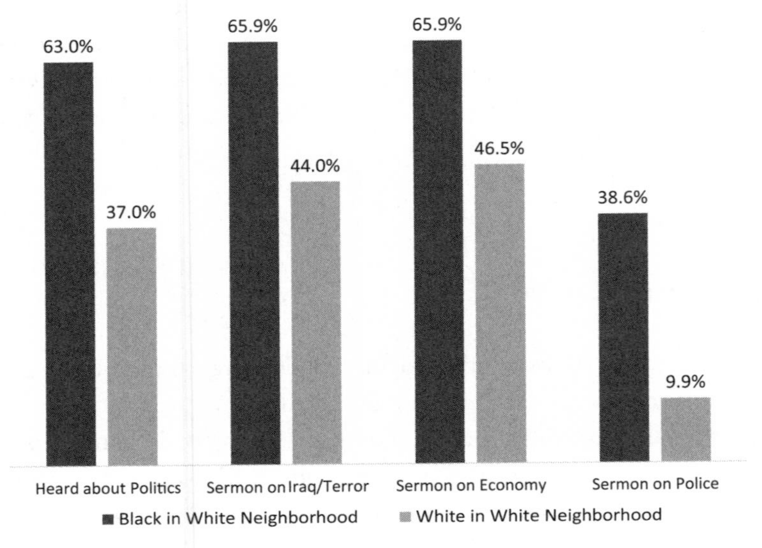

Source: 2004 National Politics Study.

Figure 3.6b. Church-Based Participation by Race and Workplace

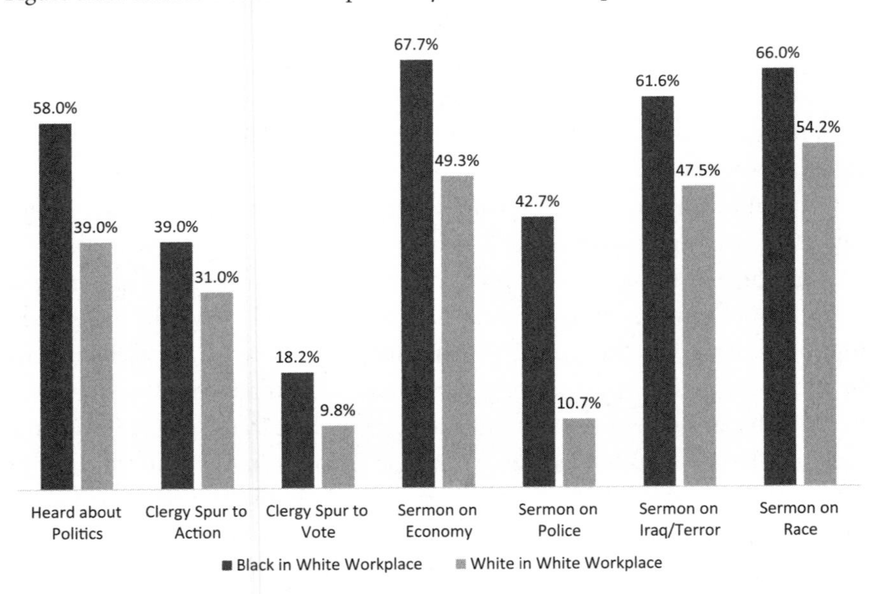

Source: 2004 National Politics Study.

There has been a strained relationship between police and African Americans for the country's entire history (in fact, since before it was a country). It would seem obvious that hearing critical commentary in church would lead to distrust. Second, the gap on hearing about race was only 12 percent for the workplace network (and not significant for the neighborhood). However, just hearing about race does not necessarily suggest the frame of the content. Given the racial views in the previous section, a negative frame or one challenging the legitimacy of claims could be just as frequent yet produce the observed differences.

COMPARISONS WITH BLACKS IN MAJORITY BLACK NETWORKS

Until now, I have not discussed the differences between blacks in white networks and blacks in black networks. The data show that there are not many. On virtually all of the questions analyzed in the previous section, the two types of African Americans are statistically indistinguishable, especially for the neighborhood network (see the appendix). This finding, or lack thereof, answers one of the major research questions for this project. To this point, it does not appear that blacks in white neighborhoods look like their white neighbors or are different from their coethnics who have majority status in their own neighborhoods.

However, when examining the different workplace networks, blacks in white workplaces do exhibit more racialized opinions. While there are no statistically significant differences between the African Americans of different workplaces in terms of institutional trust or alternative participation, the racialized opinion variables do confirm hypothesis 1. Blacks in white workplaces are less likely than blacks in black workplaces to say minorities should blame themselves for not doing well in life (51.4 percent to 58.1 percent) (see the appendix) and less likely to say blacks should overcome prejudice without special favors (47.9 percent to 55.7 percent). In an echo to Hochschild (1996), they are also more likely to say they face discrimination (67 percent to 57 percent). Blacks in white workplaces are also less likely to support racial profiling, with only 12.3 percent supporting it, compared with 21 percent of blacks in black workplaces, the same percentage as whites in white workplaces. While the p-value is slightly above the threshold (0.122), blacks in white workplaces are also more likely to say that racial groups should maintain their cultural distinctiveness (49.8 percent to 42.3 percent). There are no differences between blacks in white workplaces and blacks in black workplaces on whether blacks faced discrimination, whether whites want minorities to get a better break, or if society has treated blacks unfairly.

Blacks in white workplaces are also more pessimistic about America's commitment to equality than are blacks in black workplaces. They are less likely to say it is okay if some people have better life chances than others (37.1 percent to 44.3 percent) (see the appendix) or to agree that hard work is the only thing needed for success in America (64.2 percent to 72.4 percent). While they hold these different views, there are no statistical differences on group-based participation.

In sum, blacks in majority white networks are very different from whites in these networks on racial issues, ideology, and political participation. There are also differences between blacks in majority white networks and those in black networks, particularly on the racial opinion questions, where network minorities generally have more racialized opinions and a more pessimistic view of how American society treats the races. Again, it is not just being black that leads to more racialized opinions. It is minority status in the network that takes the extra step. The aggregate data support the hypotheses that network racial minority status matters, as does the amount of control over network partners.

The introduction of statistical controls will assess whether racial minority status in a network has an independent effect on these opinion and behavior differences while accounting for other possible influences, such as income, age, gender, education, group consciousness, party identification, ideology, and home ownership. Essentially, it strips all of those alternative explanations away to determine if being an African American in a majority white network is a determining factor in having more racialized opinions and engaging in more alternative participation. In general, all of the results from the means tests hold even after controlling for a host of alternative factors. Being an African American in a majority white network has an independent effect on the differences in opinions and behaviors found in earlier sections. The regression odds ratios will show how much more (or less) likely blacks in white networks are to answer questions in a particular way.

In order to summarize the relationships, I created additive indices for similar variables. The index allows for the modeling of variables on the same issue dimension. This method is appropriate when each of the questions deals with the same general concept. It presumes that similar respondents will answer each question in the same manner. The first index is for *institutional trust.*[5] It consists of the four institutional trust questions: trust in the government, trust in media, trust in the police, and trust in the legal system. Each question has the same four answer choices: (1) never; (2) only some of the time; (3) most of the time; and (4) just about always. If the answers to an individual's responses are added together, the index will range from 16 to 4. A person with maximum trust in all institutions will score a 16 on the scale because they answered "just about always" or "4" to each question. All respondents will fall somewhere along this continuum. When put into the ordinal regression, we will see the effect that being an African American in a majority white network has on trust in institutions when compared to whites in white networks and blacks in black networks (while controlling for various demographics that might alternatively explain the relationship). The second index deals with race opinions. The *race opinion*[6] index is comprised of five variables mentioned in various combinations previously: blacks getting less than they deserve, races being comfortable with each other, blacks not needing special favors, individual minorities being to blame for their life circumstances, and whether whites want to give blacks a break. The next indices deal with church participation. *Church participation*[7] (heard about politics in church and talked about politics in church); *church issue norms*[8] (heard a sermon about jobs/economy, police, Iraq/terrorism, immigration, and race); and *church participation norms*[9] (clergy encouraging respondent to take political action and clergy encouraging voting). Lastly, the *group participation*[10] index included questions on whether the respondent has campaigned for a minority candidate, prefers same-race leaders, and, in the past twelve months, has participated in any groups or organizations that are working to improve the conditions of racial or ethnic minorities.

There was a significant difference between blacks in white networks on all but the race opinion index. An African American in a white neighborhood is more than 2.5 times less likely to say they trust the societal institutions than a white respondent in a white neighborhood. This result holds up even when taking all of the other demographics into account (OR = 2.61) (see table 3.1). When examining the control/explanatory variable for ideology, the effect is positive (coefficient = 0.843), meaning more conservative respondents (people of "higher" ideology) will exhibit more trust (will answer "higher" on the institutional trust index) (see the appendix). The inclusion of the ideology variable means that blacks in white neighborhoods exhibit less trust than whites in white neighborhoods *of the same ideology.* The gap is even larger for workplace networks, where they are more than 3.5 times less likely to trust the institutions (OR = 3.66).

Peculiarly, the race opinion index as a whole was not statistically significant, though in the hypothesized direction. However, two of the individual questions were in the hypothesized directions and significant. Averaging between both network types, blacks in white networks are a little more than three times more likely to say blacks have gotten less than they deserve, which has been consistent with the means tests. They are also more than twice as likely to say the races will never be comfortable with each other. This is a remarkable result. The entire premise of network information transmission is being comfortable with other network members. If blacks in white networks do not think they will ever be comfortable with a majority of their network members (or that their network members will ever be comfortable with them), then the characterization of the network as disagreeable would be much more likely, especially on racial issues. If these feelings are prevalent, it could spur individuals to seek out reinforcing networks, or networks in which they feel comfortable, and this will lead to particular behaviors.

The divergent views on discrimination hold with the controls as well. In both the neighborhood and workplace, African Americans were more likely to say they personally face discrimination (neighborhood OR = 4.86; workplace OR = 6.83) and that blacks in general face discrimination (neighborhood OR = 2.55; workplace OR = 2.84). They also appear to support policies to address these disparities.

Only in the workplace network were the church participation and issue norm indices significant. Blacks in white workplaces were more than twice as likely to have heard a sermon on the topics mentioned earlier (OR = 2.19) and 65 percent more likely to have a clergy person encourage them to participate. Again, all of these are with other demographics controlled for.

In perhaps the strongest confirmation of the hypothesis, blacks in white networks were also twice as likely to engage in group-based participation (neighborhood OR = 2.34; workplace OR = 1.94). It is clear that the racial makeup of the workplace has an independent effect on opinions and behaviors beyond simple ideology or partisanship. African Americans in these majority white networks not only hold more racialized opinions, they also believe in directing their participatory resources to help the group as a whole. Both of these ideas have long-standing roots in the black counterpublic and

Table 3.1. Social Network Odds Ratios

	Neighborhood	*Workplace*
Institutional Trust Index	2.61*	3.66**
Deserve	3.51**	2.78**
Comfort	1.95+	2.32**
Personal Discrimination	4.86**	6.93**
Black Discrimination	2.55*	2.84**
Church Participation Index	1.30	1.65**
Church Issue Norm Index	1.77	2.19**
Group-Based Participation Index	2.34**	1.94**

Levels of Significance: ** = 0.01; * = 0.05; + = 0.10

Source: 2004 National Politics Study.

institutions, such as the black church, where they talk about politics, hear sermons on certain topics, and are encouraged to participate by their leaders.

As was shown with the means tests, blacks in white networks have very similar opinions and behaviors when compared to blacks in black networks, but there are some illuminating differences. For neighborhood networks, blacks in white networks were 95 percent more likely than blacks in black networks to have donated money to a campaign and they were (unexpectedly) more likely to say minorities should melt into the larger society (OR = 2.22), which is a rejection of a more radical and separatist ideology. For the workplace network, they are more likely to say they have experienced discrimination and were more likely to have discussed and heard about politics in church.

In the final evaluation, hypothesis 1 received strong confirmation. Blacks in white networks are in an information environment that does not reinforce their racial identity. If they choose to seek networks that will provide political norms, they can readily find them in the churches they attend. They are also more likely to engage in group-conscious participation.

VIEWS OF NETWORK INTERACTIONS BY NEIGHBORHOOD

The NPS questions allow an evaluation of normal opinion and behavior variables based on the racial makeup of the network. However, none of the questions deal specifically with the respondents' views of their networks, or suburban residence. Recognizing this, I included a series of questions on the

CCES survey about respondents' perceptions of certain networks. The specific questions ask whether respondents feel their views are in line with or in opposition to the majority of people in their neighborhood, job, church, or volunteer organization. These questions will test hypothesis 2: In networks where one is unable to exert control over the racial makeup (neighborhood and workplace), suburban African Americans will feel their views are not in line with the majority of network members. Essentially, they have recognized and experienced the opinion and participation differences seen in the preceding section. In the networks where they can choose the racial makeup (church and volunteer organizations) they will feel the opposite. The results prove the first part of the scenario. Fewer suburban African Americans say that their views are in line with the majority of people in their neighborhood when compared to suburban whites (49 percent to 59 percent). The gap is smaller yet persistent for the workplace (54 percent to 60 percent), and both differences are statistically significant. As to self-selected networks, the results are mixed. While suburban African Americans do not have a statistical difference with suburban whites in terms of volunteer organizations, they are more likely to think their views are more in line with their church networks (60 percent to 53 percent).

Comparing how the groups "rank" each of the networks sheds more light on these relationships. For suburban African Americans, the most consonant network is the church (60 percent), while for suburban whites it is the volunteer organization (61 percent). However, the second highest rated network for suburban whites is their job (60 percent). For suburban African Americans, the second highest rated network is the volunteer organization (59 percent). Suburban whites rate their job on par or more in agreement than the networks they have probabilistic control over. The workplace is clearly not hostile for many suburban whites; it is actually more comfortable than their churches (60 percent to 53 percent). The third most comfortable network for suburban whites is the neighborhood (59 percent), which suburban African Americans rated last (49 percent). There is no statistical difference between suburban African Americans and urban African Americans on the four questions; however, the urban African Americans mirror the rank order of the suburban African Americans.

In comparing suburban African Americans and suburban whites, African Americans were 72 percent (OR = 1.72) less likely to say their views were in line with their neighborhood and more than 2.5 times more likely to say their views are in line with others in their church, when statistical controls are included. The results for volunteer organizations and workplaces were all in the

Figure 3.7. Views In Line with the Majority by Race and Neighborhood

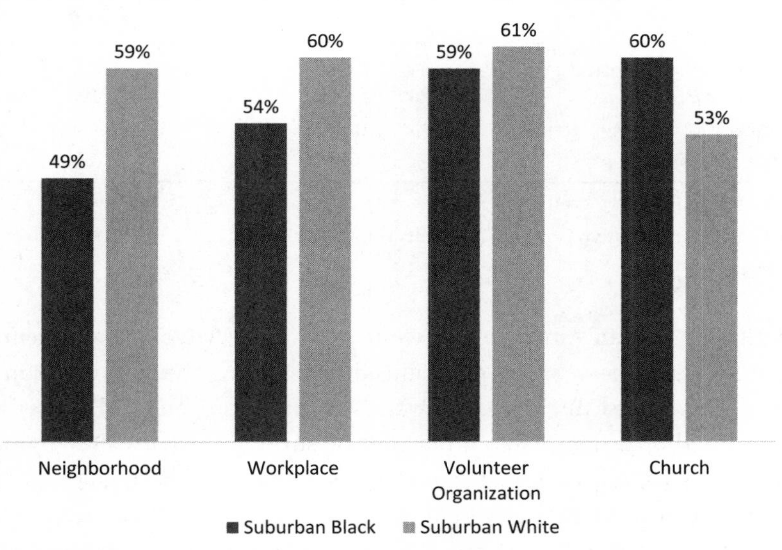

Source: 2008 Cooperative Congressional Election Study.

expected directions, and comparisons with urban African Americans were not statistically significant (see table 3.2). Therefore, we see that suburban residence, even when controlling for other factors, causes African Americans to view their networks differently than do suburban whites.

CONCLUSION

Examining the social network variables ultimately confirms the brunt of the hypotheses. Social network racial makeup does have an effect on the opinions and behaviors of African Americans in white networks when compared to those of their white counterparts. In short, minority network status matters, and matters even when accounting for things like group consciousness. That the regression results were consistently in the same direction as the means tests also suggests racial makeup and minority status have independent influences on this behavior while accounting for other demographics.

As hypothesized, there was a large difference between how blacks in white networks and whites in white networks felt about trusting the societal

Table 3.2. Network In Line Regressions

	Coefficient	*Odds Ratio*
Neighborhood Network	-0.544+	1.72
Workplace Network	-0.323	—
Volunteer Organization Network	0.073	—
Church Network	1.008**	2.74

Levels of Significance: ** = 0.01; + = 0.10
Source: 2008 Cooperative Congressional Election Study.

institutions. African Americans in white networks gave the government the lowest trust rating—a signal of disillusionment along the lines Dawson described. The largest differences between African Americans and whites were on racialized opinions. While it may not be surprising that whites' opinions were not particularly radical, it could be, as some scholars have suggested, that suburban African Americans would look more like their SES counterparts and less like their lower status coethnics. Yet they do not. These differences held on abstract questions, such as whether blacks have gotten less than they deserve, and on explicitly racialized policies, like racial profiling, again suggesting that neither government nor society has lived up to its promise. The same phenomenon may be at work in the finding that blacks in white networks are more likely than whites in white networks to campaign for a minority candidate and prefer same-race leaders, especially since the chance a coethnic is running in their personal election is quite low. The differences in ideology and political behavior were not as large.

On the question of whether whites wanted to give blacks a better break in life, hold them down, or do not care, the results are especially instructive. The prompting to think about a generic "white person" suggests this is how a respondent will view most whites by default. Once the respondent has interacted in the neighborhood, he or she can categorize a neighbor as an exception, but in thinking about random encounters, the African American resident in a white neighborhood appears to be on the defensive. It could also be the case that those in the network are racially egalitarian, but their influence is not enough to change the individual's perception of the larger racial world. Either way, being in a majority white network keeps these African Americans wary of the whites who surround them.

The differences in church type are also interesting because they track with the role of the church as a black counterpublic institution. The churches attended by African Americans in majority white neighborhoods and workplaces are much more explicitly pushing political action and speaking on topics important to the group in their sermons. While I did not stratify respondents on this question by the racial makeup of their church, it is clear that these churches are very different. There is also evidence that those who forego black churches for white ones hear a doctrine that would deemphasize racial identity (McDaniel and Ellison 2008).

The data on how respondents view their different networks also confirmed the related hypothesis 2 and are specific to suburban neighborhoods. Suburban African Americans see a separation in their proximate versus self-selecting networks, viewing the former as less in line with their views. They also rank their agreement in the expected way, while suburban whites say their job interactions are the second most agreeable out of the four. The primary difference between the jobs for these white and black respondents is that most of the people who suburban whites work with are of the same race. If suburban African Americans cannot get reinforcing information in their workplaces, or view the average white person as wanting to hold their race down, then it should come as no surprise that they find their self-selecting networks to be more in line with their views.

Perhaps the most contributory finding of the chapter is that the workplace appears to be more influential than the neighborhood. While both sets of findings are in the expected directions for both the differences in the means and the odds of choosing a particular answer in the regressions, the workplace has a stronger effect. The workplace networks were also the only ones that activated the values questions. Essentially, one can anticipate how the group will frame future ambiguous information, such as how they will react to President Obama commenting on police tactics, if they have expressed a prevailing sentiment that blacks complain too much.

While this finding surely warrants further study, it is understandable why this would be the case. While neighborhood makeup is not probabilistic, neighborhood *interaction* is. There is very little that will compel a person to interact with his or her neighbors. If one does attempt an interaction and realizes the network is disagreeable, the remainder of encounters could be superficial. This is less likely the case with workplaces. Typical office job workers spend one-third of their day around coworkers. Additionally, superiors may frown upon, or even sanction, retreating from interactions, even when one's network is disagreeable. These constant and forced interactions may make minority status—and racial differences—even more apparent to the individual and explain the gap on racialized opinions, perceptions of discrimination, and group-based participation.

The implications of this chapter are simple yet powerful. African Americans in white networks in general, and suburban African Americans in particular, spend most of their time in uncomfortable information environments with people who do not share their opinions and who believe their claims of grievance and discrimination to be illegitimate. This constant minority status and discord (even if unstated or internalized) will continue to heighten the salience and appeal of helping the group. This will be especially true of helping those coethnics with whom they share a group-based ideology and who draw the ire of the average white person in a white network. Since this aid cannot come through local voting, it is understandable that suburban African Americans would strongly support group-based participatory behaviors.

4. Suburban African American Ideology and Perception of the Cultural Community

The preceding chapter showed why suburban African Americans might consider some social networks hostile, or at least expect that proffered information will go against their preferences. African Americans in majority white networks interact with peers who hold vastly different views on race, trust in government institutions, church experiences, political ideologies, and feelings about group-based participation. Their opinions and behaviors more closely resemble those of their coethnics in majority black networks. Suburban African Americans also view their social networks differently. They are more likely to say their views are not in line with the majority of people in their neighborhood but are in line with the majority of people in their church. These differences correspond to the probabilistic chances of encountering coethnics in each network.

Having established the wide divergence of opinions between whites and blacks in majority white networks, like the suburbs, on issues directly tied to the African Americans' identity, the question that motivates this chapter is, where do they go to find reinforcing networks? I hypothesize that for suburban African Americans in metropolitan areas, the answer will be the cultural community usually found in the urban inner city. This area has been the historic settling place of blacks segregated from other neighborhoods. When the mainstream excluded them from its civil institutions, it forced them to form their own institutions in these areas, and the black counterpublic sphere was born (Baker 1995; Brown 1995; Dawson 1995, 2012; Gregory 1995; Squires 2002; Harris-Lacewell 2004; Brooks 2005). The black public sphere serves three main purposes for suburban African Americans. First, it is a place to discuss strategies for group advancement. From emancipation, it became apparent that African Americans would not be able to blend seamlessly into society (Brown 1995) and needed to work collectively to negotiate their integration. This tradition has continued throughout the decades and occurs in a variety of places, such as the church (Harris 1999), the black press (Brooks 2005), online (Greenwell 2012; Lewis 2012), and in informal settings like barbershops and beauty salons (Harris-Lacewell 2004). Second, the black public sphere institutions serve as curators of the African American critical memory, allowing African Americans to attach positive characteristics to group membership through stories of blacks overcoming adversity to succeed in a hostile society (Baker 1995). These institutions also emphasize the hostility of the mainstream in order to engender loyalty to the counterpublic and promote collective strategies for advancement (Gregory 1995). Lastly, the black public sphere takes these strategies, crafted in the institutions, and presents them as norms of behavior. Adherence to these norms is the basis for "true" racial identity, and failure to act accordingly prompts sanction (Brown 1995; Dawson 1995, 2012; Squires 2002). These norms have been pushed by different segments of the community in the past, but following the Civil Rights Act, the Voting Rights Act, and the Supreme Court's acquiescence on minority-majority gerrymandering, the primary drivers have been African American politicians (Swain 1995) and civil rights organizations (Dawson 2012).

It is one thing for suburban African Americans to travel to these areas out of necessity (for example, if the only black church or beauty salon in the area is in the cultural community or to see family), but it is quite another for them to view this community as a thought incubator where they consciously seek out these norms and find opportunities for political participation. I suspect that suburban African Americans, by virtue of their above-average education, will know about the critical memory and the historic role of the cultural community for the black collective. This recognition will spur them to travel to the majority black community, where they can receive these norms. Spending most of their time in unreceptive networks, where their minority status is made more stark and they are presented with norms contrary to their identity, will make them more likely to view this community as a norm giver than do the urban blacks who actually live there.

With this critical background in mind, the chapter will test three hypotheses. Hypothesis 1: Suburban African Americans will be more likely to frequent their cultural community than suburban whites will frequent theirs. The CCES asked respondents if there was a community similar to their culture near them.[1] The answer choices were: (1) I live in such a community; (2) there is one a short drive away; (3) there is one too far to drive; or (4) there is not one close. Those in a cultural community or with one a short drive away received a separate battery of questions about their views and uses of the community, while those without access received questions about their local community. The survey asked respondents with access to a cultural community how they used it—as a place for travel, business, or shopping. These questions comprise the *community use*[2] index.

A second battery of questions asked the same respondents about their perceptions of the cultural community by choosing as many of the terms they deemed applicable. The choices were—center of political activity; primary source of entertainment; a place of employment; a place of formal or informal education; invigorating; depressing; hostile to your views; and/or in line with your views.[3] I hypothesize that suburban African Americans will be more likely to use their cultural community and know its (counterpublic) political history. Specifically, they will view their cultural communities as centers of political activity (norm transmitter), which will correspond with an increased affinity, and therefore they will view it as invigorating.

Hypothesis 2: Suburban African Americans will hold more racially radical ideologies than suburban whites and urban African Americans. Hypothesis 2a: Suburban African Americans with strong racial identity will hold more racialized ideologies than suburban African Americans with weak racial identity. This hypothesis will test Dawson's African American ideology research and the question of whether high-SES African Americans will behave concordant with their racial or class identities. The survey asked suburban African Americans questions that range from their feelings toward political figures and where they view them ideologically to their opinions about race in America. I expect that suburban African Americans' opinions will differ from those of suburban whites in predictable ways. Dawson's ideologies follow a natural ordering from racially moderate toward more racially radical: from *radical liberalism* to *disillusioned liberalism* to *black nationalism/separatism.*[4] I expect suburban African Americans to fall closer to the black separatism end of the continuum. I believe the perceived hostility of their neighborhood and workplace will heighten their disillusionment, and the cultural community will give them norms of separatism. I believe urban African Americans will fall closer to the radical liberalism end of the continuum since their lower SES will mean more government reliance.

Figure 4.1. Community Use Index

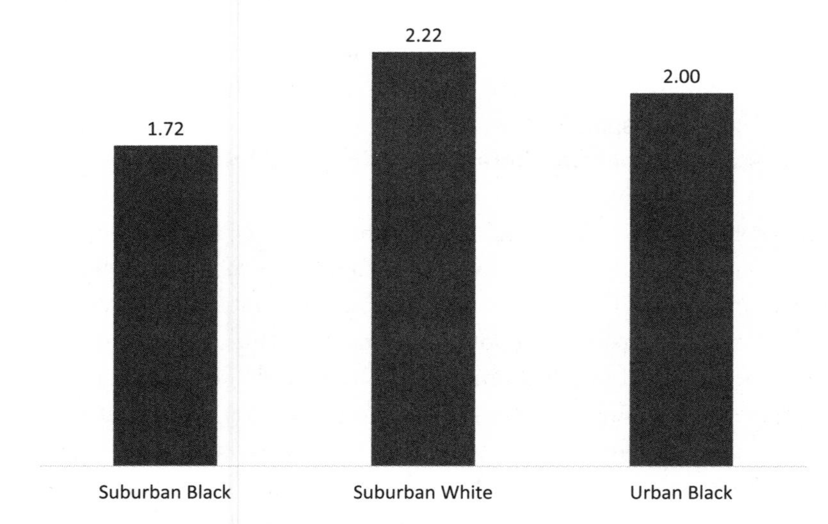

Source: 2008 Cooperative Congressional Election Study.

CULTURAL COMMUNITY USAGE AND PERCEPTION

Suburban whites and urban African Americans actually use their cultural community more frequently than suburban African Americans. On a 0–3 scale, the community use index for suburban African Americans is 1.72, compared with 2.22 for suburban whites, and 2.0 for urban African Americans (see figure 4.1). These results hold for the individual questions as well, with suburban African Americans on average being 16.5 percent less likely to use the cultural community than suburban whites and 10 percent less likely than urban African Americans. Suburban African Americans were also less likely than suburban whites to find their cultural community invigorating (5 percent to 18 percent; p-value = 0.110) and more likely to find their community depressing (18 percent to 6 percent). In a direct rejection of hypothesis 1, urban African Americans are 10 percent more likely than suburban African Americans to view their community as the center of political activity (6 percent to 16 percent) (see the appendix).

However, it may be unfair to compare suburban African Americans with suburban whites or urban African Americans about community usage. The identity question asked with which demographic the respondent most

Figure 4.2. Suburban African American Community Usage by Racial Identity

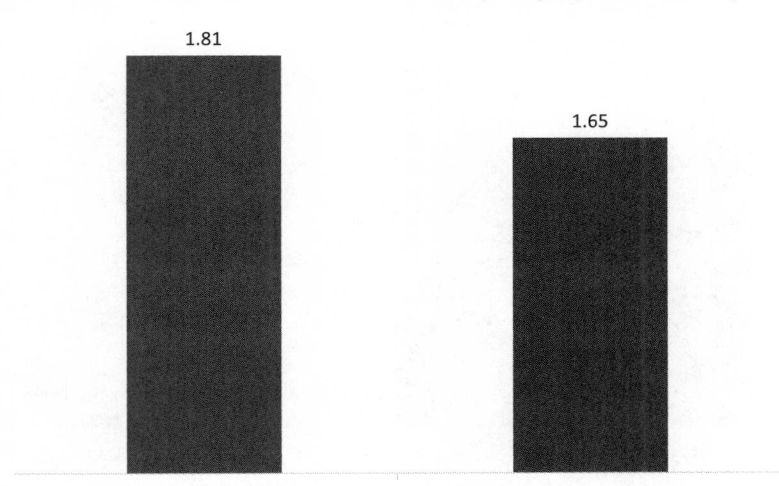

Source: 2008 Cooperative Congressional Election Study.

identifies. Only if that identity were different from the majority of their current neighborhood would the respondent be applicable to my theory, particularly the idea of increased costs to travel there. For instance, I expected that Italian American suburbanites would seek out the neighborhood with Italian cultural institutions, like authentic restaurants. However, white ethnic segregation ended more than a half-century before that of blacks. Therefore, the institutions may have dispersed along with the residents. The data also suggest whites have low levels of racial/ethnic group consciousness. For urban African Americans with high racial identity, they are likely living in their cultural community, so high levels of local participation means high community participation. That said, the fact that suburban African Americans are over the midpoint of the index (57.4 percent) shows their usage is not negligible.

There is no statistically significant difference on community use or perception between suburban African Americans who chose race as their primary identity in table 2.1 and those who did not (1.81 to 1.65; p-value = 0.453) (see figure 4.2).

In a pattern that will persist throughout the remaining chapters, the type of church one attends appears to have a strong effect on opinions and participation. The comparisons are between suburban African Americans

Figure 4.3. Suburban African American Community Usage by Church Makeup

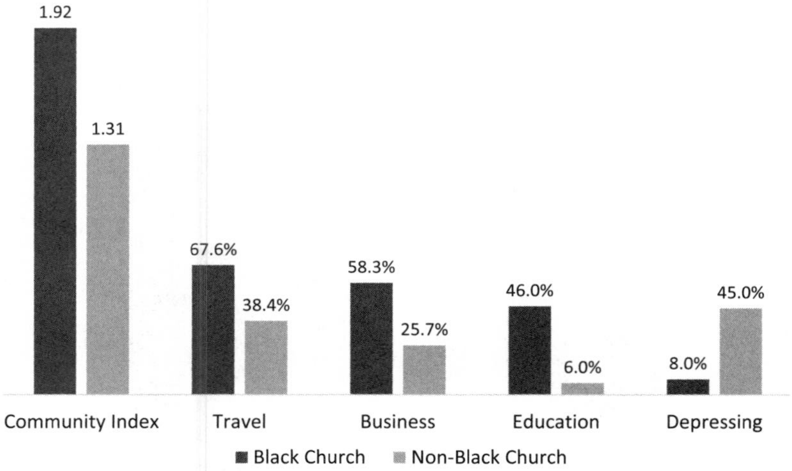

1.92
1.31
67.6%
38.4%
58.3%
25.7%
46.0%
6.0%
8.0%
45.0%
Community Index
Travel
Business
Education
Depressing
■ Black Church ■ Non-Black Church

Source: 2008 Cooperative Congressional Election Study.

who attend churches that are more than 70 percent black and suburban African Americans who attend churches that are less than 70 percent black. As expected, suburban African Americans in black churches have a higher degree of overall community usage (black church = 1.92; non-black church = 1.31). Specifically, higher proportions said they travel (67.6 percent to 38.4 percent) and do business (58.3 percent to 25.7 percent) there. The perception of the cultural community is also different, as suburban African Americans in black churches are more likely than suburban African Americans in non-black churches to view the cultural community as a place for formal or informal education (46 percent to 6 percent) and fewer find it depressing (8 percent to 45 percent) (see figure 4.3).[5]

The cultural community regressions mirror the crosstabular analysis, particularly on the use of the cultural community. Suburban whites are more than three times more likely than suburban African Americans to score higher on the usage index (OR = 3.34).[6] Urban African Americans are twice as likely to score higher (OR = 2.34). Urban African Americans are also more likely to know the history of the community (OR = 13.6) and view it as the center of political activity (OR = 5.20). (Due to the small number of respondents, I will not be able to draw firm conclusions from regression results for community usage by church type.)

In the aggregate, suburban African Americans do not use the cultural community or view it as a source of political activity, as compared to all suburban whites or urban African Americans. However, when separated by the racial makeup of one's self-selected networks, the expected differences arise. It may be that the black churches are actually located in these communities or—based on the previous chapter—that suburban African Americans attending black churches get norms that affect their views. These norms are probably not stressed in multiracial or white churches.

The second hypothesis will compare the respondents' race opinions by neighborhood type. The previous section showed that a majority of suburban African Americans use the cultural community and many feel it aligns with their views even if that usage is not appreciably more often than suburban whites and urban African Americans. If this is the case, we should expect their opinions about politics to follow the more racially radical ideologies discussed in chapter 2. The battery of race opinion questions was not as extensive in the CCES as it was in the NPS. It does, however, include feeling thermometers that represent particular aspects of Dawson's racial ideologies.

RACIAL IDEOLOGY

Feeling thermometers will assess the different ideological strands among suburban African Americans. I assume that feeling closer to political figures associated with radical ideologies indicates support for those ideas. The most radical of the thermometers (with any significant differences) was feelings toward Reverend Al Sharpton. There is the expected gap by neighborhood between suburban African Americans and suburban whites (52.7 to 27.6 on a 100 point scale) (see figure 4.4). We can again see the effect of church racial makeup, as suburban African Americans in black churches were the warmest toward the racial firebrand (56.45 to 43.84), as compared with suburban African Americans in non-black churches (see the appendix).

The next most radical figures likely would be community organizers.[7] Here, suburban African Americans feel closer than suburban whites (80.31 to 57.38) and urban African Americans (62.56). Racially identifying suburban

Figure 4.4. Feeling Thermometers by Race and Neighborhood

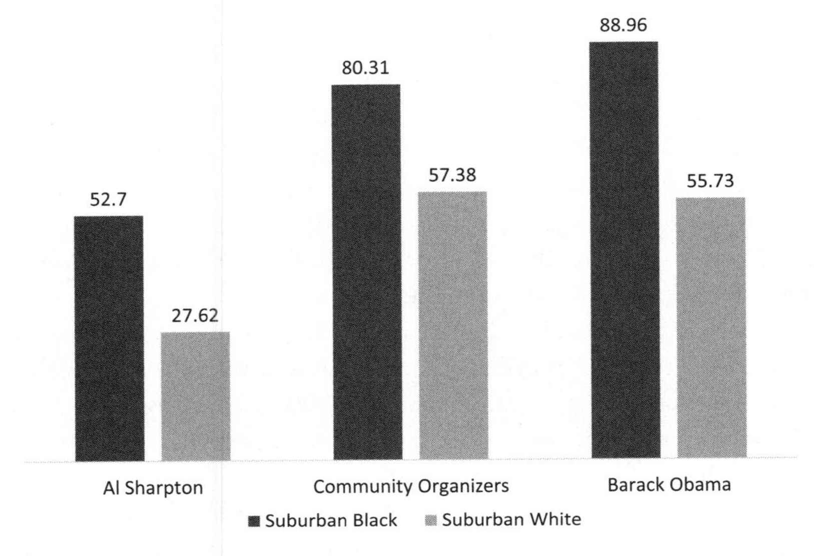

Source: 2008 Cooperative Congressional Election Study.

African Americans feel more than 20 percent closer than urban identifiers (80.73 to 59.21). One can interpret these results as a political signal or as the understandable affinity toward people working in the community on tasks more directly impactful than simple voting—tasks I hypothesize suburban African Americans will prefer. Explicit feelings for then candidate Barack Obama vary by neighborhood (suburban African Americans = 88.96; suburban whites = 55.73) and by race identification. Suburban African Americans who chose race as their primary identity score 95.6 on warmth toward Obama, compared to 83.4 for suburban African Americans who chose another demographic and 89.6 for race-identifying urban African Americans (see the appendix).

The average thermometer score for the three figures combined is 73.9 for suburban African Americans, 77.1 for racially identifying suburban African Americans, and 77.07 for suburban African Americans in black churches. This compares to their feelings toward generic "liberals" at 58.24, 57.08, and 54.27 respectively. So, not only do suburban African Americans feel more warmth toward racialized figures, they are at best lukewarm to the standard-bearers of American liberalism, echoing the findings in the Dawson research.

RACIAL OPINION

The previous chapter showed that African Americans in white networks have very different opinions on racial issues than whites in white networks. Their opinions on these issues were mostly statistically indistinguishable from African Americans in majority black networks. We can now measure the specific role of suburban residence.

In the CCES suburban African Americans were more than twice as likely as suburban whites to say blacks have gotten less than they deserve (62 percent to 30 percent), were less likely to feel blacks must work their way up without special favors (47 percent to 68 percent), and less likely to agree with the assertion that black individuals' positions are a result of not working hard (40 percent to 54 percent). When asked whether the government pays less attention to requests or complaints from blacks than whites, 36 percent more suburban African Americans than suburban whites agreed with the statement (73 percent to 37 percent). Twenty-seven percent more agreed that "generations of slavery and discrimination have created conditions that make it difficult for blacks to work their way out of the lower class" (61 percent to 34 percent) (see figure 4.5).

As hypothesized, suburban African Americans are also more in agreement with these latter two statements than urban African Americans. On government responsiveness, 15 percent more suburban African Americans than urban African Americans agreed there was racial bias (73 percent to 58 percent) and 9 percent more agreed about the effects of historic discrimination (61 percent to 52 percent) (see the appendix). In an interesting pattern that will continue throughout the chapter, urban blacks who chose race as their primary identity were 25 percent more likely to say blacks have gotten less than they deserve (63 percent to 88 percent) yet held less racialized opinions on whether special favors are necessary for equality (54 percent to 34 percent).

Perhaps the most consistent question across groups in the CCES dataset asks whether respondents favor affirmative action programs that "give preference to racial minorities and to women in employment and college admissions in order to correct for discrimination." This long question with many disparate, yet related, parts exemplifies the power of affirmative action *as a signal.* Not only is affirmative action designed to aid underrepresented groups, it does so by taking "affirmative" steps, essentially by lessening the

Figure 4.5. Race Opinion by Race and Neighborhood

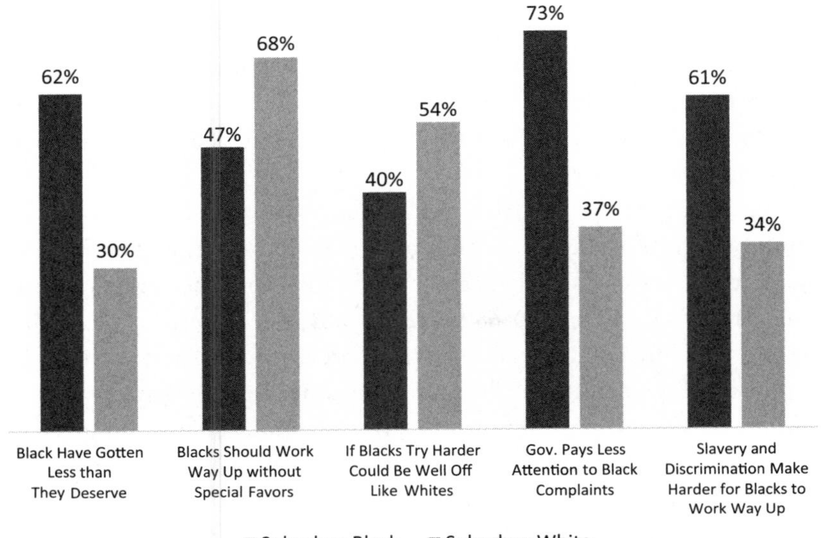

Source: 2008 Cooperative Congressional Election Study.

chances of whites (particularly white males) getting those jobs and admissions slots. The legacy of past discrimination necessitates this preferential treatment. Support for affirmative action means one believes there has been a history of discrimination (difficult to argue against), that this legacy has *caused* inequalities (as the previous data show, far from settled), and that there exists the need to take affirmative steps to correct it. This is quite a hill to climb and may explain the polarization (and why questions about affirmative action and preferential treatment in hiring and promotions produce different results).

Similar to the African Americans in white networks found in the 2004 NPS (chapter 3), suburban African Americans were 45.2 percent more likely than suburban whites to support affirmative action programs (78 percent to 32.8 percent). Among the suburban African American respondents, those who chose race as a primary identity supported affirmative action at a 16.17 percent higher rate than those who did not (86.7 percent to 70.6 percent). Those who attend a black church also appear to be more supportive than those who do not (81.5 percent to 70.6 percent; p-value = 0.125) (see figure 4.6). There is also some indication that group-conscious suburban African Americans are

Figure 4.6. Support for Affirmative Action

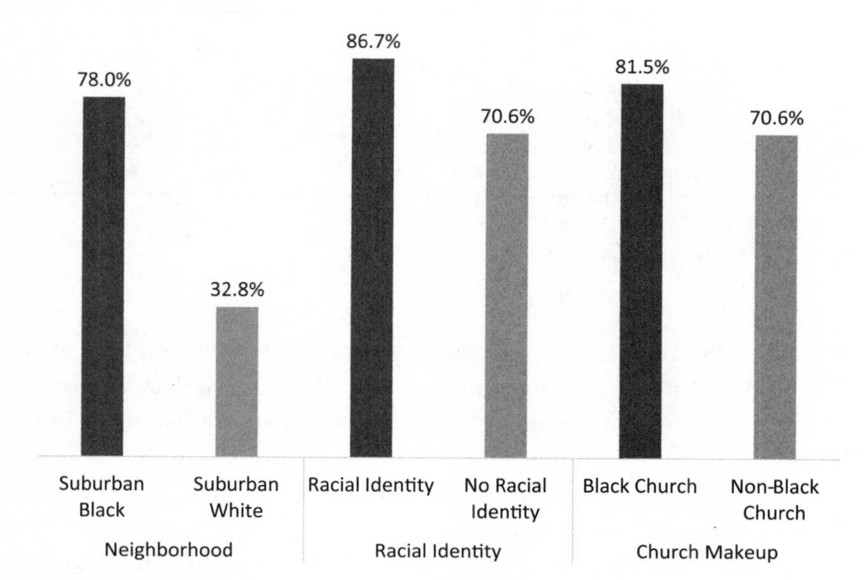

Source: 2008 Cooperative Congressional Election Study.

more racialized on this complex policy than their racially identifying urban coethnics, though the result is slightly outside of the significance threshold (86.7 to 77.3; p-value = 0.115).

The logistic regressions confirm the hypothesis that suburban African Americans hold more racialized opinions on affirmative action. Table 4.1 shows that suburban African Americans are twelve times more likely than suburban whites to support affirmative action programs (OR = 12.01) and 2.84 times more likely to support the policy than urban African Americans, when introducing statistical controls. These differences hold based on racial identity. Racially identifying suburban African Americans are 6.14 times more likely to support affirmative action than suburban African Americans who do not identify. They are also 4.47 times more likely to support it than urban African American identifiers. There was no difference based on church makeup.

The 2008 ANES also included questions on racialized opinions. Using the ANES as a supplement to the CCES is beneficial for two reasons. As stated earlier, the black and Latino oversample provides enough African Americans, after stratification by neighborhood, to get more comparable estimates between the groups and minimize the influence of outliers. Second, the strong

Table 4.1. Affirmative Action Odds Ratios

	Coefficient	*Odds Ratio*
Suburban White	-13.924**	12.01
Urban Black	1.045**	2.84
Suburban Black No Racial Identity	1.815**	6.14
Urban Black Racial Identity	1.558+	4.47

Levels of Significance: ** = 0.01; + = 0.10

Source: 2008 Cooperative Congressional Election Study.

internal validity of the ANES questions provide evidence in support of (or opposition to) the conclusions from the CCES. If the ANES data is in accord with the CCES, we can assume the CCES respondents are like those in the ANES.

The data show that suburban African American respondents in the ANES adhere to the same racial ideologies mentioned in Dawson's 2012 piece and found in the CCES. On all of the race questions, suburban African Americans hold more racially radical opinions than suburban whites. They are more likely to say blacks get less than they deserve (59 percent to 33 percent), are more likely to feel admiration for blacks (73.7 percent to 49 percent), and are more likely to feel sympathy for them (66.7 percent to 42.5 percent) (see figure 4.7). Like in the CCES, they are also more likely than suburban whites to say that the legacy of slavery has made it difficult for blacks to escape the lower class (57.9 percent to 42.1 percent) and more likely to favor preferential treatment in hiring[8]—by almost 50 percent (57.4 percent to 9.5 percent). Suburban African Americans are less likely than suburban whites to say that "if blacks would only try harder they could be just as well off as whites" (53.3 percent to 63.7 percent), that blacks should work their way up without special favors (60.4 percent to 73.4 percent), and that blacks have too much influence in American politics (15.2 percent to 39.7 percent).

Stratifying the sample by group consciousness, most of the results hold. Suburban African Americans with high group consciousness[9] are more likely to have sympathy for blacks (71.5 percent to 61.1 percent) than those with low group consciousness. Group-conscious African Americans were less likely to say blacks should try harder (45.6 percent to 59.2 percent), that blacks should do without special favors (52.2 percent to 68.6 percent), and that blacks have too much influence (10.8 percent to 23.8 percent) (see figure 4.8).

Figure 4.7. Race Opinion by Race and Neighborhood

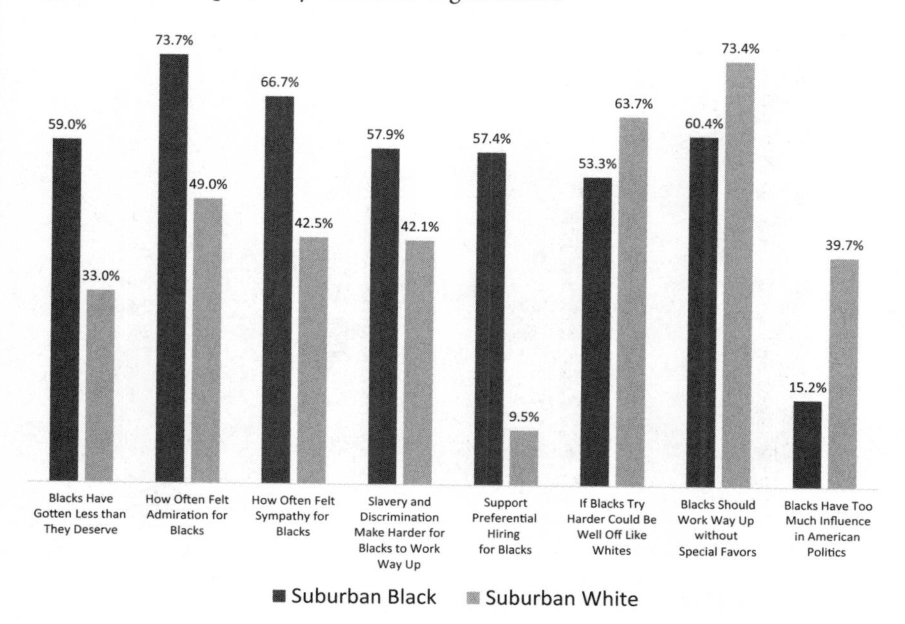

Source: 2008 American National Election Study.

The only differences with group-conscious urban African Americans were in the unexpected direction; however, they also lend credence to the CCES conclusions. The two unexpected differences come on the legacy of slavery (58.1 percent to 71.7 percent) and whether blacks have gotten less than they deserve (60 percent to 75 percent). The deserve question is particularly interesting because the CCES race battery had the same unforeseen finding for both urban group consciousness and urban black church membership. Additionally, the average agreement/disagreement on all of the race questions is right in line with those in the CCES, around 60 percent.

The regression results tell a similar story. There are major differences on these ideological questions between suburban African Americans and whites. Differences on the race questions are less consistent between suburban African Americans and urban African Americans as well as suburban African Americans with low group consciousness. Suburban African Americans were more than six times more likely to score higher than suburban whites on the race opinion index[10] (OR = 6.39) (see table 4.2). Suburban African Americans

Figure 4.8. Suburban Black Race Opinion by Group Consciousness

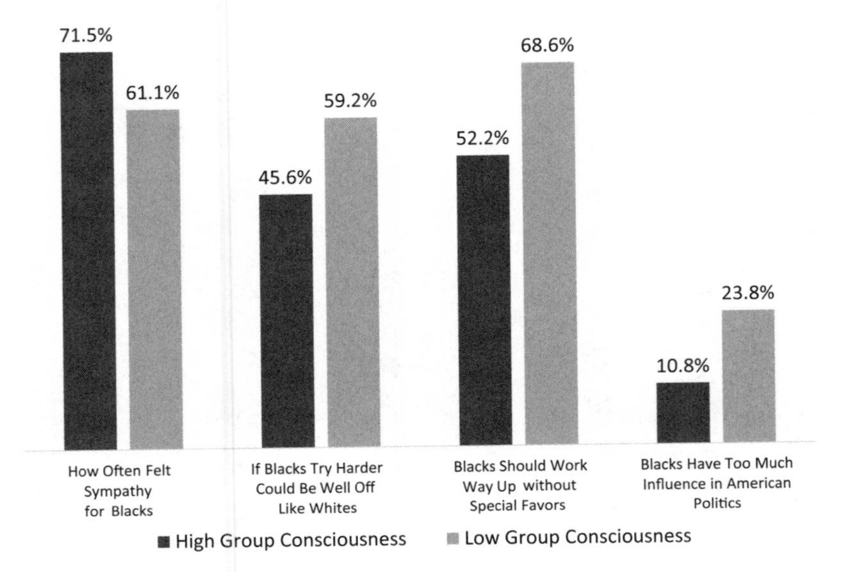

Source: 2008 American National Election Study.

Table 4.2. Race Opinion by Suburban Whites

	Coefficient	*Odds Ratio*
Race Opinion Index	1.855**	6.39
Deserve	1.357**	3.88
Admire	1.631**	5.10
Sympathy	1.626**	5.08
Slavery Effects	0.691**	1.99
Preference Treatment in Hiring	2.134**	8.44
Try Hard to Succeed	-0.802**	2.22
Special Favors	-0.887**	2.42
Too Much Influence	-1.510**	4.52

Levels of Significance: ** = 0.01

Source: 2008 American National Election Study.

were almost four times more likely than suburban whites to say blacks have gotten less than they deserve (OR = 3.88). They are also more likely to admire blacks (OR = 5.10) and have sympathy for them (OR = 5.08). They are more likely to recognize the effects of slavery and discrimination (OR = 1.99), and strongly agree with preferential treatment in hiring (OR = 8.44). They are less likely to think hard work is all blacks need to succeed (OR = 2.22), that blacks should work their way up without special favors (OR = 2.42), and that blacks have undue influence over American politics (OR = 4.52). There were no significant differences between suburban African Americans and urban African Americans on the race opinion questions or between group-conscious suburban African Americans and urbanites.

GOVERNMENT'S ROLE IN EQUALITY

The ANES also includes a battery of questions that ask about the government's role in ensuring equality in America that can shed light on the presence of Dawson's ideologies among suburban African Americans. These questions will test whether suburban African Americans believe in government solutions to race relations (radical liberalism), believe government will not fulfill its responsibilities (disillusioned liberalism), or that African Americans should take steps to help themselves (black separatism). As hypothesized, suburban African Americans and suburban whites have very different views of American society and equality. Suburban African Americans are 25 percent more likely than suburban whites to say that a big problem is that the country does not give everyone an equal chance (suburban African Americans = 77.9 percent to suburban whites = 52.5 percent) and 20 percent more likely to say the country would have fewer problems if people were treated more equally (82.7 percent to 62.9 percent) (see figure 4.9). There are smaller differences on whether it is a problem if some have more of a chance at life than others (66.6 percent to 57.8 percent) and that society should do whatever is necessary to make sure people have an equal opportunity to succeed (93.4 percent to 85 percent). On the other side of the coin, suburban African Americans are 13 percent less likely than suburban whites to say the country would be better off if people worried less about how equal people are (40.4 percent to 53.2 percent) and 10 percent fewer say America has gone too far in pushing equal rights (37.3 percent to 47.4 percent).

Figure 4.9. Government Role in Equality

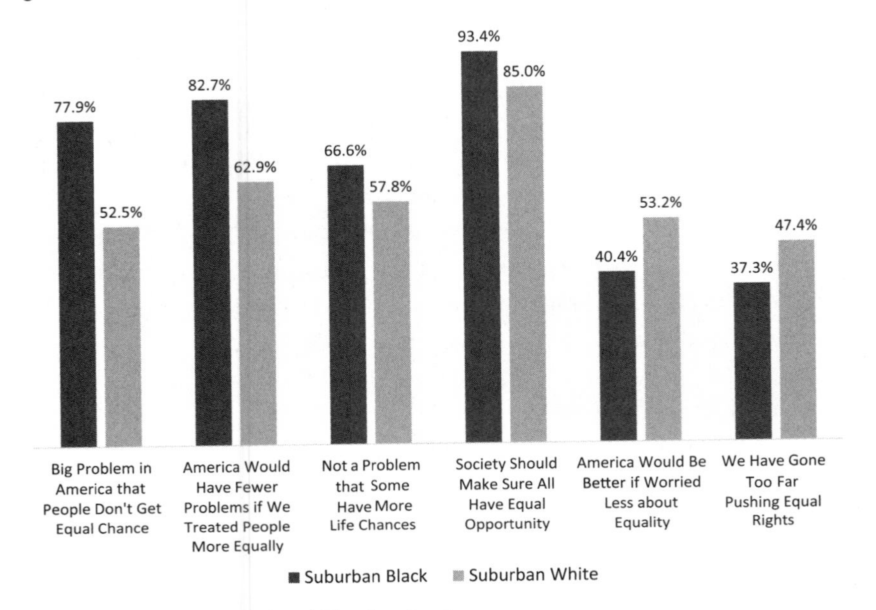

Source: 2008 American National Election Study.

Based on the previous sections, these differences should not be surprising. We can see how extreme these viewpoints and their ideologies are by aggregating across all of the questions. Assuming a score of 50 percent indicates neutrality, the farther suburban African Americans score from 50 percent on these questions the more radical their ideology. On these equality issues, suburban African Americans fall 23.8 points away from the median; this would equate to a score of 73.8 on a 100-point scale. This 23.8 points is almost two standard deviations away from the median (sd. of difference = 13.0), clearly far enough to qualify as disillusioned. The same calculation puts whites at just 10 percent from the median (less than one sd. [12.5]), still egalitarian on balance but more encouraged about how America handles race. There were no statistically significant differences on these questions between suburban African Americans and urban African Americans, and the urban distance from the median is almost identical at 23.5. Clearly, suburban residence does not temper the suburban African American's adherence to a racialized ideology, one that may not be separatist but appears very disillusioned.

Figure 4.10. Suburban Black Government Role in Equality

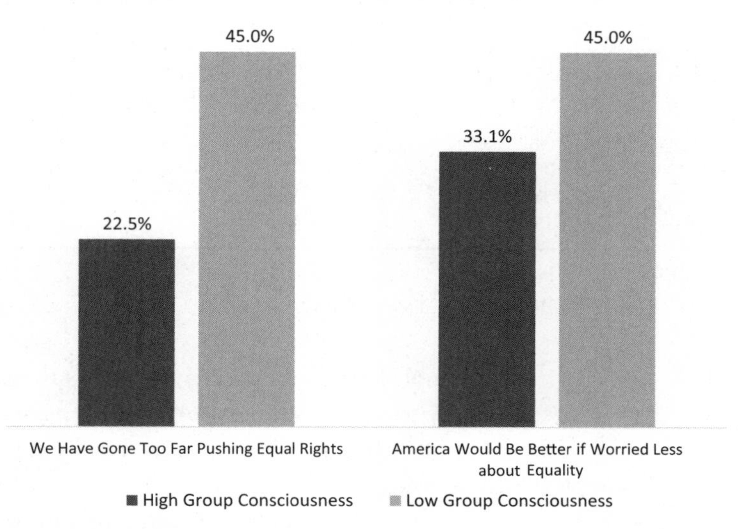

Source: 2008 American National Election Study.

Suburban African Americans with high group consciousness are 22.5 percent less likely than low group-conscious suburban African Americans to say that the country has gone too far in pushing for equal rights (22.5 percent to 45 percent) (see figure 4.10) and about 12 percent less likely to say society would be better if we worried less about equality (33.1 percent to 45 percent). Examining the median distances, high group-conscious suburban African Americans register at 29.1, more radical than all suburban African Americans combined, as should be expected. Low group-conscious suburban African Americans are only 20 points from the median, suggesting (unsurprisingly) that group consciousness relates to more racialized opinions. Again, high group-conscious urban African Americans are very close to their suburban coethnics (28.3).

The regression analysis continues to confirm the means tests and the CCES results. Compared to suburban whites, suburban African Americans are more than three times more likely to say it is a problem that people are not given an equal chance (OR = 3.60) and 2.52 times more likely to say treating people more equally would mean fewer problems. They are also 2.61 times more likely to say society should do whatever it takes to ensure equality and 2.39 times less

Table 4.3. Government Role in Equality by Suburban Whites

	Coefficient	*Odds Ratio*
Problem No Equality	1.281**	3.60
Fewer Problems if Treat Equally	0.926**	2.52
Society Ensure Equality	0.961**	2.61
Problem No Equal Life Chance	0.872**	2.39
Should Worry Less about Equal	-1.079**	2.94
Gone Too Far on Equality	-0.719**	2.05

Levels of Significance: ** = 0.01

Source: 2008 American National Election Study.

likely to say it is okay if some people have more life chances than others. They are almost three times less likely to say we should worry less about equality (OR = 2.94), and 2.05 times less likely to say society has gone too far in pushing equal rights (see table 4.3). The average of these odds ratios is 2.68. A random suburban African American would be more than two and a half times more likely to give an answer in line with a more racially radical ideology than a random suburban white respondent.

Group-conscious suburban African Americans are even more adamant society has not gone too far on equality (OR = 2.86) and should be doing more to ensure equal opportunity (OR = 3.57).

GROUP-CENTRIC POLITICAL BEHAVIOR

Having seen evidence that suburban African Americans are disillusioned with how society handles equality, we turn now to the proposed solutions. I believe the black separatist will reject race-neutral policy positions and instead focus on initiatives directed exclusively at the African American community. It should come as no surprise that most African American respondents are more supportive of these policies than most whites, but there is a question as to how much neighborhood influences differences between African Americans. As expected, suburban African Americans are less likely to say blacks should improve their social and economic position without help from the government (suburban African American = 43.1 percent; suburban white = 70.7 percent) (see figure 4.11). They more stridently believe government should see to it that blacks get fair treatment in employment (89.5 percent to

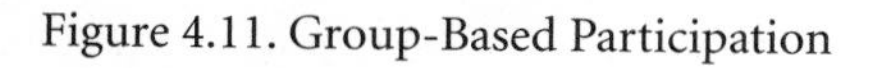

Figure 4.11. Group-Based Participation

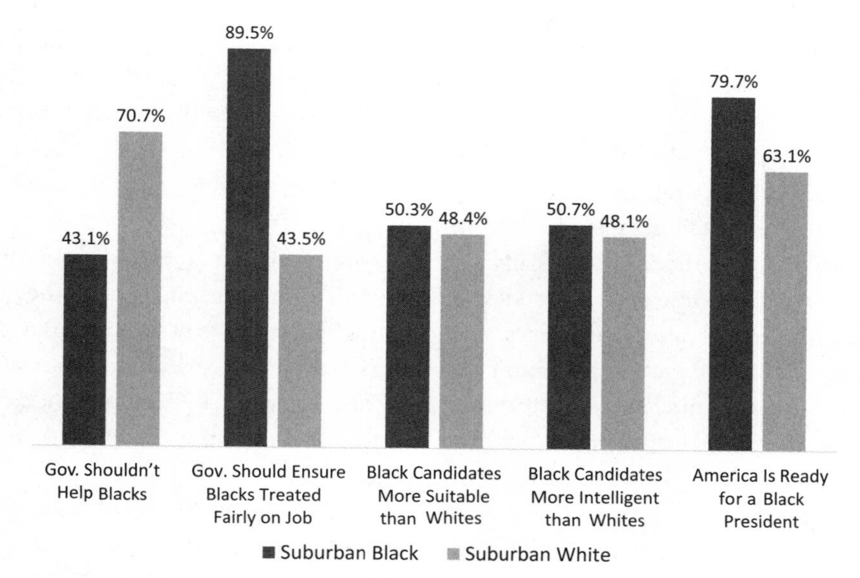

Source: 2008 American National Election Study.

43.5 percent). Suburban African Americans were also more receptive of black candidates running for office than suburban whites, finding them both better suited and more intelligent than white candidates[11] (better suited: 0.503 to 0.484; more intelligent: 0.507 to 0.481). In each instance, suburban African Americans are closer to the neutral position—"equally suited" (see the appendix). There were no differences on these questions between suburban African Americans and urban African Americans. Interestingly, suburban African Americans were more likely to say the country is ready for a black president than both suburban whites (79.7 percent to 63.1 percent) and urban African Americans (71.5 percent).

Again, racial identity moves respondents to more racially radical opinions. Group-conscious suburban African Americans were more likely to agree on the suitability of black candidates than low group-conscious suburban African Americans (0.525 to 0.492) and even group-conscious urban African Americans (0.489) (see the appendix). Respondents refusing to answer the questions dropped the number of cases very low. For that reason, I have decided not to report regression results.

CONCLUSION

Overall, the confluence of suburban residence and race does appear to have an independent effect on the racial opinions of suburban African Americans. Their opinions are much closer to their urban coethnics than their white neighbors. They also hold a more racially radical ideology. While it is not quite to the black separatism end of the spectrum, it is on the more radical side of the disillusioned liberalism midpoint.

Suburban African Americans use the community at a high rate and believe it is in line with their views; compared to their feelings about their neighborhoods and workplaces, the cultural community is a welcoming network. The logical supposition here is that suburban African Americans rely on the counterpublic history and their knowledge of it. The hypothesis only receives tacit support because they do not use the community *more* than suburban whites or urban African Americans.

There are a number of possible methodological reasons for why I did not find the expected separation. First, the numbers of suburban African Americans were much lower than suburban whites and urban African Americans and the survey further split these few residents based on whether they had a cultural community nearby. Second, these are new questions designed specifically for this dataset. In essence, they do not have the built-in internal validity the ANES questions get from decades of repetition. For example, I designed the answer choice "center of political activity" to measure a *perception* as opposed to an actual political designation. Perhaps a more extensive prompt would have engendered a different result. Third, it could be that suburban whites and urban African Americans scored higher because they actually live in their cultural community and therefore use it more often. This is definitely true for suburban whites who identify most with their class (their highest identity; see table 2.1) and urban African Americans who identify most with their race. Network type could also have an effect, suggesting a more complicated relationship than originally thought. Suburban African Americans who attend black churches were more likely to use the cultural community and viewed it with more reverence than suburban whites who attended white churches.

Ideologically, suburban African Americans feel warmer toward the racialized figures of Al Sharpton, community organizers, and Barack Obama than they do toward generic liberals. Of the three, the differences are strongest on community organizers. This is important for two reasons. First, community organizers are at the heart of disillusionment. They work to change the system with a recognition that the current patterns of participation are not working. They also are more likely than presidential candidates to advocate working to change the system from the outside, but not separate themselves from it. Second is the symbol that being a community organizer took on in the 2008 election. Much of the attack on Obama said community organizing was not a "real job" that would prepare someone to be president. However, Obama turned down a potentially more lucrative occupation to help people in the exact type of community that the suburbanite is separated from. As such, high support is understandable. The church stratification also suggests that these institutions are bastions for those with ideologies that are more radical. Suburban African Americans in black churches are more supportive of Al Sharpton than those who did not attend a black church, although his being a black preacher may suggest the result is about religious affiliation as well. The results for community organizers and Sharpton hold in the regression analysis.

On racial opinions, I believe the consistency of the affirmative action result is also illuminating since it has taken on a popular connotation more as a signal about how one wants society to evolve than a connection to any specific policy. In the CCES, suburban African Americans agree with all of the racial opinion questions at 64.1 percent, African Americans with high racial identity support at 66.9 percent, and suburban African Americans in black churches support at 64.25 percent. The averages are similar in the ANES. These results hold in the regression analysis, despite further stratification of the already small numbers of suburban African Americans based on their other demographics, suggesting that there are strong racial differences between the groups.

The black oversample in the ANES provides a supplement to my original CCES questions and confirms the results, at times on the exact same questions. Here we see large differences between suburban African Americans and suburban whites as well as differences in the expected directions between suburban African Americans based on their levels of group consciousness. Although against expectations, the fact that high group-conscious suburban African Americans were less likely than high group-conscious urban African Americans to agree that the legacy of slavery hurts blacks and that blacks get less than they deserve further proves the two datasets are compatible. In both cases, the average agreement was around 60 percent. On other questions the familiar pattern held, with suburban African Americans differing by group consciousness, but not statistically from high group-conscious urban African Americans.

The ANES also allowed for tests of other dimensions that speak directly to the racial ideologies. If we were to look at each question on a 100-point scale—with higher numbers being more pessimistic about government's desire to ensure equality—suburban African Americans score a 73.8. Suburban whites on the other hand are only at 60 percent. Such a result shows clear disillusionment (urbanites are at 73.5). Again, they may not be more disillusioned than their urban coethnics, but they do not believe the government and society have done a good job ensuring equality. When stratifying by group consciousness the number rises to 79.3, while high group-conscious urban African Americans only rise to 78.3, although this difference is not statistically significant. On the regressions, if one were to average the odds ratios of the battery, suburban African Americans are about 2.5 times more likely to give the more racially radical answer than suburban whites. Group-conscious suburban African Americans are also more likely than low group-conscious suburban African Americans to give more racialized answers on the questions of whether society has gone too far in pushing equality and whether society should be doing more to ensure equality. The results on group-centric political behavior were sporadic or inconclusive.

Ultimately, the primary hypothesis of the chapter fell short. However, it is clear that suburban residence has an independent effect on political opinions and ideologies correlating to more radical racialized ideologies and racial opinions. The next chapter will test whether these relationships hold with actual political behaviors.

5. The Suburban Political Environment and Its Effects on the Participation of Suburban African Americans

The previous chapters laid the foundation for how suburban African Americans come to their participation decisions. Suburban residence is a gift and a curse. On the positive side, these residents have the tangible benefits of nicer schools, manicured lawns, and attentive social services. Yet psychologically, they are in a neighborhood environment with a history of hostility to their presence and which lacks institutions that reinforce their racial identity. There is a certain duality to their political environment as well. On balance, suburban African Americans' political preferences should be no different from those of their neighbors. The cleavages of their *residential* identity should not break along ideological or racial lines. One neighbor may want speed humps on the street while another may protest landscaping fees. This competition plays itself out in venues like homeowners' associations and county commissions, where neighbors of all backgrounds and demographics may find themselves as allies or adversaries. However, some issue dimensions pique identities beyond the neighborhood. When the focus is race, a suburban African American has a choice of whether or not to act in a group-conscious way. The literature suggests this reaction is a product of the individual's racial identity and experiences with race in the world.

Say a suburban African American's only encounter with racialized discourse comes through the conservative media outlets he consumes once a week. Hence, he spends the majority of his time thinking about things other than race. Now imagine another suburban African American with a stronger racial identity and history of group-conscious behavior. She views much of life through a racial lens, seeking out reinforcing information through websites like theroot.com and never misses the Al Sharpton show on Sirius XM's "Urban View" channel while at work. Both suburban African Americans live in the same neighborhood, have access to the same municipal services, and have to vote for the same school bond this November. The suburban African American with a low racial identity may find this environment very engaging, while the other may see few avenues for group-conscious participation. Both individuals may feel the desire to participate locally. For the low identifier, this local participation may be sufficient, as it fulfills the duty to the primary identity—possibly his class or neighborhood. For the high identifier, there will be the draw for additional participation (even at a higher cost) directed toward the group.

The literature finds that environment has a strong influence on one's political behavior. It both structures one's choices of things like candidates and can engender a psychological attachment to an area—for example, people saying they are from a Blue State or Red State. With politics being a communal pursuit and success being contingent on persuading others to join your "side," people frequently talk politics and try to get others to behave as they do. This could mean informing a political ally about an upcoming election or trying to convince an uncommitted friend to vote against a tax increase. Many of these quasi-political encounters happen in social settings like side conversations before a PTA meeting (Rosenstone and Hansen 1993; Zuckerman, Valentino, and Zuckerman 1994; Mutz 2002). This "low cost" information is a benefit to an agreeable individual as it saves the receiver the time of collecting it. To one that disagrees, the reaction to a constant stream of dissonant information could foment mild annoyance, trigger contentious discussion, or possibly serve as a source of inferiority feelings. The outstanding question is whether this disagreeable environment will spur the individual to seek out compatible information (Scheufele et al. 2004) or cause a retreat from political life (Mutz 2002).

This chapter asks whether being in a disagreeable environment has an independent influence on participation for African Americans in suburban neighborhoods. Specifically, it will examine four aspects of political behavior to determine how the suburban environment affects the participation of the African Americans who live there: the political choices that confront suburban African Americans, whether they are more or less likely to seek out confirmatory information, their voting behavior, and whether they engage in political participation that could more directly benefit their groups. Specifically, I test four hypotheses. The first hypothesis is: Suburban African Americans will have a lower approval of their congressional representative than suburban whites and urban blacks. The CCES survey asked respondents how much they approved of their specific candidates for the 2008 House election. I expect suburban African Americans to feel neither candidate will speak positively to their racial identity and therefore to rate them lower than do suburban whites and urban African Americans, who have likely had their districts drawn to maximize their demographics. Indeed, the previous chapters have shown us exactly what the majority of suburban residents think about racial issues. A related hypothesis (1a) states: Suburban African Americans will also rate the Democratic congressional candidate as being more conservative on the ideological spectrum than they find themselves. The CCES asked respondents to place themselves ideologically on a scale of 0 to 100, with 0 being extremely liberal and 100 being extremely conservative. Respondents placed their congressional candidate on the same ideological scale. I calculate the "candidate thermometer distance" by subtracting the respondent's ideology from that of each House candidate. Larger absolute scores will indicate more ideological distance from the respondent and therefore less support. Negative numbers indicate a respondent perceives the congressional candidate as more conservative, positive numbers mean the candidate is perceived as more liberal. It is expected that suburban African Americans will give their Democratic candidate larger and more negative scores than do suburban whites and urban African Americans.

Hypothesis 2: Suburban African Americans will be more likely than suburban whites and urban African Americans to seek out group-specific information. The CCES asked respondents if they had used a variety of media in the past twenty-four hours, how interested they were in the news, and how interested they were in politics. If suburban African Americans are in disagreeable networks, most of the (racial) information they receive will not be actionable. Without this shortcut, the suburban African American will have to find it from other, relatively easily accessed outlets.

Hypothesis 3: Suburban African Americans will be more likely to vote than the average urban African American, but less likely than the average suburban white. Participation is contingent on resources like income and education. Suburban African Americans will have higher SES than their urban coethnics and lower political resources than suburban whites. Urban African Americans have been shown to overcome resource deficiencies through group consciousness and are enticed to participate by group-based appeals from political elites. Suburban African Americans steeped in counterpublic institutions or with high group consciousness will receive the same boost. Hypothesis 3a: Suburban African Americans will vote less in their local elections. Both the CCES and ANES asked respondents if they voted in the presidential and House elections. I hypothesize suburban African Americans will be more likely to vote in the presidential election and skip the House vote. They will be less likely to participate if the election does not speak to their primary identity.[1]

Hypothesis 4: Suburban African Americans will be more likely to engage in group-based participation. Suburban African Americans are not in a local political environment where participation reinforces their racial identity, or advances the group. The data in previous chapters show they are also in networks where most participants are indifferent to or hostile to black uplift. This should make alternative participation—behaviors that can be more specifically directed at a particular group or goal (as opposed to electing a candidate that will make decisions on a variety of unrelated issues) more important, even if they come at a higher resource cost. A native Chicagoan that moved to the outskirts of Dallas may get more relevant news from the websites of the *Chicago Tribune* than by watching the local 6 p.m. news. During the election, he or she may read the endorsement of a coethnic for mayor and donate to the campaign. Both surveys asked respondents about a variety of participatory behaviors beyond voting, such as attending political meetings, posting signs in their yards, donating money, etc. I hypothesize that suburban African Americans will engage in these behaviors with more frequency than suburban whites and urban African Americans, who can participate locally in ways that speak to their primary identity.[2]

POLITICAL CHOICE

Suburban African Americans in the CCES were surprisingly more likely to think their congressional district was in line with their views. Fifty-eight percent of suburban African Americans agree with the statement, compared to 45 percent of suburban whites (p-value = 0.124) and only 38 percent of urban African Americans (see the appendix). That said, suburban African Americans who chose race as their primary identity are 33 percent less likely than those who chose some other demographic to say their congressional district is in line (44 percent to 77 percent) (see figure 5.1). There was no statistical difference in the ideological distances between suburban African American voters and their Democratic House candidates. Yet suburban African Americans do think the Democratic candidates are more conservative and are further away from them than do urban African Americans. The unexpected finding is for suburban whites. They also view the Democratic candidates as more conservative than themselves and have the largest distance from the candidates (see the appendix).

Figure 5.1. Suburban African American District Views In Line by Race Identity

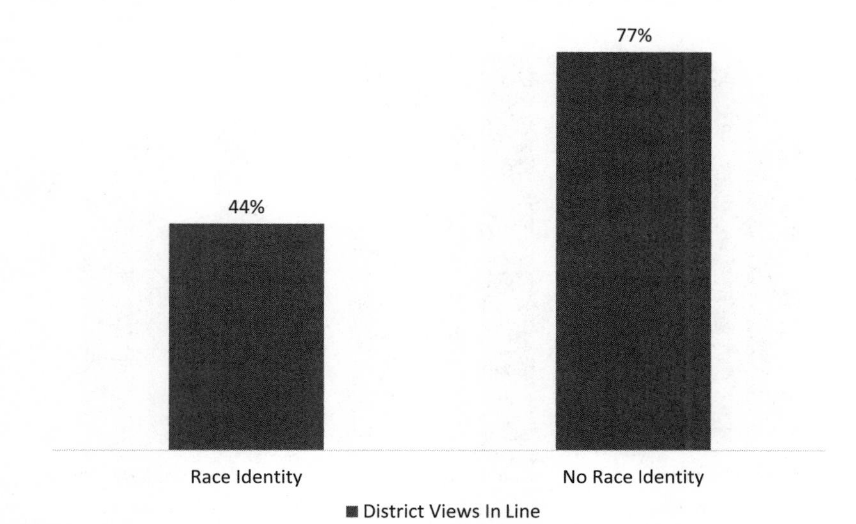

Source: 2008 Cooperative Congressional Election Study.

POLITICAL INFORMATION ACQUISITION

Turning to the second hypothesis, the average suburban African American is less interested in politics than the average suburban white (65 percent to 77.9 percent) or urban African American (76.4 percent) (see figure 5.2). However, racial identity again changes the behavioral calculus. Suburban African Americans who chose race as their primary identity were more interested in politics than those who did not by almost 30 percent (80.2 percent to 52.2 percent) (see figure 5.3). They are also more attentive to general news and public affairs than suburban African Americans who chose a different demographic (88.2 percent to 73.5 percent) and racially identifying urban African Americans (76 percent). For specific media sources, racially identifying suburban African Americans are more likely to read the newspaper than their suburban coethnics who identified with a different demographic (73 percent to 67.3 percent).

Church makeup also seems related to media usage. Suburban African Americans were divided by church racial makeup, with those attending churches that are 70 percent black or greater being more likely to have read a blog (26.5 percent to 8.8 percent) or watched television news (86.7 percent

Figure 5.2. Political Information Acquisition by Race and Neighborhood

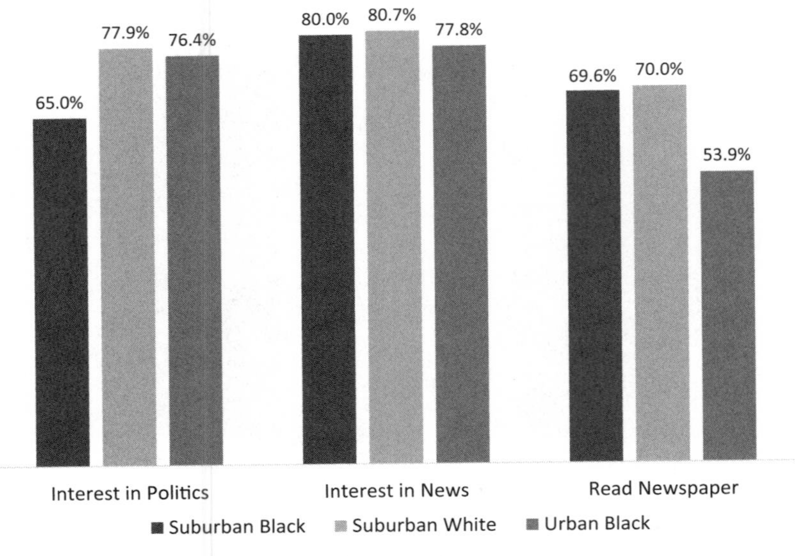

Source: 2008 Cooperative Congressional Election Study.

Figure 5.3. Political Information Acquisition by Racial Identity

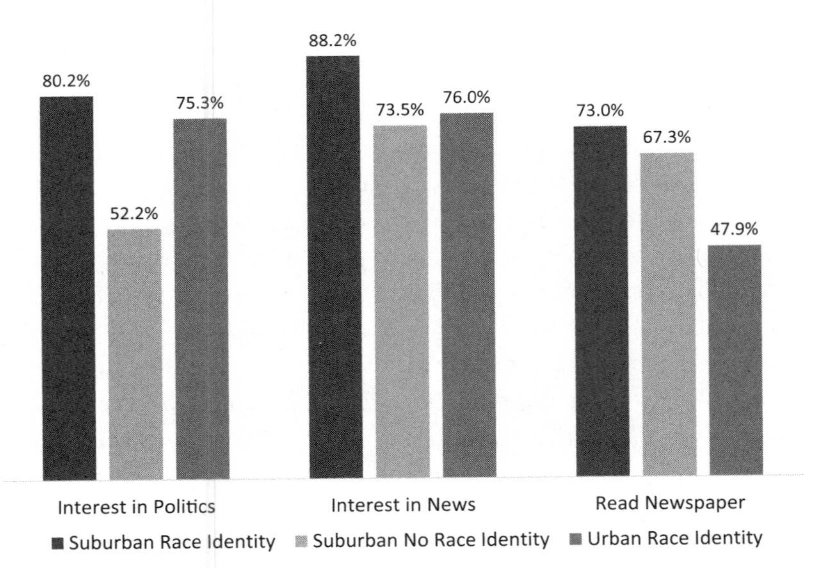

Source: 2008 Cooperative Congressional Election Study.

to 69.7 percent) than suburban African Americans at churches that are less than 70 percent black. The largest gap in media usage was on radio usage, at 25 percent (58 percent to 33 percent) (see the appendix). This logic extends to the church as well. Choosing a particular church could signal a quest for a particular set of norms. However, church attendance is not daily, so they will still have to seek out reinforcing information.

While there are no statistical differences between groups in the aggregate, the identity and church network findings fit right in line with the theory of this project. If suburban African Americans are in majority white networks, but race is not their most salient identity, they may receive an acceptable amount of agreeable information through the normal network channels. However, if racial identity is high and physical connection to the reinforcing networks is low (as the previous chapter showed), and the network is dissonant, then acquiring reinforcing information from these media channels is necessary.

POLITICAL PARTICIPATION

Turning to voting participation, there are perceptible differences based on racial neighborhood makeup and group consciousness. Using the ANES, the data show no difference between suburban African Americans and any of the other groups on turnout or voting for a candidate of a particular party. This is likely because voting is a low-cost activity, even given resource disparities. However, the data confirm one of the major outstanding questions of this project. Suburban African Americans do not find their local House political environment stimulating. I proposed that suburban African Americans would not be very interested in their House elections because candidates will not discuss racial issues in a positive way, if they are discussed at all. This is exactly the case. Suburban African Americans have significantly lower House turnout (74 percent) than both suburban whites (88 percent) and urban African Americans (83 percent) (see figure 5.4).

Not only do they skip the House races, they are more likely to do so after having just voted for president! More than a quarter of suburban African Americans rolled off their ballot (25.3 percent) compared to just 10.9 percent of suburban whites and 15.7 percent of urban African Americans (see figure 5.4). This result confirms that not only do suburban African Americans feel their views are not in line with their districts, they do not even participate in

Figure 5.4. ANES Suburban Black House Participation by Race and Neighborhood

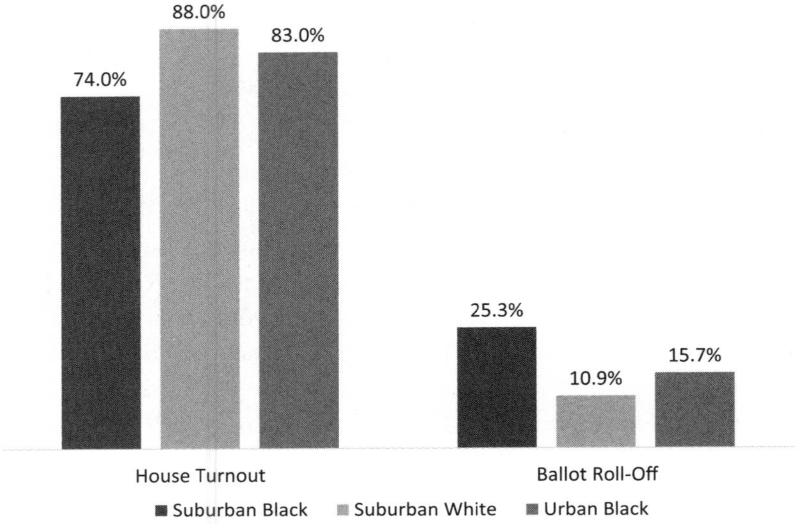

Source: 2008 American National Election Study.

the election, even though the cost is beyond negligible and presumably just voting for the Democrat would advance *some* of their preferred issues.

While there is no statistically significant difference between suburban African Americans in terms of group consciousness, they are less likely than high group-conscious urban African Americans to vote in the House election (68 percent to 89 percent) and more likely to roll off by more than 21 percent (31.5 percent to 9.7 percent) (see figure 5.5). All told, suburban African American political behavior is influenced by resources and environment. The cost of voting is so low that we should rightfully expect high resourced and high group-conscious respondents to vote at similar rates. It does appear, however, that suburban African Americans do not feel House elections are worth their vote.

The regression analysis confirms that suburban residence has an independent effect on the decision to vote in the House election for African Americans living there, even when accounting for various other demographics. The relationship between suburban African Americans and suburban whites is in the hypothesized direction, even though the coefficient for the model does not reach statistical significance (beta = 0.589, p-value = 0.176). Suburban African Americans are 2.62 times more likely to roll off their ballots than urban

Figure 5.5. ANES Suburban Black House Participation by Group Consciousness

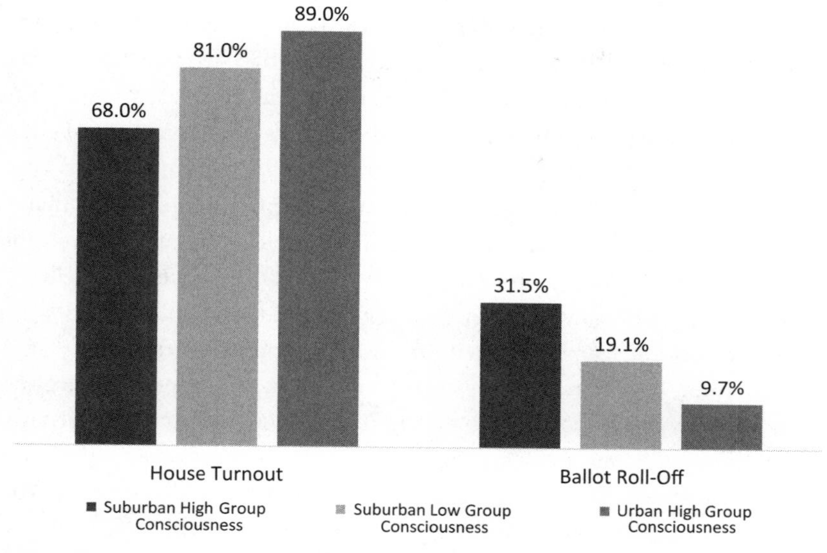

Source: 2008 American National Election Study.

Table 5.1. NES Roll-Off Regressions

	Coefficient	*Odds Ratio*
Suburban White	0.586	—
Urban Black	0.964*	2.62
Suburban Black No Group Consciousness	1.753+	5.77
Urban Black Group Consciousness	2.708*	14.99

Levels of Significance: * = 0.05; + = 0.10

Source: 2008 American National Election Study.

African Americans. High group-conscious suburban African Americans are 5.77 times more likely to roll off their ballot than their low group-conscious suburban African American neighbors, which is an astounding number (see table 5.1). Examining the predicted probabilities, more than a third (34.1 percent) of suburban African Americans are expected to vote for president and skip the congressional race, even accounting for a host of other demographics. Low group-conscious suburban African Americans are predicted to roll off at a rate of 9.7 percent.

ALTERNATIVE PARTICIPATION

Finally, we consider whether suburban African Americans seek alternative forms of participation. We have observed that suburban African Americans in majority white networks have very different opinions compared with whites about things like trusting the police, whether blacks complain too much, or if success in America only requires hard work. These individuals find comfort in institutions like the black church, with norms and practices that fit into their more racially radical ideologies. The previous chapter showed that church membership shapes opinions and even behaviors, such as traveling to the central community. Even if they do not view the area as a place for political activity, they do not seem that warm toward their local congressional district elections either. So where do they expend all of this untapped political energy? In a strong confirmation of hypothesis 4, they channel it into alternative participation.

Suburban African Americans not only engage in more alternative participation, their racial identity has a tremendous influence. The ANES alternative participation questions are in three categories: activities the respondent has *ever* done, activities they would do in the *future,* and activities they have done in the *past twelve months.* The temporal qualifier of twelve months is important because one can presume the activity was directed toward the 2008 election. Future participation may indicate that the 2008 electoral climate or network situation is pushing the respondent toward certain behaviors.

Suburban African Americans were more likely to say they would attend a meeting of a town or city government or school board in the future when compared to suburban whites (48 percent to 36.3 percent) or attend a meeting to talk about particular social concerns (35.5 percent to 25.6 percent). They were also more likely to engage in political social network behavior, being 13 percent more likely to invite someone to attend a meeting about political or social concerns (29.8 percent to 17.1 percent) and "distribute information or advertising supporting a political or social interest group" (28.8 percent to 16.4 percent). They were also more likely than suburban whites to give money to a religious organization (59.9 percent to 50.4 percent). Perhaps most interesting is that suburban African Americans were 8 percent more likely to attend a protest (21 percent to 13.2 percent) (see figure 5.6). This may be one of the most directed and costly political behaviors, and that one-fifth of suburban African Americans say that they may do so in the future is very interesting. This may

Figure 5.6. Alternative Future Participation by Race and Neighborhood

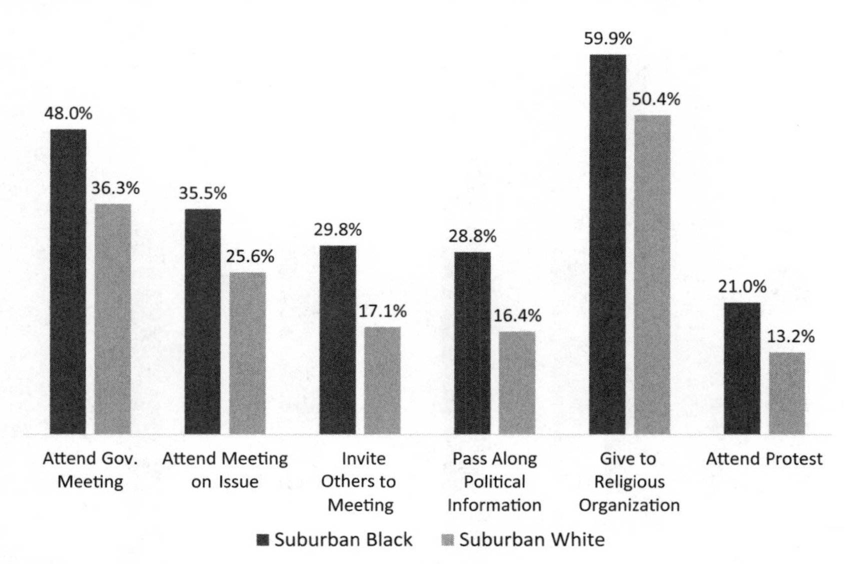

Source: 2008 American National Election Study.

also mirror the SES gains discussed in chapter 1. As resources increase, so does participation, especially types that require more resources.

Racial identity clearly plays a part in the suburban African American's choice of alternative participation. High group-conscious suburban African Americans were nearly 29 percent more likely than suburban African Americans with low group consciousness to have ever "given money to an organization concerned with a political or social issue" (excluding religious organizations) (37.7 percent to 9.2 percent). On average, 44.5 percent of high group-conscious suburban African Americans have signed a petition, compared to only 20.9 percent of low group-conscious suburban African Americans. To further the point, they are 26 percent more likely than low group-conscious suburban African Americans to have ever attended a meeting about political or social concerns (31.1 percent to 6.1 percent) and 16 percent more likely to have distributed political or social interest information (23.9 percent to 7.6 percent). They are also more likely to have ever protested (21.7 percent to 10.7 percent; p-value = 0.116), but no more likely to have given to a religious organization (see figure 5.7).

These relationships also hold when discussing future participation. Framing the question prospectively changes the two variables just discussed in the

Figure 5.7. Suburban Black Alternative Participation (Ever in Past)

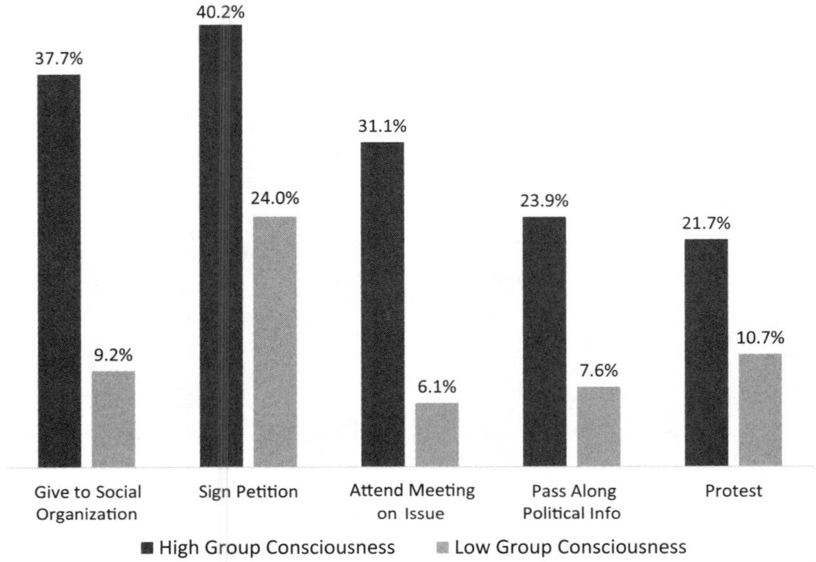

37.7%
9.2%
40.2%
24.0%
31.1%
6.1%
23.9%
7.6%
21.7%
10.7%
Give to Social Organization
Sign Petition
Attend Meeting on Issue
Pass Along Political Info
Protest
■ High Group Consciousness ■ Low Group Consciousness

Source: 2008 American National Election Study.

expected directions with significant differences. High group-conscious suburban African Americans are now more likely than low group-conscious suburban African Americans to protest (27.1 percent to 16.9 percent), and almost three-fourths say they will give to a religious organization (72.7 percent to 52.6 percent). They are also more likely to do so than high group-conscious urban African Americans (58.4 percent). Again, they are more likely to sign a petition, with an average of 44.5 percent saying they would do so compared to only 20.9 percent of suburban African Americans with low group consciousness. They are also more likely to attend a government meeting (57.6 percent to 41.9 percent) or a meeting about an issue (44 percent to 28 percent) (see figure 5.8).

The survey asked slightly different questions about recent participation, but, as hypothesized, suburban African Americans who adhere strongly to the norm of group consciousness are more likely to have engaged in alternative political behaviors. Figure 5.9 summarizes the alternative participation by group consciousness. Group-conscious suburban African Americans were more than twice as likely to have "talked to any people and try to show them why they should vote for or against one of the parties or candidates" (61 percent to 29

Figure 5.8. Suburban Black Alternative Future Participation

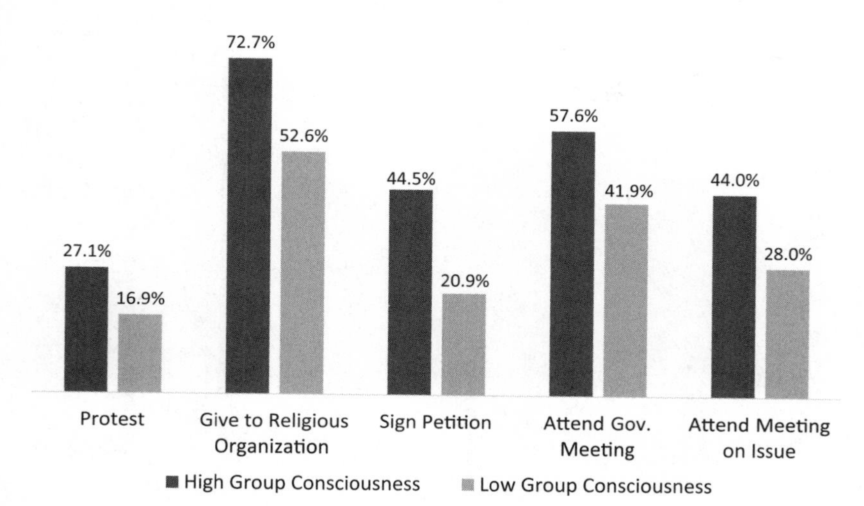

Source: 2008 American National Election Study.

percent), and were 21 percent more likely to have donated to a candidate, party, and/or PAC (22.2 percent to 1.5 percent). Suburban African Americans with high group consciousness were more likely to "wear a campaign button, put a campaign sticker on your car, or place a sign in your window or in front of your home" (41 percent to 23 percent). These suburban African Americans are more likely than low group-conscious suburban African Americans to have attended a political meeting, rally, or speech (20 percent to 2 percent) and to have actually worked for a candidate (11 percent to 2 percent), which is a very effort-costly activity. They were more likely to have donated to charity than both low group-conscious suburban African Americans (84.4 percent to 61.5 percent) and high group-conscious urban African Americans (71.4 percent). They were also more likely than low group-conscious suburban African Americans to have attended a meeting about community issues or schools (34.7 percent to 4.6 percent). There is little doubt racial identity plays a large role in the political behaviors of suburban African Americans.

When adding the extra hurdle of statistical controls, the variables on each of the issue dimensions still show significant differences. An index of all the "Have you ever"[3] participation questions includes the following questions: signed an Internet or paper petition, attended a government meeting, attended

Figure 5.9. Suburban Black Alternative Participation (Past 12 Months)

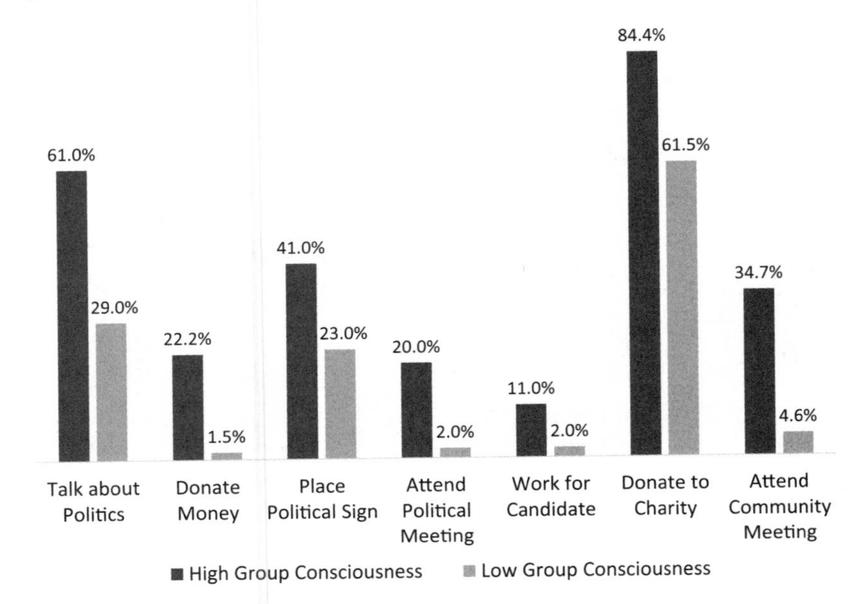

Source: 2008 American National Election Study.

a meeting about an issue, distributed information, given to a social or political organization, protested, and given to a religious organization. Suburban African Americans are actually 2.35 times less likely to score high (engage in more of the activities) on the scale than suburban whites.

However, a look within suburban African Americans tells a different story. Since the only difference between these respondents is their racial identity (not age, income, ideology, partisanship, or education level), one can say that this identity is an independent driver of participation, particularly behaviors that can be directed toward that identity. A look at the predicted probability of a suburban African American engaging in these behaviors provides more insight into this relationship. Most group-conscious suburban African Americans engaged in two activities (probability of the average group-conscious African American scoring 2 on the Ever Participate index = 27.3 percent), while low group-conscious suburban African Americans had the highest probability of having engaged in just one activity (37 percent). The largest separation comes at the four activities or higher range. High group-conscious suburban African Americans have an average probability of 7.5 percent of engaging in

Table 5.2. ANES Alternative Participation Regressions

	Coefficient	*Odds Ratio*
Suburban Whites		
Ever Participate	-0.857**	2.35
Future Participate	0.563*	1.75
Suburban African Americans by Group Consciousness		
Ever Participate	1.717**	5.56
Future Participate	1.542**	4.67
12 Months Participate	1.901**	6.69

Levels of Significance: ** = 0.01

Source: 2008 American National Election Study.

four or more activities, while the low group-conscious respondents' probability of doing so was just 2.5 percent.

This entire project has revolved around the question of how do suburban African Americans with strong racial identities and adherence to group-conscious behaviors navigate their daily environment. How do those traits affect their relationships? What kinds of activities and places carry more meaning? What kind of political behaviors become more attractive, and what kind become perfunctory? Where are the scarce resources of time and money expended? The *future participation* index[4] consisted of the same questions (except protest). Suburban African Americans were slightly more likely to engage in future participation than suburban whites (OR = 1.75) (see table 5.2). High group-conscious suburban African Americans are more than four times as likely to engage in future alternative participation (OR = 4.67) compared to those with low group consciousness. Group-conscious suburban African Americans had their highest predicted probability of engaging in 3.75 future behaviors (8.2 percent), low group-conscious suburban African Americans had the highest probability of engaging in just 1.5 future behaviors.

Finally, the *recent participation* index[5] further confirms the theory. The index consisted of the following questions detailing political activity in the past twelve months: persuading others to vote for or against parties or candidates, attending political events, placing a sign or bumper sticker, working for a candidate, donating money, contacting a government official, attending a community meeting, doing volunteer work, and donating to charity. Suburban African Americans appear to be more likely to engage in the alternative behaviors than suburban whites (beta = 0.379, p-value = 0.124), but less likely than urban African Americans (beta = -0.400, p-value = 0.119). Yet, there is no equivocation between group-conscious suburban African Americans. High group-conscious suburban African Americans are almost seven times more likely to have recently engaged in these behaviors (OR = 6.69)! This is even when controlling for other demographics. Group-conscious suburban African Americans were most likely to have engaged in three activities (34.7 percent), while those with lower group consciousness were most likely to have engaged in only one activity (34.3 percent).

CONCLUSION

The results presented confirm the hypotheses of this chapter and the overall thesis of the book. Suburban African Americans are more likely to seek out information and are less likely to vote in their (relatively costless) local congressional election than suburban whites. Instead, they choose more resource-costly alternative behaviors that can be more easily directed at their group. The previously researched exhibitions of group consciousness and the data presented in this book suggest that their choices are spurred by a desire to reinforce their racial identity and work toward the group uplift norms taught since childhood and reinforced by counterpublic institutions.

Specifically, the first two hypotheses did not receive general confirmation by either the CCES or ANES data. Suburban African Americans in the CCES actually felt their congressional districts were more in line with their views until racial identity was taken into account. But when racial identity was factored in, then we find very different views of the district. There are no significant differences in their evaluation of the House candidates' ideology, nor do they rate them as more conservative in the ideological placements. It does not appear that they view their political choices any more negatively than do their neighbors or coethnics.

Suburban African Americans who identify with their race do in fact have more interest in the news and politics. This could be because they are constantly searching for information that will counteract the dissonant information from their network. If we build on the NPS findings, group-conscious suburban African Americans will be the most keen to reject the information transmitted in majority white networks; therefore, it makes sense that they are the ones to seek out more—most likely confirmatory—information. Overall, I would not feel confident either challenging or supporting Scheufle et al.'s (2004) findings that suburban African Americans in disagreeable networks indirectly participate more by seeking out more information.

As to political participation, there is very little difference between the groups on turnout. This is not totally unexpected, since the suburbanites have high political resources due to their SES and the urbanites have been shown to participate at high rates because mobilization efforts are more efficient, the counterpublic institutions intentionally work to lower the costs of voting, and the group-conscious norm of helping the group through voting is strong. That said, the main focus of hypothesis 3 was the roll-off measure. It was in the expected direction and robust throughout all of the group comparisons and regression models for the ANES. Suburban African Americans view their congressional race very differently, likely because they are in the minority of their district, just as they are in their proximate networks, and they may not want to support either candidate.

The ANES data show us that group consciousness matters for alternative participation. High group-conscious suburban African Americans' being more likely to give to a religious organization is the epitome of resource-costly but group-based political activity. Possibly an even more costly activity is protesting, and high group-conscious suburban African Americans are the most likely to do that as well. Protesting in 2008 undoubtedly harkens back to the critical memory of the civil rights movement and may be more costly because if the protest turns violent, the individual could be harmed or even arrested for exercising his or her right to assemble and petition the state. The regression analysis confirms all of the previous findings and is even more impressive because the indices are comprised of some variables that did not have significant differences when analyzed alone.

Ultimately, group consciousness has a tremendous influence on suburban African American participation, especially the choice to forego voting in the local jurisdiction for more resource-costly forms of alternative participation. While this in and of itself is not a new finding, the fact that this population holds such strong levels of racial identity and behaviors while interacting with people very similar to them in terms of income, education, and occupation most of the time is important. And while they may not hold more racialized opinions than their urban coethnics, the fact that they clearly choose self-selecting networks that reinforce this identity in an explicit way proves that the draw of a better life in the suburbs will push certain types of African Americans back into the arms of their counterpublic and its group-conscious participatory norms.

6. Conclusion

The data have shown that suburban African Americans truly do live in a unique environment. Their opinions and political behaviors are not in line with those of their white neighbors and coworkers—people they spend the most time with and with whom they have similar SES. Instead, they appear to adhere to group-conscious norms. In addition to the differences based on race, there is also an interesting separation between suburban African Americans with strong racial identities and suburban African Americans who do not closely identify with their race. On its face, this finding may seem obvious; however, there is no reason to think *ceteris paribus* that any African American should maintain group-conscious norms when the primary structuring of their life is not race. As far as America is from being a color-blind society, there are virtually zero formal negative distinctions based on race. Unlike when African American status would exclude one from participation in society, and even open one's self up to physical harm, the contemporary suburban African American can go through life without race being as much of a detriment. Indeed, some suburban African Americans feel as though their class status, gender, or occupation are more pertinent identities in their lives. As such, that a majority of these suburban African Americans do identity with their race and maintain this separation from whites, and some suburban coethnics, is informative.

In general, the data confirmed most of the hypotheses, both the general ones laid out in chapter 2 and the more specific ones based on the particular datasets. The racial makeup of one's social network was particularly elucidating. African Americans in majority white networks hold very different racial opinions than whites in majority white networks. Previous research has shown the effect of minority status when dealing with religious affiliation and partisanship; now we can add race to the equation. The African American in a majority white neighborhood and workplace should not view those social networks as information cost cutters on racial dimensions.

These suburban African Americans have much lower trust in government institutions than their white counterparts. They are also more likely to feel the government has not done enough for race relations and equality. Much like in the findings of Hochschild (1996), they do in fact view race as the main indexing of their life and believe they are treated differently because of it, as evidenced by the fact that they believe African Americans face high levels of racial discrimination and that they personally face more discrimination than suburban whites and urban African Americans.

One of the most interesting findings was the large difference in the churches African Americans and whites in majority white neighborhoods and workplaces attend. The churches these African Americans attend are much more political, as these attendees were more likely to have explicitly heard about politics in church and were more likely to have heard a sermon or lecture in church about key issues of the day, like the economy, the police, and improving racial relations.

The difference in proximate versus self-selecting networks was made explicit using the CCES instrument, as it specifically asked respondents if they felt their views were in line with the majority of people in their neighborhood, workplace, church, and volunteer organization networks. Suburban whites actually felt their workplaces were more in line with their views than their churches, whereas suburban African Americans felt that their churches were the most receptive. Given the place the church has served in the counterpublic sphere, this finding is understandable for African Americans; however, the fact that suburban whites actually feel their church is the least receptive of the four is very interesting. Less than half of suburban African Americans felt their neighborhood was in line with their views, the lowest score of all the groups. Clearly, they do not feel their neighborhoods are receptive to their views based on their racial makeup, and given the fact that their white neighbors and coworkers hold racial opinions that are indifferent, if not hostile, to their group identity, this is not unexpected.

The question is whether these racial differences extend to the suburbs specifically. I expected that suburban African Americans would be the most likely to seek out their cultural community because they could not find the reinforcing norms in the networks they frequent most often. I also expected their information acquisition would be higher, as found by Scheufele et al. (2004) for the same reason. In short, the data did not confirm these hypotheses. Indeed, suburban African Americans did have high rates of using the cultural community and believed it to be a source for political norms, just not more than suburban whites or urban African Americans. In hindsight, this should be expected. If the suburban neighborhood is structured based on class, and the urban neighborhood is structured on race, the fact that most whites identify with their class, and most African Americans identify with their race, would mean that both of those groups actually live in their cultural communities and therefore should use them most often. That said, there is evidence that the choice of networks is again informative, especially the racial makeup of the networks one self-selects: suburban African Americans attending churches that are more than 70 percent African American are more likely to use the community than suburban African Americans who attend churches with lower black concentrations.

While their uses and perceptions of the cultural community may not have gone in the expected direction, the suburbs do have an independent effect on racial opinions, with suburban African Americans, again, being very different from suburban whites and showing a clear separation from other African American suburban neighbors based on racial identity and group consciousness. The means tests largely confirm the results from the social network chapter, in that suburban African Americans are more likely to think African Americans do not get a fair chance in society, primarily based on the legacy of slavery and history of discrimination. They are also more likely to support racially directed policies, such as affirmative action and preferential treatment in job hiring. Again, their view of American society is more pessimistic and they consistently differ from their white neighbors on whether or not society has lived up to its promise of equality. They also appear to adhere to more group-conscious opinions, having the most belief that the country is ready for a black president and that black candidates are more suited for office than white candidates. The regressions show that these findings hold even when controlling for a host of demographic variables, including the level of group consciousness to which the suburban African American adheres.

These findings, along with the fact that African Americans in white neighborhoods and workplaces feel as though whites want to hold them back in society and that suburban African Americans rate black figures like Barack Obama, Al Sharpton, and community organizers with more affinity, speak to the research on black ideologies conducted by Dawson (2001, 2012) and Harris-Lacewell (2004). While suburban African Americans hold racially radical opinions, they never reach the level of actual separatism from mainstream society, as one would expect if suburban African Americans in fact said cultures should remain distinct. Instead, they are in a more disillusioned posture. They clearly do not think society will work toward their progress without affirmative steps. The question for the final chapter was whether the suburban African American will take these affirmative steps in the form of alternative participatory behaviors that are better able to aid the racial group.

The answer to that question is a clear and consistent yes. The final hypothesis posited that suburban African Americans who have rejected their proximate networks and sought out majority African American networks in the cultural community will behave in accordance with the latter's norms. The basis for this belief is rooted in the fact that suburban neighborhoods will present undesirable political choices to the suburban African American with high racial identification. In fact, group-conscious suburban African Americans are less likely than suburban African Americans with lower levels of group consciousness to feel their congressional district is actually in line with their views; they are also more likely to have interest in politics and the news in general, and more likely to have read a newspaper recently. Therefore, there is some confirmation that suburban residence increases the information pursuit, but the NPS data that made up the bulk of the social network chapter did not duplicate this finding.

While suburban African Americans' perceptions of their neighborhood political choices may not have shown significant differences, their behaviors did. Suburban African Americans were more likely to vote in the presidential election and skip the congressional election than suburban whites and urban African Americans. Those with high group consciousness were also more likely to roll off than suburban African Americans with low group consciousness and group-conscious urban African Americans. Clearly, they are not expending their participatory energies in their local races, yet they are more likely to have engaged in alternative behaviors, such as donating money to candidates, inviting others to political meetings, attending the meetings themselves, protesting, and giving to religious organizations. Again, suburban African Americans with high group consciousness are more likely than those with low group consciousness to have engaged in the behaviors in the past, during the 2008 election, and in the future.

In sum, suburban African Americans are in a brave new world and they behave that way. Their closest network members do not share their identity, worldview, or policy prescriptions for how to aid other blacks. They believe African American claims to be illegitimate, likely because blacks lack a commitment to individualism. Living in the suburban environment is the fruit of their labor, yet advancement actually brings discomfort. Fortunately, access to racial norms and networks is attainable, and those that do seek them out—by attending black churches—can find welcoming environments. These suburban African Americans not only show an ideological commitment to black uplift, but a behavioral one as well. They are literally putting their money where their mouths are, expressing a commitment to ideas like having black candidates and then showing the highest rates of activities, such as donating money and volunteering. I suggest, and the data show, that living in that unique suburban environment and the social networks it produces is the main driver of this behavior.

DISCUSSION

Going forward, I believe this and related projects will be aided by a more directed sample that focuses on African Americans generally and suburban African Americans specifically. Combing for relevant variables in samples that are designed, and post-weighted, for things like congressional competitiveness will always limit the explanatory power of the analysis and the ability to run more data-taxing tests that can better tease out these hypothesized relationships. The community use questions could also use more validity. Split-sample tests could achieve this, where different variations are posed, including iterations with much longer prompts to eliminate any confusion and deal with the fact that certain respondents may actually live in these areas and therefore travel there more often. Finally, one could improve the design with a mixed method approach. One could target specific suburban African American communities for focus groups or interviews to better contextualize the motivations behind these participation decisions, as opposed to simple observations of their rates.

Politically, this project has shed light on a population that can be a resource and take the lead on black uplift. The stereotypes that have dogged their inner-city coethnics do not hinder suburban African Americans as much. In fact, because of their education levels and ability to fit into the mainstream, some people make a separation between "good blacks" and "bad blacks," to the further detriment of those ascribed with a "ghetto" pathology. The data show that there is no real separation on worldview or opinions. Therefore, questions of police tactics or mass incarceration will have a highly resourced and politically connected ally to pick up the mantel. Suburban African Americans may be moving farther from their inner-city brethren, but the racial solidarity we have seen through the history of blacks in America appears to be just as strong, as does the continued evolution and normative strength of the African American counterpublic. Class has not trumped race, and as long as the opinion differences between whites and blacks of the same SES are as large and consistent, it will not. Suburban African Americans cannot work toward their aims simply by voting, but as long as resources are high and alternative participatory avenues are available, they can continue to find some comfort in reinforcing their racial identity and exercising their group consciousness.

Appendix

Levels of Significance: ** = 0.01; * = 0.05; + = 0.10

Institutional Trust by Neighborhood

	Government	*Media*	*Police*	*Legal System*
Black in White Neighborhood	36% (0.216) 49	36% (0.219) 48	47% (0.271) 49	43% (0.218) 48
White in White Neighborhood	49%** (0.239) 464	39% (0.199) 456	66%** (0.210) 462	55%** (0.222) 456
Black in Black Neighborhood	33% (0.234) 404	36% (0.205) 406	43% (0.229) 407	41% (0.221) 405

Source: 2004 National Politics Study.

Institutional Trust by Workplace

	Government	*Media*	*Police*	*Legal System*
Black in White Workplace	33% (0.235) 186	36% (0.210) 186	43% (0.243) 185	38% (0.222) 185
White in White Workplace	48%** (0.239) 463	39%* (0.194) 459	67%** (0.209) 466	54%** (0.223) 462
Black in Black Workplace	32% (0.230) 175	35% (0.211) 177	44% (0.235) 179	41% (0.222) 177

Source: 2004 National Politics Study

American Values by Neighborhood

	Work Hard	*Chance at Equality*	*Ashamed of America*
Black in White Neighborhood	69% (0.296) 48	39.2% (0.346) 48	67.7% (0.333) 49
White in White Neighborhood	76%+ (0.286) 461	43.7% (0.333) 456	60.6% (0.360) 463
Black in Black Neighborhood	71.5% (0.332) 409	40.6% (0.384) 403	70.2% (0.340) 405

Source: 2004 National Politics Study.

American Values by Workplace

	Work Hard	*Chance at Equality*	*Ashamed of America*
Black in White Workplace	64.2% (0.336) 187	37.1% (0.346) 180	72.6% (0.331) 184
White in White Workplace	74.5%** (0.288) 466	43%* (0.327) 464	62%** (0.342) 467
Black in Black Workplace	72.4%* (0.331) 178	44.3%* (0.393) 175	70.7% (0.340) 178

Source: 2004 National Politics Study.

Race Opinion by Neighborhood (1)

	Deserve	*Comfort*	*Blame Self*	*Special Favors*	*Work Hard*
Black in White Neighborhood	70% (0.276) 49	25.6% (0.347) 49	49.6% (0.321) 48	48.2% (0.362) 49	69% (0.296) 49
White in White Neighborhood	38%** (0.343) 444	17.7%* (0.266) 461	60%* (0.320) 460	65.9%** (0.347) 451	76%+ (0.286) 461
Black in Black Neighborhood	67% (0.343) 400	34.6%+ (0.355) 404	58.1% (0.363) 407	58.1% (0.363) 399	71.5% (0.332) 409

Source: 2004 National Politics Study.

Race Opinion by Neighborhood (2)

	Personal Discrim.	*Black Discrim.*	*Better Break*	*Blacks Treated Unfairly*	*Affirmative Action*	*Preference in Hiring*
Black in White Neighborhood	62% (0.272) 45	82% (0.197) 48	15.9% (0.369) 48	70.5% (0.327) 48	81.9% (0.382) 47	51.6% (0.290) 48
White in White Neighborhood	20%** (0.272) 422	68%** (0.234) 458	42.6%** (0.495) 413	16.4%** (0.280) 458	61.6%* (0.478) 421	23.1%** (0.281) 454
Black in Black Neighborhood	58% (0.319) 4394	82% (0.224) 409	24.6% (0.431) 373	74.4% (0.281) 403	89.2% (0.298) 376	50.6% (0.332) 394

Source: 2004 National Politics Study.

Race Opinion by Workplace (1)

	Deserve	*Comfort*	*Blame Self*	*Special Favors*	*Maintain Culture*	*Same-Sex Marriage*
Black in White Workplace	69% (0.331) 180	35.1% (0.366) 184	51.4% (0.358) 185	47.9% (0.403) 176	49.8% (0.445) 173	2.18% (0.807) 173
White in White Workplace	41%** (0.351) 442	17.7%** (0.267) 462	57.9%* (0.335) 458	63.5%** (0.351) 454	41.3%* (0.404) 444	1.97%* (0.786) 453
Black in Black Workplace	67% (0.355) 169	35.1% (0.357) 176	58.1%+ (0.366) 177	55.7%+ (0.394) 172	42.3% (0.443) 163	2.30% (0.773) 167

Source: 2004 National Politics Study.

Race Opinion by Workplace (2)

	Personal Discrim.	*Black Discrim.*	*Better Break*	*Blacks Treated Unfairly*	*Affirmative Action*	*Preference in Hiring*	*Racial Profiling*
Black in White Workplace	67% (0.277) 173	84% (0.208) 186	24% (0.428) 175	77.4% (0.295) 184	88.3% (0.308) 180	52% (0.341) 177	12.3% (0.258) 183
White in White Workplace	21%** (0.279) 424	70%** (0.234) 461	41.8%** (0.493) 416	16.7%** (0.282) 455	60.1%** (0.481) 422	24.2%** (0.286) 463	21.2%** (0.307) 462
Black in Black Workplace	57%** (0.319) 177	84% (0.208) 186	22% (0.415) 159	77.2% (0.278) 176	85.4% (0.340) 165	51.8% (0.336) 172	21%** (0.361) 178

Source: 2004 National Politics Study.

Alternative Behavior by Neighborhood

	Campaign for Candidate	*Talk about Voting*	*Attend Meeting*	*Donate Money*	*Campaign for Minority*	*Prefer Same-Race Leaders*
Black in White Neighborhood	22% (0.422) 49	65% (0.505) 48	19% (0.394) 48	35% (0.481) 49	13% (0.334) 48	49% (0.301) 47
White in White Neighborhood	25% (0.436) 465	52% (0.500) 462	16% (0.370) 464	24%+ (0.428) 465	5%* (0.222) 463	42% (0.332) 452

Black in Black Neighborhood	26% (0.439) 407	42% (0.495) 408	21% (0.410) 407	18%** (0.381) 409	13% (0.334) 407	50% (0.345) 404

Source: 2004 National Politics Study.

Alternative Behavior by Workplace

	Campaign for Candidate	*Talk about Voting*	*Attend Meeting*	*Donate Money*	*Campaign for Minority*	*Prefer Same-Race Leaders*
Black in White Workplace	28% (0.453) 186	51% (0.501) 186	21% (0.409) 185	24% (0.425) 187	13% (0.341) 187	51% (0.327) 182
White in White Workplace	28% (0.450) 467	54% (0.499) 464	19% (0.391) 467	27% (0.445) 467	5%** (0.225) 467	42%** (0.321) 460
Black in Black Workplace	23% (0.425) 179	42% (0.495) 177	17% (0.379) 179	17% (0.379) 179	40.4% (0.375) 172	50% (0.344) 175

Source: 2004 National Politics Study.

Church-Based Participation by Neighborhood (1)

	Religiosity	*Attend Church*	*Heard Political Discussions*	*Clergy Spur to Action*	*Clergy Spur to Vote*
Black in White Neighborhood	78.1% (0.193) 46	51.8% (0.419) 375	63% (0.489) 43	37% (0.489) 43	16.2% (0.373) 43
White in White Neighborhood	67.5%* (0.286) 418	41.9%* (0.309) 375	37%** (0.482) 367	28% (0.451) 372	10.4% (0.306) 372
Black in Black Neighborhood	75.4% (0.242) 373	45.7% (0.296) 357	54% (0.499) 353	35% (0.478) 351	22.1% (0.415) 353

Source: 2004 National Politics Study.

Church-Based Participation by Neighborhood (2)

	Sermon on Economy	*Sermon on Iraq/Terror*	*Sermon on Legal System/Police*	*Sermon on Race*
Black in White Neighborhood	65.9% (0.479) 44	65.9% (0.479) 44	38.6% (0.492) 44	47.7% (0.505) 44
White in White Neighborhood	46.5%* (0.499) 372	44%* (0.497) 370	9.9%** (0.299) 372	52.2% (0.500) 371
Black in Black Neighborhood	63.5% (0.482) 351	57.9% (0.494) 354	37.6% (0.485) 353	60.1% (0.490) 354

Source: 2004 National Politics Study.

Church-Based Participation by Workplace (1)

	Religiosity	*Attend Church*	*Heard Political Discussions*	*Clergy Spur to Action*	*Clergy Spur to Vote*
Black in White Workplace	78.3% (0.233) 170	49.8% (0.302) 159	58% (0.495) 158	39% (0.488) 159	18.2% (0.387) 159
White in White Workplace	68.1%** (0.293) 413	42.7%* (0.303) 365	39%** (0.489) 360	31% (0.465) 363	9.8%* (0.298) 364
Black in Black Workplace	76.8% (0.256) 165	46.9% (0.314) 160	52% (0.501) 157	29%+ (0.457) 156	27.3%* (0.447) 157

Source: 2004 National Politics Study.

Church-Based Participation by Workplace (2)

	Sermon on Economy	*Sermon on Iraq/Terror*	*Sermon on Legal Sytem/Police*	*Sermon on Race*
Black in White Workplace	67.7% (0.469) 158	61.6% (0.487) 159	42.7% (0.496) 159	66% (0.475) 159
White in White Workplace	49.3%** (0.500) 363	47.5%* (0.500) 362	10.7%** (0.310) 363	54.2%* (0.498) 363
Black in Black Workplace	59.4% (0.492) 158	52.8% (0.500) 159	32.4%+ (0.469) 157	57.8% (0.495) 159

Source: 2004 National Politics Study.

Neighborhood Regressions (1) (compared to whites in white neighborhoods)

	Institutional Trust Index	*Deserve*	*Comfort*	*Personal Discrim.*	*Black Discrim.*
Black in White Neighborhood	-0.963* (0.328)	1.258** (0.345)	0.670+ (0.364)	1.583** (0.343)	0.940* (0.371)
Income	0.030+ (0.019)	-0.023 (0.020)	-0.044* (0.021)	-0.021 (0.020)	0.004 (0.021)
Education	0.275** (0.082)	0.238* (0.087)	-0.166+ (0.096)	-0.177* (0.089)	0.090 (0.093)
Gender	-0.184 .180	0.104 (0.191)	-0.118 (0.212)	0.412* (0.196)	0.042 (0.206)
Age	-0.001 (006)	0.009 (0.006)	0.021** (0.007)	-0.010+ (0.006)	0.004 (0.006)
Group Consciousness	0.110 (0.236)	-0.075 (0.250)	0.537* (0.277)	0.289 (0.258)	0.528* (0.271)
Party Identification	0.113* (0.274)	-0.086* (0.045)	-0.092+ (0.050)	-0.046 (0.047)	-0.078 (0.050)
Ideology	0.843* (0.376)	-1.822** (0.404)	1.216* (0.437)	1.048* (0.413)	-1.562** (0.436)
Home Ownership	-0.139 (0.274)	0.075 (0.290)	0.150 (0.333)	-0.078 (0.297)	0.426 (0.312)
N	399	392	398	399	399
-2 Log Likelihood	96.359**	946.723+	747.633	947.009	735.849

Source: 2004 National Politics Study.

Neighborhood Regressions (2) (compared to whites in white neighborhoods)

	Church Partic. Index	*Church Issue Norm Index*	*Group Partic. Index*
Black in White Neighborhood	0.263 (0.380)	0.571 (0.359)	0.852** (0.326)
Income	0.007 (0.023)	0.014 (0.022)	0.003 (0.019)
Education	0.174+ (0.101)	0.144 (0.094)	0.096 (0.082)
Gender	-0.473* (0.222)	-0.239 (0.205)	-0.338+ (0.181)
Age	-0.012+ (0.007)	-0.009 (0.006)	0.006 (0.006)

	Church Partic. Index	*Church Issue Norm Index*	*Group Partic. Index*
Group Consciousness	0.391 (0.292)	0.448+ (0.270)	0.451* (0.237)
Party Identification	-0.087+ (0.052)	-0.171** (0.049)	0.009 (0.043)
Ideology	0.729 (0.470)	0.618 (0.435)	-0.659+ (0.375)
Home Ownership	0.045 (0.351)	0.339 (0.359)	0.115 (0.274)
	371 619.600	318 996.342	399 1624.177

Source: 2004 National Politics Study.

Workplace Regressions (1) (compared to whites in white workplaces)

	Institutional Trust Index	*Deserve*	*Comfort*	*Personal Discrim.*	*Black Discrim.*
Black in White Workplace	-1.299** (0.206)	1.024** (2.14)	0.842** (0.220)	1.937** (0.223)	1.047** (0.228)
Income	0.019 (0.016)	-0.034* (0.017)	-0.034+ (0.018)	-0.039* (0.017)	0.007 (0.018)
Education	0.222** (0.074)	0.288** (0.079)	-0.160+ (0.085)	-0.174* (0.080)	0.201* (0.054)
Gender	-0.092 (0.160)	-0.098 (0.170)	0.121 (0.182)	0.360* (0.172)	0.024 (0.180)
Age	0.004 (0.005)	0.004 (0.005)	0.018** (0.006)	-0.016** (0.005)	-0.004 (0.005)
Group Consciousness	-0.454* 0.214	0.443* (0.227)	0.604* (0.247)	0.582* (0.232)	0.314 (0.240)
Party Identification	0.030 (0.040)	-0.137** (0.042)	-0.069 (0.046)	-0.033 (0.044)	-0.067 (0.045)
Ideology	1.043** (0.329)	-0.987** (0.347)	1.011** (0.372)	0.505 (0.352)	-1.045** (0.370)
Home Ownership	-0.158 (0.211)	-0.050 (0.224)	-0.311 (0.237)	0.281 (0.228)	0.281 (0.237)
	518 1660.756**	502 1246.684	514 1063.432	518 1064.389	518 962.074

Source: 2004 National Politics Study.

Workplace Regressions (2) (compared to whites in white workplaces)

	Church Partic. Index	*Church Issue Norm Index*	*Group-Based Partic. Index*
Black in White Workplace	0.502* (0.245)	0.785** (0.231)	0.663** (0.200)
Income	0.038* (0.020)	0.032+ (0.018)	0.014 (0.016)
Education	0.287** (0.092)	0.172* (0.085)	0.057 (0.074)
Gender	-0.374+ (0.197)	0.049 (0.182)	-0.372* (0.160)
Age	-0.012+ (0.006)	-0.010+ (0.006)	0.005 (0.005)
Group Consciousness	-0.019 (0.264)	0.118 (0.247)	0.315 (0.214)
Party Identification	-0.074 (0.049)	-0.069 (0.046)	-0.038 (0.040)
Ideology	0.012 (0.402)	-0.022 (0.373)	-0.788* (0.328)
Home Ownership	-0.047 (0.267)	-0.121 (0.248)	0.194 (0.211)
N	411	413	518
-2 Log Likelihood	818.013	1348.998	2102.066

Source: 2004 National Politics Study.

Network Views In Line

	Neighborhood	*Workplace*	*Volunteer Organization*	*Church*
Suburban Black	49% (0.292) 83	54% (0.253) 83	59% (0.287) 82	60% (0.296) 86
Suburban White	59%** (0.230) 580	60%+ (0.261) 553	61% (0.270) 568	53%+ (0.327) 571
Urban Black	53% (0.268) 66	58% (0.269) 67	59% (0.303) 65	59% (0.329) 63

Source: 2008 Cooperative Congressional Election Study.

Network Views In Line Regressions

	Neighborhood	*Workplace*	*Volunteer Org.*	*Church*
Suburban Blacks	-0.544+	-0.323	0.073	1.008**
	(0.284)	(0.283)	(0.288)	(0.272)
Income	0.041	0.041	0.069**	0.053*
	(0.028)	(0.027)	(0.027)	(0.025)
Education	-0.078	0.596+	0.611+	0.152
	(0.331)	(0.326)	(0.325)	(0.303)
Gender	-0.286	-0.149	0.276	0.203
	(0.181)	(0.177)	(0.177)	(0.166)
Age	0.030**	-0.004	0.021**	0.026**
	(0.007)	(0.006)	(0.006)	(0.006)
Party Identification	0.113*	0.051	0.050	0.274**
	(0.054)	(0.052)	(0.052)	(0.051)
Ideology	0.187	0.464	-0.031	0.989*
	(0.429)	(0.421)	(0.422)	(0.398)
Home Ownership	0.011	0.118	-0.150	-0.215
	(0.228)	(0.222)	(0.224)	(0.211)
Racial Identity	0.295	0.166	0.093	0.476*
	(0.242)	(0.235)	(0.237)	(0.224)
N	537	516	524	531
-2 Log Likelihood	979.044**	1072.559	1041.537**	1226.096+

Source: 2008 Cooperative Congressional Election Study.

Cultural Community Usage

	Cultural Community Index	*Use for Travel*	*Use for Business*	*Use for Shopping*	*Know Community History*
Suburban Black	1.72	56.3%	49.9%	66.2%	58%
	(0.794)	(0.360)	(0.338)	(0.244)	(0.254)
	57	57	57	57	24
Suburban White	2.22**	78.4%**	66.5%**	77.2%**	61%
	(0.693)	(0.274)	(0.316)	(0.244)	(0.298)
	396	402	398	403	396
Urban Black	2.00*	77.8%**	47.8%	74.8%+	63.7%
	(0.557)	(0.286)	(0.338)	(0.257)	(0.246)
	49	49	49	49	23

Source: 2008 Cooperative Congressional Election Study.

Cultural Community Perception (1)

	Center of Political Activity	*Primary Source of Entertainment*	*Place of Employment*	*Place of Education*
Suburban Black	6%	22%	27%	39%
	(0.240)	(0.424)	(0.452)	(0.498)
	57	24	24	24
Suburban White	11%	21%	31%	36%
	(0.314)	(0.410)	(0.465)	(0.482)
	410	202	202	202
Urban Black	16%+	22%	13%	53%
	(0.368)	(0.424)	(0.341)	(0.510)
	49	23	23	23

Source: 2008 Cooperative Congressional Election Study.

Cultural Community Perception (2)

	Invigorating	*Depressing*	*Hostile to Your Views*	*In Line with Views*
Suburban Black	5%	18%	9%	42%
	(0.222)	(0.393)	(0.286)	(0.504)
	24	24	24	24
Suburban White	18%	6%*	8%	45%
	(0.384)	(0.239)	(0.276)	(0.499)
	202	202	202	202
Urban Black	11%	13%	29%+	34%
	(0.322)	(0.343)	(0.464)	(0.483)
	23	23	23	23

Source: 2008 Cooperative Congressional Election Study.

Suburban African American Cultural Community Usage

	Cultural Community Index	*Use for Travel*	*Use for Business*	*Use for Shopping*	*Know Community History*
Racial Identity	1.81	62.4%	54.4%	64.1%	60.3%
	(0.798)	(0.311)	(0.319)	(0.280)	(0.264)
	27	27	27	27	14
No Racial Identity	1.65	50.8%	46%	68.1%	54.6%
	(0.797)	(0.396)	(0.355)	(0.211)	(0.248)
	30	30	30	30	9

Source: 2008 Cooperative Congressional Election Study.

Suburban African American Cultural Community Perception (1)

	Center of Political Activity	*Primary Source of Entertainment*	*Place of Employment*	*Place of Education*
Racial Identity	6%	22%	28%	33%
	(0.239)	(0.432)	(0.467)	(0.488)
	27	14	14	14
No Racial Identity	6%	22%	24%	48%
	(0.246)	(0.436)	(0.454)	(0.528)
	30	9	9	9

Source: 2008 Cooperative Congressional Election Study.

Suburban African American Cultural Community Perception (2)

	Invigorating	*Depressing*	*Hostile to Your Views*	*In Line with Views*
Racial Identity	6%	27%	11%	33%
	(0.236)	(0.462)	(0.330)	(0.488)
	14	14	14	14
No Racial Identity	4%	4%	4%	54%
	(0.212)	(0.212)	(0.212)	(0.527)
	9	9	9	9

Source: 2008 Cooperative Congressional Election Study.

Suburban African American Cultural Community Usage

	Cultural Community Index	*Use for Travel*	*Use for Business*	*Use for Shopping*	*Know Community History*
Black Church	1.92	67.6%	58.3%	66.5%	57.7%
	(0.783)	(0.320)	(0.316)	(0.279)	(0.245)
	34	34	34	34	15
Non-Black Church	1.31*	38.4%**	25.7%**	67.7%	56.5%
	(0.758)	(0.405)	(0.324)	(0.172)	(0.324)
	15	15	15	15	7

Source: 2008 Cooperative Congressional Election Study.

Suburban African American Cultural Community Perception (1)

	Center of Political Activity	*Primary Source of Entertainment*	*Place of Employment*	*Place of Education*
Black Church	8%	19%	27%	46%
	(0.272)	(0.407)	(0.457)	(0.516)
	34	15	15	15
Non-Black Church	5%	6%	6%	6%+
	(0.228)	(0.251)	(0.251)	(0.251)
	15	7	7	7

Source: 2008 Cooperative Congressional Election Study.

Suburban African American Cultural Community Perception (2)

	Invigorating	*Depressing*	*Hostile to Your Views*	*In Line with Views*
Black Church	5%	8%	6%	46%
	(0.232)	(0.284)	(0.237)	(0.516)
	15	15	15	15
Non-Black Church	6%	45%*	18%	44%
	(0.251)	(0.537)	(0.412)	(0.536)
	7	7	7	7

Source: 2008 Cooperative Congressional Election Study.

Cultural Community Usage Regression—Race by Neighborhood

	Suburban Whites	*Urban Blacks*		
	Community Usage Index	*Community Usage Index*	*Center of Political Activity*	*Know Comm. History*
Suburban Blacks	-1.206**	-0.869*	-1.649+	-2.616**
	(0.310)	(0.403)	(0.972)	(1.011)
Income	0.069**	0.229**	-0.047	-0.045
	(0.027)	(0.076)	(0.149)	(0.185)
Education	-0.071	1.095	2.885+	4.403*
	(0.327)	(0.932)	(1.769)	(2.031)
Gender	-0.129	-0.434	-0.833	3.809**
	(0.184)	(0.398)	(0.896)	(1.292)
Age	-0.013*	0.008	0.051+	0.046
	(0.007)	(0.014)	(0.029)	(0.042)
Racial Identity	0.035	-0.016	0.428	-0.998
	(0.242)	(0.413)	(0.852)	(0.980)
Party Identification	0.037	0.268	-0.084	2.326**
	(0.055)	(0.173)	(0.401)	(0.729)
Ideology	-0.629	-1.663*	-1.580	3.763*
	(0.438)	(0.763)	(1.922)	(1.877)
Home Ownership	0.662**	-0.255	0.685	-0.838
	(0.238)	(0.461)	(0.927)	(1.278)
N	379	92	93	37
-2 Log Likelihood	1384.490**	106.297**	46.024	41.916

Source: 2008 Cooperative Congressional Election Study.

Cultural Community Usage Regression—
Suburban African American by Church Makeup

	Community Usage Index
Black Church	4.036**
	(1.040)
Income	0.351*
	(0.156)
Education	2.729+
	(1.528)
Gender	-0.097
	(0.668)
Age	-0.025
	(0.028)
Racial Identity	0.781
	(0.780)
Party Identification	0.845**
	(0.324)
Ideology	-4.794**
	(1.582)
Home Ownership	-1.440
	(0.982)
N	42
-2 Log Likelihood	144.491

Source: 2008 Cooperative Congressional Election Study.

Feeling Thermometers by Neighborhood

	Al Sharpton	*Community Organizers*	*Barack Obama*
Suburban Black	52.70	80.31	88.96
	(25.87)	(20.52)	(20.22)
	82	33	85
Suburban White	27.62**	57.38**	55.73**
	(22.84)	(28.16)	(29.53)
	448	259	521
Urban Black	49.42	62.56**	85.10
	(27.34)	(31.86)	(23.54)
	57	34	66

Source: 2008 Cooperative Congressional Election Study.

Feeling Thermometers Suburban African American by Racial Identity

	Al Sharpton	*Community Organizers*	*Barack Obama*
Race Identity	55.11 (28.45) 38	80.73 (20.44) 20	95.64 (6.39) 39
No Race Identity	50.67 (23.62) 45	79.67 (21.43) 13	83.42** (25.53) 47
Urban Race Identity	59.44 (25.92) 14	59.21* (27.31) 14	89.62* (14.85) 30

Source: 2008 Cooperative Congressional Election Study.

Feeling Thermometers Suburban African American by Church Makeup

	Al Sharpton	*Community Organizers*	*Barack Obama*
Black Church	56.45 (27.27) 47	81.81 (14.84) 22	92.97 (15.87) 49
Non-Black Church	43.84* (21.73) 26	78.86 (33.87) 9	88.73 (21.43) 26

Source: 2008 Cooperative Congressional Election Study.

Race Opinion

	Deserve	*Special Favors*	*Try Hard to Succeed*	*Black Complaints*	*History of Discrimination*
Suburban Black	62% (0.320) 37	47% (0.313) 37	40% (0.364) 37	73% (0.337) 37	61% (0.342) 38
Suburban White	30%** (0.292) 302	68%** (0.325) 304	54%* (0.337) 301	37%** (0.321) 301	34%** (0.334) 304
Urban Black	63% (0.389) 35	45% (0.326) 33	39% (0.366) 32	58%+ (0.340) 35	52%+ (0.379) 33

Source: 2008 Cooperative Congressional Election Study.

Affirmative Action Opinion

Suburban Black	78% (0.285) 87	Race Identity	86.7% (0.245) 40
Suburban White	32.8%** (0.316) 593	No Race Identity	70.6%** (0.297) 47
Urban Black	72.8% (0.255) 67	Black Church	81.5% (0.278) 49
		Non-Black Church	70.6% (0.323) 27

Source: 2008 Cooperative Congressional Election Study.

Affirmative Action Regressions

	Suburban White	*Urban Black*	*Suburban No Racial Identity*	*Urban Racial Identity*
Suburban Black/ Racial Identity	-13.924** (7.435)	1.045** (0.382)	1.815** (0.593)	1.558+ (0.827)
Income	0.883 (1.500)	-0.133+ (0.070)	-0.177 (0.110)	-0.152 (0.160)
Education	41.979** (15.638)	2.112** (0.876)	0.023 (1.343)	1.380 (1.798)
Gender	6.184 (8.568)	-0.781** (0.392)	-0.233 (0.577)	-0.266 (0.635)
Age	-0.612+ (0.329)	0.008 (0.014)	-0.015 (0.022)	0.047+ (0.027)
Racial Identity	-1.930 (7.763)	0.789* (0.371)	—	—
Party Identification	-7.432* (3.366)	-0.356* (0.143)	-0.289 (0.193)	-0.201 (0.280)
Ideology	29.676* (14.408)	-1.248+ (0.715)	-1.231 (0.993)	-2.156 (1.338)
Home Ownership	-6.935 (10.315)	-0.389 (0.428)	0.538 (0.766)	0.409 (0.827)
N	379	136	75	57
-2 Log Likelihood	1384.490**	192.676**	114.935	61.146*

Source: 2008 Cooperative Congressional Election Study.

Race Opinion

	Deserve	*Admiration*	*Sympathy*	*Effects of Slavery Remain*
Suburban Black	59% (0.316) 169	73.7% (0.291) 168	66.7% (0.312) 168	57.9% (0.344) 170
Suburban White	33%** (0.281) 426	49%** (0.262) 418	42.5%** (0.264) 417	42.1%** (0.329) 426
Urban Black	66%* (0.305) 238	73.3% (0.294) 235	68.1% (0.333) 238	66.6%** (0.328) 241

Source: 2008 American National Election Study.

Race Opinion (2)

	Pref. Treatment in Job	*Try Hard to Succeed*	*Special Favors*	*Too Much Influence*
Suburban Black	57.4% (0.496) 148	53.3% (0.357) 171	60.4% (0.361) 167	15.2% (0.243) 167
Suburban White	9.5%** (0.294) 397	63.7%** (0.299) 424	73.4%** (0.281) 426	39.7%** (0.311) 384
Urban Black	53.8% (0.499) 223	57.5% (0.351) 236	63.6% (0.352) 238	12.2% (0.243) 237

Source: 2008 American National Election Study.

Race Opinion by Group Consciousness

	Deserve	*Sympathy*	*Slavery*	*Try Hard*	*Special Favors*	*Too Much Influence*
High Group Consciousness	68% (0.298) 156	71.5 (0.301) 44	68.1% (0.341) 156	45.6 (0.354) 46	52.2 (0.391) 45	10.8 (0.208) 46
Low Group Consciousness	60% (0.323) 183	61.1+ (0.304) 65	58.4% (0.339) 186	59.2+ (0.368) 65	68.6* (0.344) 63	23.8** (0.281) 63

Source: 2008 American National Election Study.

Race Opinion Regressions

	Race Opinion Index	*Deserve*	*Admire*	*Sympathy*	*Slavery*
Suburban Black	1.855**	1.357**	1.631**	1.626**	0.691**
	(0.260)	(0.257)	(0.276)	(0.272)	(0.252)
Income	-0.028+	-0.038*	-0.025	-0.029+	-0.036*
	(0.017)	(0.017)	(0.018)	(0.018)	(0.017)
Education	0.299**	0.093*	0.132**	0.197**	0.173**
	(0.048)	(0.046)	(0.049)	(0.050)	(0.047)
Gender	-0.092	-0.179	0.303	0.161	-0.389*
	(0.188)	(0.186)	(0.197)	(0.197)	(0.187)
Age	0.010*	0.003	0.023**	0.030**	0.007
	(0.005)	(0.005)	(0.006)	(0.006)	(0.005)
Party Identification	-1.353**	-1.013**	-0.748*	-0.949**	-1.379**
	(0.327)	(0.326)	(0.341)	(0.344)	(0.330)
Ideology	-0.656*	-0.415	0.031	0.112	-0.096
	(0.297)	(0.297)	(0.314)	(0.315)	(0.298)
N	401	414	407	407	414
-2 Log Likelihood	1207.543*	1160.765	882.967**	877.443**	1180.008*

Source: 2008 American National Election Study.

Race Opinion Regressions (2)

	Pref. Treatment in Jobs	*Try Hard to Succeed*	*Special Favors*	*Too Much Influence*
Suburban Black	2.134**	-0.802**	-0.887**	-1.510**
	(0.374)	(0.251)	(0.254)	(0.302)
Income	-0.044	-0.003	0.013	0.014
	(0.033)	(0.017)	(0.017)	(0.020)
Education	-0.161+	-0.273**	-0.280**	-0.129*
	(0.085)	(0.048)	(0.049)	(0.054)
Gender	-0.025	0.132	0.472*	-0.073
	(0.342)	(0.186)	(0.191)	(0.220)
Age	0.020*	-0.001	0.012*	0.003
	(0.010)	(0.005)	(0.006)	(0.006)
Party Identification	-1.427*	0.394	0.449	0.711+
	(0.613)	(0.325)	(0.333)	(0.374)
Ideology	-0.830	0.842**	0.307	0.991**
	(0.532)	(0.300)	(0.305)	(0.349)
N	381	413	414	384
-2 Log Likelihood	248.500	1180.358*	1084.342**	634.963

Source: 2008 American National Election Study.

Government Role in Equality

	Problem not Equal	*Treat Equal*	*Life Chance*	*Society Make Equal*	*Less Worry*	*Too Far on Rights*
Suburban Black	77.9%	82.7%	66.6%	93.4%	40.4%	37.3%
	(0.288)	(0.237)	(0.345)	(0.161)	(0.368)	(0.370)
	171	170	170	171	170	170
Suburban White	52.5%**	62.9%**	57.8%**	85%**	53.2%**	47.4%**
	(0.314)	(0.285)	(0.291)	(0.227)	(0.314)	(0.331)
	426	425	425	426	426	425
Urban Black	78.5%	85.1%	65.2%	94.5%	45.6%	34.9%
	(0.273)	(0.240)	(0.365)	(0.141)	(0.377)	(0.376)
	242	242	240	242	242	242

Source: 2008 American National Election Study.

Suburban African American Government Role in Equality by Group Consciousness

	Too Far on Equality	*Worry Less about Equality*
High Group Consciousness	25.5%	33.1%
	(0.355)	(0.369)
	46	46
Low Group Consciousness	45%**	45%+
	(0.362)	(0.364)
	65	65

Source: 2008 American National Election Study.

Government Role in Society Regressions

	Problem not Equal	*Treat Equal*	*Society Ensure Equal*	*Life Chance*	*Worry Too Much about Equal*	*Too Far on Equality*
Suburban Black	1.281**	0.926**	0.961**	0.872**	-1.079**	-0.719**
	(0.264)	(0.266)	(0.346)	(0.257)	(0.254)	(0.254)
Income	-0.030+	-0.027	-0.010	0.020	0.000	-0.003
	(0.017)	(0.017)	(0.019)	(0.017)	(0.017)	(0.017)
Education	-0.028	-0.048	0.049	0.088+	-0.141**	-0.195**
	(0.047)	(0.048)	(0.055)	(0.046)	(0.046)	(0.047)
Gender	-0.100	0.018	-0.151	0.387*	-0.198	-0.136
	(0.188)	(0.191)	(0.218)	(0.188)	(0.185)	(0.186)
Age	0.006	0.009+	0.017**	-0.019**	-0.005	0.013*
	(0.005)	(0.005)	(0.006)	(0.005)	(0.005)	(0.005)
Party Identification	-1.732**	-1.761**	-1.898**	-0.895**	0.937**	1.006**
	(0.335)	(0.340)	(0.398)	(0.327)	(0.324)	(0.326)
Ideology	-0.294	-0.297	0.497	-0.449	0.582*	1.158**
	(0.302)	(0.306)	(0.346)	(0.298)	(0.296)	(0.300)
N	414	413	414	413	414	414
-2 Log Likelihood	1149.332	1085.733	756.656	1155.288	1125.816	1204.026

Source: 2008 American National Election Study.

Group-Based Participation

	Gov. Shouldn't Help Blacks	*Gov. Ensure Job Help*	*Black Candidates More Suitable*	*Black Candidates More Intelligent*	*Ready for Black President*
Suburban Black	43.1% (0.339) 162	89.5% (0.307) 105	.503 (0.069) 168	.507 (0.072) 170	79.7% (0.402) 183
Suburban White	70.7%** (0.257) 394	43.5%** (0.496) 223	.484** (0.078) 422	.481** (0.083) 421	63.1%** (0.482) 429
Urban Black	38.8% (0.339) 218	89.1% (0.311) 157	.495 (0.093) 238	.507 (0.111) 235	71.5%** (0.452) 260

Source: 2008 American National Election Study.

Group-Based Participation

	Black Candidate Suitable
High Group Consciousness	0.525 (0.106) 45
Low Group Consciousness	0.492* (0.062) 64
Urban High Group Consciousness	0.489+ (0.119) 76

Source: 2008 American National Election Study.

Group-Based Opinion Regressions

	Gov. Shouldn't Help Blacks	*Gov. Help Black Jobs*	*Black Cand. Intelligent*
Suburban Black	-1.608** (0.258)	1.761** (0.494)	1.910+ (1.161)
Income	0.033* (0.017)	-0.027 (0.030)	0.041 (0.048)
Education	-0.145** (0.048)	0.104 (0.081)	0.240+ (0.129)
Gender	0.147 (0.188)	-0.424 (0.312)	0.352 (0.534)
Age	-0.004 (0.005)	0.014 (0.009)	-0.035* (0.014)
Party Identification	0.758* (0.319)	-1.568** (0.560)	-1.899* (0.974)
Ideology	0.722* (0.293)	0.072 (0.545)	-0.681 (0.862)
N	396	239	411
-2 Log Likelihood	1208.101	271.288	122.244

Source: 2008 American National Election Study.

Political Choice

	District In Line	*Democratic Candidate Ideology Distance*
Suburban Black	58% (0.500) 39	-13.74 (28.75) 46
Suburban White	45% (0.498) 305	-22.33 (36.42) 302
Urban Black	38%+ (0.491) 36	-7.54 (31.62) 27

Source: 2008 Cooperative Congressional Election Study.

Political Choice

	District In Line
Race Identity	44% (0.508) 44
No Race Identity	77%* (0.437) 16

Source: 2008 Cooperative Congressional Election Study.

Information Acquisition

	Interest in Politics	*Interest in News*	*Read Newspaper*
Suburban Black	65% (0.388) 83	80% (0.279) 85	69.9% (0.461) 87
Suburban White	77.9%** (0.320) 588	80.7% (0.295) 587	70% (0.458) 594
Urban Black	76.4%+ (0.345) 64	77.8% (0.269) 67	53.9%* (0.502) 67

Source: 2008 Cooperative Congressional Election Study.

Information Acquisition by Racial Identity

	Interest in Politics	*Interest in News*	*Read Newspaper*
Suburban Race Identity	80.2% (0.297) 38	88.2% (0.193) 37	73% (0.449) 40
Suburban No Race Identity	52.2%** (0.412) 45	73.5%* (0.318) 47	67.3%* (0.474) 47
Urban Race Identity	75.3% (0.337) 30	76%* (0.294) 37	47.9% (0.508) 30

Source: 2008 Cooperative Congressional Election Study.

Information Acquisition by Church Makeup

	Blog	*TV News*	*Radio*
Suburban Black Church	26.5% (0.446) 49	86.7% (0.342) 49	58% (0.498) 49
Suburban Non-Black Church	8.8%+ (0.288) 27	69.7%+ (0.467) 27	33%* (0.479) 27
Urban Black Church	29.7% (0.465) 27	86.6% (0.346) 27	44.1% (0.506) 27

Source: 2008 Cooperative Congressional Election Study.

Voting Participation

	Pres. Turnout	*House Turnout*	*Ballot Roll-Off*
Suburban Black	82% (0.386) 171	74% (0.441) 138	25.3% (0.436) 138
Suburban White	79% (0.405) 426	88%** (0.320) 338	10.9%** (0.331) 338
Urban Black	82% (0.386) 242	83%* (0.374) 197	15.7%* (0.365) 197

Source: 2008 American National Election Study.

Voting Participation by Group Consciousness

	Pres. Turnout	*House Turnout*	*Ballot Roll-Off*
Suburban Race Identity	85% (0.363) 46	68% (0.471) 38	31.5% (0.471) 38
Suburban No Race Identity	75% (0.434) 65	81% (0.398) 47	19.1% (0.397) 47
Urban Race Identity	94% (0.248) 77	89%** (0.316) 72	9.7%** (0.298) 72

Source: 2008 American National Election Study.

Ballot Roll-Off Regressions

	Suburban White	*Urban Black*
Suburban Black	0.589 (0.435)	0.964* (0.462)
Income	-0.058+ (0.030)	-0.035 (0.042)
Education	-0.226** (0.089)	-0.315** (0.112)
Gender	-0.103 (0.349)	0.341 (0.450)
Age	-0.022* (0.010)	-0.043** (0.016)
Party Identification	0.211 (0.625)	-0.048 (1.028)
Ideology	-0.185 (0.547)	-0.385 (0.717)
N -2 Log Likelihood	346 246.954	164 136.261

Source: 2008 American National Election Study.

Ballot Roll-Off Regressions by Group Consciousness

	Suburban Low Group Consciousness	*Urban High Group Consciousness*
Ballot Roll-Off	1.753+ (0.942)	2.708* (1.090)
Income	-0.082 (0.094)	-0.193+ (0.107)
Education	-0.272 (0.243)	-0.283 (0.275)
Gender	0.587 (0.915)	1.376 (0.910)
Age	-0.021 (0.036)	0.006 (0.033)
Party Identification	-4.878 (3.763)	1.862 (2.090)
Ideology	0.192 (1.314)	0.606 (1.419)
N -2 Log Likelihood	46 39.105	64 35.254

Source: 2008 American National Election Study.

Alternative Future Participation

	Attend Gov. Meeting	*Attend Meeting on Issue*	*Invite Others to Meeting*	*Pass Along Political Information*	*Give to Religious Organization*	*Attend Protest*
Suburban Black	48%	35.5%	29.8%	28.8%	59.9%	21%
	(0.325)	(0.319)	(0.331)	(0.327)	(0.344)	(0.290)
	170	169	169	169	168	169
Suburban White	36.3%**	25.6%**	17.1%**	16.4%**	50.4%**	13.2%**
	(0.307)	(0.291)	(0.263)	(0.262)	(0.390)	(0.232)
	426	426	426	426	426	426
Urban Black	43.1%	32.5%	27.4%	27.7%	59.3%	22.3%
	(0.350)	(0.324)	(0.321)	(0.328)	(0.360)	(0.298)
	241	241	241	241	242	242

Source: 2008 American National Election Study.

Suburban Black Alternative Participation (Ever in Past)

	Give to Social Org.	*Sign Petition*	*Attend Meeting on Issue*	*Pass Political Info*	*Protest*
High Group Consciousness	37.7% (0.490) 45	40.2% (0.778) 46	31.1% (0.468) 45	23.9% (0.431) 46	21.7% (0.417) 46
Low Group Consciousness	9.2%** (0.291) 65	25%** (0.436) 64	6.1%** (0.242) 65	7.6%** (0.268) 65	10.7% (0.312) 65

Source: 2008 American National Election Study.

Suburban Black Alternative Participation (Future)

	Protest	*Give to Religious Org.*	*Sign Petition*	*Attend Gov. Meeting*	*Attend Meeting on Issue*
High Group Consciousness	27.1% (0.324) 46	72.7% (0.340) 45	44.5% (0.670) 46	57.6% (0.341) 46	44% (0.350) 46
Low Group Consciousness	16.9%+ (0.269) 65	52.6%** (0.345) 65	20.9%** (0.509) 65	41.9%* (0.325) 65	28%* (0.317) 65

Source: 2008 American National Election Study.

NES Suburban Black Alternative Participation (Past 12 Months)

	Talk about Politics	*Donate Money*	*Place Political Sign*	*Attend Political Meeting*	*Work for Candidate*	*Donate to Charity*	*Attend Community Meeting*
High Group Consciousness	61%	22.2%	41%	20%	11%	84.4%	34.7%
	(0.493)	(0.420)	(0.498)	(0.401)	(0.315)	(0.366)	(0.481)
	46	45	46	46	46	45	46
Low Group Consciousness	29%**	1.5%**	23%*	2%*	2%*	61.5%**	4.6%**
	(0.458)	(0.124)	(0.425)	(0.124)	(0.124)	(0.490)	(0.211)
	65	65	65	65	65	65	65

Source: 2008 American National Election Study.

Alternative Participation Regressions

	Ever Participate Index	*Future Participate Index*	*12 Months Participate Index*
Suburban Blacks	-0.857**	0.563*	0.379
	(0.248)	(0.242)	(0.247)
Income	0.049**	0.020	0.052**
	(0.016)	(0.016)	(0.017)
Education	0.371**	0.225**	0.279**
	(0.048)	(0.045)	(0.047)
Gender	0.519**	0.340+	0.548**
	(0.184)	(0.180)	(0.185)
Age	0.008	-0.007	0.012*
	(0.005)	(0.005)	(0.005)
Party Identification	-0.262	-0.764*	-0.324
	(0.318)	(0.314)	(0.320)
Ideology	0.294	0.855**	0.952**
	(0.293)	(0.289)	(0.296)
N	410	413	411
-2 Log Likelihood	1488.178	1698.390	1514.377

Source: 2008 American National Election Study.

Alternative Participation Regressions by Group Consciousness

	Ever Participate Index	*Future Participate Index*	*12 Months Participate Index*
Suburban Group Consciousness	1.717** (0.545)	1.542** (0.511)	1.901** (0.552)
Income	0.054 (0.052)	-0.032 (0.049)	0.064 (0.052)
Education	0.583** (0.157)	-0.009 (0.134)	0.169 (0.142)
Gender	1.268* (0.532)	0.515 (0.489)	1.557** (0.543)
Age	0.032+ (0.020)	-0.016 (0.018)	0.017 (0.019)
Party Identification	1.167 (1.222)	-0.208 (1.139)	-1.898 (1.230)
Ideology	-0.105 (0.784)	0.214 (0.743)	0.844 (0.281)
N	58	58	58
-2 Log Likelihood	150.411	354.129	145.201

Source: 2008 American National Election Study.

Notes

CHAPTER 1. THE UNIQUE STORY OF THE SUBURBAN AFRICAN AMERICAN

1. For this study, socioeconomic status will refer to the combination of such characteristics as income, education, occupation, etc.

2. In the extant literature, the definition of a suburb is fluid and ranges from physical geographic determinations to self-reporting. The Census Bureau does not have a formal designation for a suburb. The definition I will use will also be somewhat fluid throughout this project and ultimately will be dependent on the data available and its level of precision. I will use three definitions: (1) self-reported suburban residence, (2) interviewer designations of neighborhood type, and (3) statistical analysis of census data where I designate the suburbs as all areas in the metropolitan statistical area (MSA) that are outside the boundaries of the central city (the largest city in the MSA).

3. Racially radical in this sense means advocating for policies specifically directed toward their race to correct for historical discrimination and segregation. They are "radical" in the sense that they go beyond the current liberal ideas of how to address these disparities.

4. The Brookings Institution uses a slightly different designation of suburbs than I do. They count all areas outside of the central city as suburbs, but they include all principal cities in their measure of the urban area. While I believe the measure I employ is better, an examination of the black and white racial proportions for each measure show similarities. For example, in analyzing the Philadelphia MSA, I define the suburbs as all areas outside of Philadelphia proper. Brookings would define the suburbs as all areas outside of Philadelphia, Pennsylvania, Camden, New Jersey, and Wilmington, Delaware. The racial makeup of the Philadelphia suburbs (2012 American Community Survey) for this project is 77 percent white and 13 percent black; in the Frey article the makeup of the same area (2010 Census) is 75 percent white and 13 percent black.

5. However, according to Frey's numbers, African Americans' proportion of the national suburbs is smaller than their share of the total population (10 percent of suburbs compared to 12.6 percent of the population). My measure has the African American share of the suburbs at 15 percent, likely because I truncated my data to the top twenty-five MSAs by black population proportion with a population over 1 million.

6. The years included are 1990, 1995, 2000, 2005, and 2010.

7. All education data come from the Current Population Survey conducted by the U.S. Census, "Percent of People 25 Years and Over Who Have Completed High School or College, by Race, Hispanic Origin and Sex: Selected Years 1940 to 2013." All income data come from the Current Population Survey conducted by the U.S.

Census, "Race and Hispanic Origin of People (Both Sexes Combined) by Median and Mean Income 1947 to 2012, People 15 Years or Older." Income is in 2012 CPI-U-RS adjusted dollars. Comparisons were made to all races as opposed to whites because the inclusion of Asian Americans raises the aggregate SES levels for all categories. Hence, the threshold is more rigorous and highlights the impressiveness of the relative increases.

8. Comparisons based on the same criteria as the income and education data were not possible. The data only begin in 1995 and the categorization of industries changes. Data for 2000 were not available. The data come from the Labor Force Statistics from the Current Population Survey, "Employed Persons by Detailed Industry, Sex, Race, and Hispanic Origin: 2010 and 2013," www.census.gov.

9. Data are from the 2012 American Community Survey (ACS). The total universe of MSAs for this chapter is based on the top twenty-five MSAs in terms of black population proportion, with total populations over 1 million, from the 2012 Census Statistical Abstract.

10. For simplicity's sake, the term urban will refer to all people living within the boundaries of the largest principal city of the MSA and will serve as the geographic counterpart to the suburbs.

11. 2013 Current Population Survey, listed as Professional and Related occupations.

12. 2013 Current Population Survey, listed as Management, Business, and Financial Operations occupations.

13. 2012 American Community Survey, "Occupation for Employed Civilian Population 16 Years and Over."

14. Zip Code 19010 Profile, http://www.zipdatamaps.com/19010 (accessed January 2016).

15. Via Sharp (2012), thesocietypages.org/socimages/2012/04/25/1934-philadelphia-redlining-map/ (accessed January 2016).

16. These traditional black belt suburbs would be designated as urban areas in my analysis because they are within the central city.

17. This is a point with which I am in total agreement and which I will test in subsequent chapters.

18. Internal validity is the requirement that a survey question elicits a causal response on the part of the respondent. Major validity issues are unclear or overly complex concepts that the respondent may not be familiar with or has not thought a lot about.

19. This means that external validity is again sacrificed and introduces the additional bias that people will refer others of similar demographics and ideologies.

20. That is not to say qualitative researchers do not take great pains to ensure the strongest possible validity and make administration as procedural as possible. There is simply a trade-off between the depth of probing and representativeness.

21. While this number may be roughly equivalent to suburban African American population proportions, and therefore adequate for external validity/generalizability, it presents problems for statistical analysis. Since tests of statistical significance are

based on the spread of responses on a question and their deviation from the mean, outlier responses are particularly punitive on the statistical tests. When the number of respondents for a certain group is low, these outliers exert an unduly detrimental influence on estimates.

CHAPTER 2. HOW SUBURBAN AFRICAN AMERICANS FIT INTO OUR SOCIAL SCIENCE THEORIES

1. Here, salient means influential to one's sense of self.

2. American society's use of phenotype to ascribe race means there may be constraints on these choices.

3. Mainstream versus marginalized status does not always correspond to one's proportion of the population. Southern whites in the mid-twentieth century held in-group status even though blacks outnumbered them in many jurisdictions.

4. This is as opposed to other choices that identity influences, but which do not necessarily affect the fate of other group members, such as marriage partners or children's names.

5. Friedman uses the dissimilarity index, which compares the racial proportions in one jurisdiction with the proportions in a nested area to see if the pattern holds or differs. For example, a city's makeup may be 80 percent white and 20 percent black. A neighborhood in that city that is also 80/20 matches the norm. A neighborhood with a 50/50 makeup is more diverse.

6. This is not to say a person will not have agreeable neighbors, but this will be more by chance than by self-selection.

7. This is not to say that this standard of behavior is set in an effort to perpetuate or benefit from the racial hierarchy. In keeping with the probabilistic theory, it is understandable that the majority opinion will be the norm of the network. In a group of four, where two people agree, the third person has a choice to have an alternative view or be persuaded to go with the two original people who agreed. For this third person only one person *potentially* agrees with them while two clearly disagree. In an effort to lessen discomfort, the person could be more likely to accept the new information and adjust their position toward the majority. Hence, the prevailing norm of the group may move toward larger majorities.

8. As the scope of one's voluntary target narrows, so will control over the probabilistic makeup of the environment. The number of outlets for "any community service" will be much larger than fundraising for the city zoo. In fact, the same applies to workplace networks. If one's aim were simply to have a job, or have a job at, say, a fast food restaurant, then it would be much easier to leave a disagreeable work environment than it would be if one's expertise were information technology maintenance of a computer program only utilized in municipal human resources offices.

9. There is an extensive history of slaves using songs with coded meanings to discuss escape attempts or clandestine gatherings.

10. Class refers to socioeconomic status (in other words, income, education, occupation, neighborhood prestige). The major socioeconomic difference throughout the lineage of black politics research on this subject has been between the black middle class and the black working class, hence my references to "class differences" primarily in the recounting of this literature and periodically throughout the book.

11. Distinguishing these complex ideologies into two groups named for their most famous adherents is admittedly simplistic. There is a long lineage of research on both sides of this debate; however, it is not completely relevant to the crux of this project.

12. These would be considered Dawson's (2001, 2012) radical liberalism and black conservatism, respectfully. A full recounting of black ideologies and their main proponents follows in the next section.

13. Of course, the state only deemed some organizations acceptable. Radical groups such as the Universal Negro Improvement Association, the Nation of Islam, and the Black Panther Party were targets of official surveillance, intimidation, and coercion.

14. Popular recollection has oversimplified the idea of a major split between King and Malcolm X in a narrative pushed by black conservatives (Baker 1995). Indeed, most studies of the era suggest King had become increasingly radicalized and embracing of the combative strategies at the end of his life.

15. As mentioned earlier, Dawson's post-1995 works walk back some of these claims about the black public sphere decline.

16. At the time of this writing, a spate of unarmed black males being shot and killed by white police officers was galvanizing the counterpublic and its institutions to protest. The protests, ranging from coordinated efforts to shut down highways in Oakland to somewhat riotous protests in Baltimore, have continued the legacy of civil disobedience.

17. This is not to say that all majority black institutions are located in the inner city. Historically, African Americans founded them because they were not welcomed in any other areas. Contemporarily, some of these institutions have moved outside of the neighborhood for cheaper property costs, more available space (like some of the black megachurches), and to be closer to the few suburban black neighborhoods, like in Prince George's County, Maryland. The draw of finding a majority institution is still there and suburban blacks should still seek them out regardless of their physical location. The major mechanism is that minority status in immediate networks will lead to a desire for majority status in other networks and desired norms.

18. The labels changed slightly between the studies. When in conflict, the 2012 versions are used.

19. This was called radical egalitarianism in Dawson 2001.

20. This was called black Marxism in Dawson 2001.

21. This also leads to the paradox of voting, which theorizes that an individual will only undertake a behavior if one's inaction would result in the benefit being lost. If the individual can still realize the benefit without expending any resources, then any costs associated with the behavior will turn the calculus negative. This has led to an

operationalization of the participatory formula where the chance that one's behavior results in the gain/loss of the benefit is negligible (especially since the most well-known formula introduces this as a multiplicative) and therefore the rational actor should never participate (vote). However, the simplest form of the model does not account for intangible (and therefore unquantifiable) benefits, such as feelings of civic duty (Riker and Ordeshook 1968). In the case of suburban African Americans, this intangible benefit could be aiding the racial group.

22. Actually, 2012 was the first time African American presidential turnout by percentage was higher than that of whites.

23. Scholars define ballot roll-off as voting in top-of-the-ballot elections but skipping lower races, even if voters cast votes in some and not others. In this project, I define roll-off as voting for president but not voting in the U.S. Congressional race.

CHAPTER 3. SUBURBAN AFRICAN AMERICANS AND SOCIAL NETWORKS

1. As is convention, most variables were scaled to be between 0 and 1. This allows for an easy interpretation of the result as a percentage. A result like "suburban African Americans had 50 percent support" could mean everyone registered 50 percent or equal amounts registered 0 or 100. In the first scenario, the standard deviation would be 0, in the second it would be 50. For the standard deviations, see the specific tables in the appendix.

2. Here, chance means the sample being measured is producing a result that would not be found in the larger population.

3. The full tables with the number of cases and standard deviations are included in the appendix.

4. p-value = 0.11.

5. Cronbach's Alpha = 0.736.

6. Cronbach's Alpha = 0.127.

7. Cronbach's Alpha = 0.615.

8. Cronbach's Alpha = 0.711.

9. Cronbach's Alpha = 0.518.

10. Cronbach's Alpha = 0.091.

CHAPTER 4. SUBURBAN AFRICAN AMERICAN IDEOLOGY AND PERCEPTION OF THE CULTURAL COMMUNITY

1. The designation of a "similar culture" is based on the identity chosen in table 2.1.

2. Cronbach's Alpha = 0.645.

3. The survey administration randomized these choices along with most of the other questions in the survey.

4. Other ideologies are not easily represented by specific questions in any of the three datasets employed for this project.

5. One should exercise caution in extrapolating these church-based relationships to the larger population, as the number of respondents is very low.

6. Again, this means that they will use the community more often.

7. The fact that Barack Obama was a community organizer and the frequent mockery and skepticism of the job by Republicans, like vice presidential nominee Sarah Palin, undoubtedly adds an additional layer to feelings about the position beyond simply organizing community members.

8. The ANES has no specific question on affirmative action.

9. Group consciousness is measured in the ANES by the question: "what happens to black people in [this country has] something to do with what happens in my life." There were four answer choices. "High" group-conscious respondents said that it did matter and that it mattered a lot. "Low" group-conscious respondents said it mattered a little or not at all.

10. ANES race opinion index: blacks have too much influence over government, feel admiration for blacks, feel sympathy for blacks, blacks should work their way up without special favors, slavery has made it difficult for blacks to get out of the lower class, blacks have gotten less than they deserve, and blacks would be as well off as whites if they tried harder. Cronbach's Alpha = 0.049.

11. A score of zero indicates whites are "a great deal better suited" and a score of 1 indicates blacks are "a great deal better suited."

CHAPTER 5. THE SUBURBAN POLITICAL ENVIRONMENT AND ITS EFFECTS ON THE PARTICIPATION OF SUBURBAN AFRICAN AMERICANS

1. There are usually multiple elections on the ballot and they may activate different identities (a Democratic parent in a heavily Republican state will likely be less enthusiastic about the gubernatorial race than a local school bond issue). For a high-resourced, group-conscious, suburban African American, the likelihood of skipping the House race, which only costs the pushing of an extra button, may be very low, especially since one of the candidates is likely of the same party.

2. This is primary identity as selected in table 2.1 or by their level of group consciousness in the ANES.

3. Cronbach's Alpha = 0.777.

4. Cronbach's Alpha = 0.763.

5. Cronbach's Alpha = 0.699.

Bibliography

Adelman, Robert M. 2005. "The Roles of Race, Class, and Residential Preferences in the Neighborhood Racial Composition of Middle-Class Blacks and Whites." *Social Science Quarterly* 86 (1): 209–228.

Alba, Richard D., John R. Logan, and Brian J. Stults. 2000. "How Segregated Are Middle-Class African Americans?" *Social Problems* 47 (4): 543–558.

Baker, Houston A. 1995. "Critical Memory and the Black Public Sphere." In *The Black Public Sphere,* edited by The Black Public Sphere Collective. Chicago: Univ. of Chicago Press.

Berelson, Bernard R., Paul F. Lazarsfeld, and William N. McPhee. 1954. *Voting.* Chicago: Univ. of Chicago Press.

Blumer, Herbert. 1958. "Race Prejudice as a Sense of Group Position." *Pacific Sociological Review* 1 (1): 3–7.

Bobo, Lawrence. 1983. "Whites' Opposition to Busing: Symbolic Racism or Realistic Group Conflict?" *Journal of Personality and Social Psychology* 45 (6): 1196–1210.

Bobo, Lawrence, Camille Z. Charles, Maria Krysan, and Alicia D. Simmons. 2012. "The *Real* Record on Racial Attitudes." In *Social Trends in American Life: Findings from the General Social Survey since 1972,* edited by Peter V. Marsden, 38–83. Princeton, N.J.: Princeton Univ. Press.

Bobo, Lawrence, and Franklin D. Gilliam Jr. 1990. "Race, Sociopolitical Participation, and Black Empowerment." *American Political Science Review* 84 (2): 377–393.

Bobo, Lawrence, and Vincent L. Hutchings. 1996. "Perceptions of Racial Group Competition: Extending Blumer's Theory of Group Position to a Multiracial Social Context." *American Sociological Review* 61 (6): 951–972.

Branton, Regina P., and Bradford S. Jones. 2005. "Reexamining Racial Attitudes: The Conditional Relationship Between Diversity and Socioeconomic Environment." *American Journal of Political Science* 49 (2): 359–372.

Brief, Arthur P., Elizabeth E. Umphress, Joerg Dietz, John W. Burrows, Rebecca M. Butz, and Lotte Scholten. 2005. "Community Matters: Realistic Group Conflict Theory and the Impact of Diversity." *Academy of Management Journal* 48 (5): 830–844.

Brooks, Joanna. 2005. "The Early American Public Sphere and the Emergence of a Black Print Counterpublic." *William and Mary Quarterly* 62 (1): 67–92.

Brown, Elsa Barkley. 1995. "Negotiating and Transforming the Public Sphere: African American Political Life in the Transition from Slavery to Freedom." In *The Black Public Sphere,* edited by The Black Public Sphere Collective. Chicago: Univ. of Chicago Press.

Chong, Dennis, and Reuel Rogers. 2005. "Racial Solidarity and Political Participation." *Political Behavior* 27 (4): 347–374.

Clark, William A. V. 2007. "Race, Class, and Place: Evaluating Mobility Outcomes for African Americans." *Urban Affairs Review* 42 (3): 295–314.
Cohen, Cathy J., and Michael C. Dawson. 1993. "Neighborhood Poverty and African American Politics." *American Political Science Review* 87 (2): 286–302.
Cross, William, Jr. 1991. *Shades of Black: Diversity in African American Identity.* Philadelphia: Temple Univ. Press.
Dawson, Michael C. 1994. *Behind the Mule: Race and Class in African-American Politics.* Princeton, N.J.: Princeton Univ. Press.
———. 1995. "A Black Counterpublic?: Economic Earthquakes, Racial Agenda(s), and Black Politics." In *The Black Public Sphere,* edited by The Black Public Sphere Collective. Chicago: Univ. of Chicago Press.
———. 2001. *Black Visions.* Chicago: Univ. of Chicago Press.
———. 2012. "The Black Public Sphere and Black Civil Society." In *The Oxford Handbook of African American Citizenship, 1865–Present,* edited by Lawrence D. Bobo, Lisa Crooms-Robinson, Linda Darling-Hammond, Michael C. Dawson, Henry Louis Gates, Gerald Jaynes, and Claude Steele. Oxford: Oxford Univ. Press.
Dawson, Michael, Ronald Brown, and James S. Jackson. 2008. *National Black Politics Study, 1993.* ICPSR. Distributed by Inter-University Consortium for Political and Social Research, 2008. http://doi.org/10.3886/ICPSR02018.v2.
Dixon, Jeffrey C. 2006. "The Ties that Bind and Those that Don't: Toward Reconciling Group Threat and Contact Theories of Prejudice." *Social Forces* 84 (4): 2179–2204.
Downs, Anthony. 1957. *An Economic Theory of Democracy.* New York: Harper.
Eveland, William P., Jr., and Myiah Hutchens Hively. 2009. "Political Discussion Frequency, Network Size, and Heterogeneity of Discussion as Predictors of Political Knowledge and Participation." *Journal of Communication* 59 (2): 205–224.
Eveland, William P., Jr., and Steven B. Kleinman. 2011. "Comparing General and Political Discussion Networks within Voluntary Organizations Using Social Network Analysis." *Political Behavior* 35 (1): 65–87. doi:10.1007/s11109-011-9187-4.
Festiger, Leon. 1957. *A Theory of Cognitive Dissonance.* Stanford: Stanford Univ. Press.
Fischer, Mary J. 2008. "Shifting Geographies: Examining the Role of Segregation in Blacks' Declining Suburbanization." *Urban Affairs Review* 43 (4): 475–496.
Fraser, Nancy. 1992. "Rethinking the Public Sphere: A Contribution to the Critique of Actually Existing Democracy." *Social Text* 25 (26): 56–80.
Frasure-Yokley, Lorrie. 2015. *Racial and Ethnic Politics in American Suburbs.* Cambridge: Cambridge Univ. Press.
Frey, William. 2011. "Melting Pot Cities and Suburbs: Racial and Ethnic Change in Metro America in the 2000s." Brookings Institute Metropolitan Policy Program. 1–16.
Friedman, Samantha. 2008. "Do Declines in Residential Segregation Mean Stable Neighborhood Racial Integration in Metropolitan America? A Research Note." *Social Science Research* 37 (3): 920–933.
Gates, Henry Louis, Jr. "Who Was the 1st Black Millionairess." *The Root,* June, 24, 2013. Accessed December 3, 2014. http://www.theroot.com/articles/history/2013/06/who_was_the_first_black_millionairess/.

Gay, Claudine. 2004. "Putting Race in Context: Identifying the Environmental Determinants of Black Racial Attitudes." *American Political Science Review* 98 (4): 547–562.

Gilens, Martin. 1996. "Race and Poverty in America: Public Misperceptions and the American News Media." *Public Opinion Quarterly* 60 (4): 515–541.

———. 2009. *Why Americans Hate Welfare: Race, Media, and the Politics of Antipoverty Policy.* Chicago: Univ. of Chicago Press.

Glynn, Carroll J., Andrew F. Hayes, and James Shanahan. 1997. "Perceived Support for One's Opinions and Willingness to Speak Out: A Meta-Analysis of Survey Studies on the 'Spiral of Silence.'" *Public Opinion Quarterly* 61 (3): 452–463.

Gosnell, Harold F. 1967. *Negro Politicians: The Rise of Negro Politics in Chicago.* 1935. Reprint, Chicago: Univ. of Chicago Press.

Greenwell, Ava Thompson. 2012. "Twentieth-Century Ideology Meets Twenty-First-Century Technology: Black News Websites and Racial Uplift." *Fire!!!* 1 (2): 111–138.

Gregory, Steven. 1995. "Race, Identity and Political Activism: The Shifting Contours of the African American Public Sphere." In *The Black Public Sphere,* edited by The Black Public Sphere Collective. Chicago: Univ. of Chicago Press.

Harris, Fredrick C. 1999. *Something Within: Religion in African-American Political Activism.* New York: Oxford Univ. Press.

Harris-Lacewell, Melissa. 2004. *Barbershops, Bibles, and BET: Everyday Talk and Black Political Thought.* Princeton, N.J.: Princeton Univ. Press.

Haynes, Bruce. 2001. *Red Lines, Black Spaces.* New Haven, Conn.: Yale Univ. Press.

Hochschild, Jennifer L. 1996. *Facing Up to the American Dream: Race, Class, and the Soul of the Nation.* Princeton, N.J.: Princeton Univ. Press.

Huckfeldt, Robert, Paul Allen Beck, Russell J. Dalton, and Jeffrey Levine. 1995. "Political Environments, Cohesive Social Groups, and the Communication of Public Opinion." *American Journal of Political Science* 39 (4): 1025–1054.

Huckfeldt, R., P. E. Johnson, and J. Sprague. 2004. *Political Disagreement: The Survival of Diverse Opinions within Communication Networks.* Cambridge: Cambridge Univ. Press.

Huckfeldt, Robert, and Jeanette Morehouse Mendez. 2008. "Moths, Flames, and Political Engagement: Managing Disagreement within Communication Networks." *Journal of Politics* 70 (1): 83–96.

Huckfeldt, Robert, Eric Plutzer, and John Sprague. 1993. "Alternative Contexts of Political Behavior: Churches, Neighborhoods, and Individuals." *Journal of Politics* 55 (2): 365–381.

Huckfeldt, Robert, and John Sprague. 1987. "Networks in Context: The Social Flow of Political Information." *American Political Science Review* 81 (4): 1197–1216.

———. 1988. "Choice, Social Structure, and Political Information: The Information Coercion of Minorities." *American Journal of Political Science* 32 (2): 467–482.

———. 1995. *Citizens, Politics, and Social Communication: Information and Influence in an Election Campaign.* New York: Cambridge Univ. Press.

Huddy, Leonie. 2003. "Group Identity and Political Cohesion." In *Oxford Handbook of*

Political Psychology, 1st ed., edited by David Sears, Leonie Huddy, and Robert Jervis, 511–556. New York: Oxford Univ. Press.

———. 2013. "From Group Identity to Political Cohesion and Commitment." In *Oxford Handbook of Political Psychology,* 2nd ed., edited by Leonie Huddy, David O. Sears, and Jack S. Levy, 737–773. Oxford: Oxford Univ. Press.

Hutchings, V. L., and N. A. Valentino. 2004. "The Centrality of Race in American Politics." *Annual Review of Political Science* 7:383–408.

Ibarra, Herminia. 1995. "Race, Opportunity, and Diversity of Social Circles in Managerial Networks." *Academy of Management Journal* 38 (3): 673–703.

Jackson, Byran O. 1987. "The Effects of Racial Group Consciousness on Political Mobilization in American Cities." *Western Political Quarterly* 40 (4): 631–646.

Johnson, V. C. 2002. *Black Power in the Suburbs: The Myth or Reality of African American Suburban Political Incorporation.* New York: State Univ. of New York Press.

Joslyn, Mark R. 1997. "The Public Nature of Personal Opinion: The Impact of Collective Sentiment on Individual Appraisal." *Political Behavior* 19 (4): 337–363.

Kaufmann, Karen M. 2004. *The Urban Voter: Group Conflict and Mayoral Voting Behavior in American Cities.* Ann Arbor: Univ. of Michigan Press.

Kinder, D. R., and L. M. Sanders. 1996. *Divided by Color: Racial Politics and Democratic Ideals.* Chicago: Univ. of Chicago Press.

Kossinets, Gueorgi, and Duncan J. Watts. 2009. "Origins of Homophily in an Evolving Social Network." *American Journal of Sociology* 115 (2): 405–450.

Lewis, R. L'Heureux. 2012. "The Root and the Black Public Sphere." *Humanity and Society* 36 (2): 171–174.

Mayhew, Bruce H., J. Miller McPherson, Thomas Rotolo, and Lynn Smith-Lovin. 1995. "Sex and Race Homogeneity in Naturally Occurring Groups." *Social Forces* 74 (1): 15–52.

McAdam, Doug. 1982. *Political Process and the Development of Black Insurgency, 1930–1970.* Chicago: Univ. of Chicago Press.

McClurg, Scott D. 2003. "Social Networks and Political Participation: The Role of Social Interaction in Explaining Political Participation." *Political Research Quarterly* 56 (4): 449–464.

———. 2006. "Political Disagreement in Context: The Conditional Effect of Neighborhood Context, Disagreement and Political Talk on Electoral Participation." *Political Behavior* 28 (4): 349–366.

McDaniel, Eric L. 2008. *Politics in the Pews: The Political Mobilization of Black Churches.* Ann Arbor: Univ. of Michigan Press.

McDaniel, Eric L., and Christopher G. Ellison. 2008. "God's Party? Race, Religion, and Partisanship Over Time." *Political Research Quarterly* 61 (2): 180–191.

McPherson, Miller, Lynn Smith-Lovin, and James M. Cook. 2001. "Birds of a Feather: Homophily in Social Networks." *Annual Review of Sociology* 27:415–444.

Mendelberg, T. 2001. *The Race Card: Campaign Strategy, Implicit Messages, and the Norm of Equality.* Princeton, N.J.: Princeton Univ. Press.

Miller, Arthur H., Patricia Gurin, Gerald Gurin, and Oksana Malanchuk. 1981. "Group

Consciousness and Political Participation." *American Journal of Political Science* 25 (3): 494–511.

Morris, Aldon D. 1984. *Origins of the Civil Rights Movement: Black Communities Organizing for Change.* New York: Free Press.

Mutz, Diana C. 2002. "Cross-Cutting Social Networks: Testing Democratic Theory in Practice." *American Political Science Review* 96 (1): 111–126.

Nir, Lilach. 2005. "Ambivalent Social Networks and Their Consequences for Participation." *International Public Opinion Research* 17 (4): 422–442.

Oliver, J. Eric. 2001. *Democracy in Suburbia.* Princeton, N.J.: Princeton Univ. Press.

———. 2010. *Paradoxes of Integration: Race, Neighborhood, and Civic Life in Multiethnic America.* Chicago: Univ. of Chicago Press.

Oliver, J. Eric, and Tali Mendelberg. 2000. "Reconsidering the Environmental Determinants of White Racial Attitudes." *American Journal of Political Science* 44 (3): 574–589.

Pantoja, Adrian D., and Gary M. Segura. 2003. "Fear and Loathing in California: Contextual Threat and Political Sophistication Among Latino Voters." *Political Behavior* 25 (3): 265–286.

Pattillo-McCoy, Mary. 2000. *Black Picket Fences.* Chicago: Univ. of Chicago Press.

Peffley, Mark, and Jon Hurwitz. 2002. "The Racial Components of Race-Neutral Crime Policy Attitudes." *Political Psychology* 23 (1): 59–75.

Philpot, Tasha S. 2007. *Race, Republicans, and the Return of the Party of Lincoln.* Ann Arbor: Univ. of Michigan Press.

Raphael, Steven, and Michael A. Stoll. 2010. "Job Sprawl and the Suburbanization of Poverty." Brookings Institute Metropolitan Policy Program. 1–21.

Riker, William H., and Peter C. Ordeshook. 1968. "A Theory of the Calculus of Voting." *American Political Science Review* 62 (1): 25–42.

Rosenstone, Steven, and John Hansen. 1993. *Mobilization, Participation, and Democracy in America.* New York: Macmillan.

Scheufele, Dietram A., Matthew C. Nisbet, Dominique Brossard, and Erik C. Nisbet. 2004. "Social Structure and Citizenship: Examining the Impacts of Social Setting, Network Heterogeneity, and Informational Variables on Political Participation." *Political Communication* 21 (3): 315–338.

Schneider, Mark, and Thomas Phelan. 1993. "Black Suburbanization in the 1980s." *Demography* 30 (May): 269–279.

Scott, J. 2012. *What Is Social Network Analysis?* London: Bloomsbury Publishing.

Sears, David O., and Christia Brown. 2013. "Childhood and Adult Political Development." In *The Oxford Handbook of Political Psychology,* 2nd ed., edited by Leonie Huddy, David O. Sears, and Jack S. Levy. Oxford: Oxford Univ. Press.

Shapiro, Thomas, Tatjana Meschede, and Sam Osoro. 2013. "The Roots of the Widening Racial Wealth Gap: Explaining the Black-White Economic Divide." Institute on Assets and Social Policy. 1–8.

Simpson, Andrea Y. 1998. *The Tie That Binds: Identity and Political Attitudes in the Post–Civil Rights Generation.* New York: New York Univ. Press.

Smith, Jeffrey A., Miller McPherson, and Lynn Smith-Lovin. 2014. "Social Distance in the United States: Sex, Race, Religion, Age, and Education Homophily Among Confidants, 1985 to 2004." *American Sociological Review* 79 (3): 432–456.

Squires, Catherine R. 2002. "Rethinking the Black Public Sphere: An Alternative Vocabulary for Multiple Public Spheres." *Communication Theory* 12 (4): 446–468.

Staerklé, Christian, Alain Clémence, and Dario Spini. 2011. "Social Representations: A Normative and Dynamic Intergroup Approach." *Political Psychology* 32 (5): 759–768.

Swain, Carol M. 1993. *Black Faces, Black Interests: The Representation of African Americans in Congress.* Cambridge: Harvard Univ. Press.

Tajfel, Henri. 1981. *Human Groups and Social Categories.* Cambridge: Cambridge Univ. Press.

Tate, Katherine. 1994. *From Protest to Politics.* Cambridge, Mass.: Harvard Univ. Press.

———. 2004. *National Black Election Study, 1996.* ICPSR. Columbus: Ohio State University, 1997. Distributed by Inter-University Consortium for Political and Social Research, 2004.

Ulbig, Stacy G., and Carolyn L. Funk. 1999. "Conflict Avoidance and Political Participation." *Political Behavior* 21 (3): 265–282.

U.S. Census Bureau. 2012. 2012 American Community Survey (1-Year Estimates). http://www.census.gov/programs-surveys/acs/data.html.

———. 2012. 2012 Statistical Abstract of the United States. http://www.census.gov/library/publications/2011/compendia/statab/131ed.html.

U.S. Census Bureau Current Population Survey. 2015. Table A-2. "Percent of People 25 Years and Over Who Have Completed High School or College, by Race, Hispanic Origin and Sex: Selected Years 1940 to 2013." https://www.census.gov/hhes/socdemo/education/data/cps/historical/.

U.S. Census Bureau Current Population Survey. 2016. Table P-4. "Race and Hispanic Origin of People (Both Sexes Combined) by Median and Mean Income." http://www.census.gov/data/tables/time-series/demo/income-poverty/historical-income-people.html.

Vanderleeuw, James M. and Thomas E. Sowers. 2007. "Race, Roll-off, and Racial Transition: The Influence of Political Change on Racial Group Voter Roll-off in Urban Elections." *Social Science Quarterly* 88 (4): 937–952.

Verba, Sidney, Kay L. Schlozman, and Henry E. Brady. 1995. *Voice and Equality: Civic Voluntarism in American Politics.* Cambridge, Mass.: Harvard Univ. Press.

Weare, Christopher, Juliet Musso, and Ann Crigler. 2008. "Networks for Civic Engagement? Neighbourhood Councils and Faith-Based Organizations in Los Angeles." *Journal of Civil Society* 4 (3): 211–232.

Wilson, William J. 1978. *The Declining Significance of Race: Blacks and Changing American Institutions.* Chicago: Univ. of Chicago Press.

———. 2011. "The Declining Significance of Race: Revisited and Revised." *Daedalus* 140 (2): 55–69.

Winter, David G. 2003. "Personality and Political Behavior." In *Oxford Handbook of Political Psychology,* 1st ed., edited by David Sears, Leonie Huddy, and Robert Jervis, 110–145. New York: Oxford Univ. Press.

Zuckerman, Alan S., Nicholas A. Valentino, and Ezra W. Zuckerman. 1994. "A Structural Theory of Vote Choice: Social and Political Networks and Electoral Flows in Britain and the United States." *Journal of Politics* 56 (4): 1008–1033.

Index